Helping Students Succeed
in the Regular Classroom

Joseph E. Zins
Michael J. Curtis
Janet L. Graden
Charlene R. Ponti

Helping Students Succeed in the Regular Classroom

A Guide for Developing Intervention Assistance Programs

Jossey-Bass Publishers

San Francisco • London • 1988

HELPING STUDENTS SUCCEED IN THE REGULAR CLASSROOM
A Guide for Developing Intervention Assistance Programs
by Joseph E. Zins, Michael J. Curtis, Janet L. Graden,
and Charlene R. Ponti

Copyright © 1988 by: Jossey-Bass Inc., Publishers
350 Sansome Street
San Francisco, California 94104

&

Jossey-Bass Limited
28 Banner Street
London EC1Y 8QE

Library of Congress Cataloging-in-Publication Data

Helping students succeed in the regular classroom.

(Jossey-Bass social and behavioral science series)
(Jossey-Bass education series)
Bibliography: p.
Includes index.
1. Problem children—Education.   2. Mainstreaming
in education.   3. Teacher participation in personnel
service.   4. Behavior modification.   I. Zins, Joseph E.
II. Series.   III. Series: Jossey-Bass education series.
LC4801.H445   1988   371.9   87-46350
ISBN 1-55542-096-6 (alk. paper)

Manufactured in the United States of America

The paper in this book meets the guidelines for
permanence and durability of the Committee on
Production Guidelines for Book Longevity of the
Council on Library Resources.

JACKET DESIGN BY WILLI BAUM

FIRST EDITION

Code 8823

A joint publication in

THE JOSSEY-BASS
SOCIAL AND BEHAVIORAL SCIENCE SERIES

Psychoeducational Interventions:
Guidebooks for School Practitioners

and

THE JOSSEY-BASS EDUCATION SERIES

Consulting Editors

Charles A. Maher
Rutgers University

Joseph E. Zins
University of Cincinnati

Contents

**Part Two: Developing and Implementing Programs to Help
Teachers Solve Problems in the Classroom**

Tables and Figures

Preface

There is a growing interest in alternative methods of providing services to students with school-related problems. One procedure gaining increasing popularity is intervention assistance. Essentially this process uses collaborative consultation as the overarching framework for the delivery of special services. The goal is to expand instructional options for all students and to do so in the least restrictive setting. Thus, intervention assistance has a strong preventive orientation. Because intervention assistance programs are implemented on a systemic basis, they are an integral component of the educational system and not a tangential or disjointed addition.

A growing number of states and school districts are adopting similar approaches through programs referred to by terms such as prereferral intervention, teacher-assistance teams, and building-level support teams. Although the specific procedures used in these programs may vary, they all address the significant problems that exist in the special services systems currently operating in many schools. However, most of these programs have not been thoroughly conceptualized, and they do not adequately or thoroughly address all of the issues necessary for effective implementation in the schools.

As intervention assistance programs are promoted, adopted, and even mandated, there is a danger that they could become education's latest bandwagon, only to fade out of existence after a short and ineffectual stay. Yet, the consultation component of intervention assistance is a conceptually and empirically sound way to provide services to all students and teachers. The framework we advocate is not an entirely different type of service but rather an effective means of integrating consultation and intervention assistance into the existing services delivery system.

This book encompasses all the ingredients for understanding and effectively implementing and operating an intervention assistance program in a school or district. In our experience, two to three years are required to build a program and integrate it fully. Our orientation is practical, but we also present the necessary conceptual background to understand the intervention assistance process. Our goal is to provide sufficient detail to enable practitioners to make intervention assistance programs integral components of their current educational systems. We discuss the development of interventions for individual students as well as the implementation of the intervention assistance program in a school organization.

This book is intended for various professionals practicing in the schools, as well as students in training, who are interested in understanding and implementing an intervention assistance program. Special services personnel—such as school psychologists, special education teachers, counselors, speech and language clinicians, nurses, and special services administrators—as well as regular education teachers, supervisors, and principals will all find the book helpful. In fact, use of the book across disciplines will be beneficial in enhancing professional collaboration, which will ultimately facilitate the learning and adjustment of all students.

Overview

Chapter One introduces the concept of intervention assistance and provides a discussion of need, important aspects, goals, and benefits. Next, a comprehensive and detailed rationale is presented through an overview of relevant theory and research; this overview explains why educators should consider implementing intervention assistance programs (Chapter Two). Key aspects of consultation, which provides the basic foundation for an intervention assistance approach, are thoroughly discussed in Chapter Three. In Chapter Four, the stages in the intervention assistance process are described, including the specific problem-solving steps. Special issues associated with group problem solving are also addressed.

Next, Chapters Five and Six provide extensive coverage of intervention design for common academic and behavioral problems experienced by students. Chapter Five includes a review of affective and socialization interventions, and Chapter Six describes academic and cognitive treatments to improve academic performance. These two chapters provide a general framework for designing interventions as well as numerous specific examples of effective interventions that might be implemented through the intervention assistance process.

In the second part of the book, the focus shifts to how an intervention assistance program can be incorporated as a system of services delivery. Assessing the readiness of the school organization to implement such an approach is the topic of Chapter Seven, and specific strategies for implementation are included in Chapter Eight. Pragmatic issues are addressed in the next chapters with regard to removing barriers to the intervention assistance approach (Chapter Nine) and dealing with practical problems (Chapter Ten). Procedures for evaluating the effectiveness of an intervention assistance program are presented in Chapter Eleven, while important legal and ethical principles that relate to the approach are discussed in Chapter Twelve. Finally, conclusions and suggested directions for future activities to effectively implement the approach are covered in the last chapter.

Acknowledgments

We would like to acknowledge the many individuals who were instrumental in the completion of this book. Our colleagues at the University of Cincinnati, as usual, provided significant intellectual stimulation and challenged our thinking. To them we express our gratitude. Vicki Curtis reviewed early drafts of several chapters and made a number of practical suggestions. Frances Floyd, our secretary, changed our word-processing program in the middle of this project but nevertheless helped us through numerous revisions and stuck with us to the end.

Each of us helped develop intervention assistance programs in a number of schools. We appreciate the learning experiences that we have been fortunate to share with those institutions. The idea for this book, which is based largely on those experiences, originated with Joseph E. Zins, who also took responsibility for coordinating the overall project. The other three authors contributed equally to its development and completion.

An endeavor of this magnitude is never confined to normal "office hours." It occupies innumerable evenings and weekends and, in doing so, inevitably takes its toll on the normalcy of family life. Vicki Curtis and Ken Graden provided unwavering understanding and support for their respective spouses, Michael Curtis and Janet Graden. Joseph Zins and Charlene Ponti, husband and wife, also acknowledge each other's unfaltering support and willingness to share pressures and responsibilities during the development of this project. All of the authors gratefully recognize the goodwill of all concerned that made this book possible.

Cincinnati, Ohio　　　　　　　　　　Joseph E. Zins
March 1988　　　　　　　　　　　　Michael J. Curtis
　　　　　　　　　　　　　　　　　　Janet L. Graden
　　　　　　　　　　　　　　　　　　Charlene R. Ponti

The Authors

J oseph E. Zins is professor of school psychology at the University of Cincinnati and has served for five years as consulting psychologist with the Beechwood (Kentucky) Independent Schools. He received his Ed.D. degree in school psychology from the University of Cincinnati in 1977. Zins has served as a consultant to school districts in several states, and for more than eight years before coming to his current position worked as a school psychologist in public schools and as a staff psychologist in a community mental health center.

Zins has conducted research and published more than fifty chapters, articles, and reviews on consultation, prevention, and the delivery of psychological services in educational settings. In addition to this volume, Zins has coedited five books and is consulting editor of the Psychoeducational Interventions: Guidebooks for School Practitioners series, published by Jossey-Bass. He has been a member of the editorial boards of five journals, including the *School Psychology Review, Special Services in the Schools,* and *Professional School Psychology.*

Zins is a fellow of the American Psychological Association, former secretary of the National Association of School Psychologists, and past president of the Kentucky Association for Psychology in the Schools. He has been the recipient of a number of awards recognizing his scholarship and leadership in school psychology.

Michael J. Curtis is professor and director of school psychology at the University of Cincinnati. He received his Ph.D. degree in school psychology from the University of Texas, Austin, in 1974. He has worked in schools in both New York and Texas and continues to serve schools and school districts as a consulting psychologist.

Curtis has published widely and has been a frequent speaker at state, national, and international meetings on topics relating to consultation, organizational development, legal and ethical issues, and the delivery of psychological services in the schools. He has served on the editorial boards of *Professional School Psychology* and *School Psychology Review*. He has also been a member of the board of directors and vice-president of the *Journal of School Psychology*.

Curtis has served as president of the National Association of School Psychologists, president of the Ohio School Psychologists Association, chair of the Council of Directors of School Psychology Programs, and is a fellow of the American Psychological Association. He has received several awards for outstanding contributions and service to school psychology.

Janet L. Graden is assistant professor of school psychology at the University of Cincinnati. She received her Ph.D. degree in school psychology from the University of Minnesota in 1984. Graden was a school psychologist for four years in Indiana and Minnesota, where she implemented consultative approaches to services delivery, and she continues to consult in schools.

Graden is coeditor of *Alternative Educational Delivery Systems: Enhancing Instructional Options for All Students.* She has written many articles on alternative referral approaches and on services for students with learning disabilities. Graden serves on the editorial boards of *School Psychology Review* and *Exceptional Children* and is an associate editor of *Special Services Digest.* She has given numerous presentations to professional organizations and school districts on implementing intervention assistance approaches. In addition, she is active in professional associations as committee co-chair for the National Association of School Psychologists and for the Ohio School Psychologists Association.

Charlene R. Ponti has served as a school psychologist with the Hamilton County (Ohio) Office of Education for four years. She is also adjunct assistant professor of school psychology at the University of Cincinnati. Ponti received her Ph.D. degree in school psychology from the University of Cincinnati in 1985. Previous appointments included serving as a school psychologist in the Kenton County (Kentucky) public schools, as a visiting assistant professor of school psychology at Miami University (Ohio), and as a social worker at Giuffre Medical Center in Philadelphia.

Ponti's primary research interests are in consultation, behavioral and cognitive behavioral interventions, and the delivery of psychological services in schools. Her work has appeared in journals including the *School Psychology Review* and *Special Services in the Schools,* and she is a frequent presenter at national professional conferences. She also serves on the editorial board of *School Psychology Review* and as a contributing editor for *Special Services Digest.*

Ponti has been active in the Division of School Psychology of the American Psychological Association and in the National Association of School Psychologists. She has served as membership chair of the Ohio School Psychologists Association and program chair for the Kentucky Association for Psychology in the Schools.

Dedicated, with love,
to our children
Lauren,
Matt,
Matthew,
and
Adam

Helping Students Succeed in the Regular Classroom

CHAPTER ONE

Introduction:
Special Education
Is Not Always the Answer

C riticism continues to mount regarding services for students with special needs. Practitioners and researchers have noted significant problems with almost every aspect of these services: assessment, decisions regarding placement, and the special education process itself, particularly education of the mildly handicapped (for example, learning disabled and educable mentally retarded) (Reynolds, Wang, and Walberg, 1987). These problems also pertain to education for students who have not been identified as handicapped but who nevertheless experience learning or behavioral difficulties (or both).

Need for New Approaches

Under the current educational system in many districts, students who experience problems in school are referred for a multidisciplinary psychoeducational assessment, with the expected outcome being placement in a special education program. Research suggests that those expectations are usually met (Algozzine, Christenson, and Ysseldyke, 1982). Furthermore, with 3 to 5 percent of the entire school population being referred each year, the special education population is expanding at an alarming rate (Algozzine, Ysseldyke, and Christenson, 1983). As a result, special education is expected to serve increasing numbers of students at a level substantially beyond that for which resources are presently available. And these already limited resources are not expected to increase significantly in the foreseeable future, at least not enough for them to meet currently escalating demands.

This general overreliance on special education results from a variety of factors, many not directly associated with students' classroom performance and behavior. For example, people often believe that the needs of children who are experiencing learning or behavioral problems cannot be met by the regular classroom teacher because of a lack of knowledge or skills. Although we acknowledge that the problems experienced by students have many causes, some of which regular teachers cannot deal with, the widespread notion that pupils' individual needs can be met only through special education programs and not in the regular classroom is mistaken.

The belief of many classroom teachers that they are unable to intervene effectively with these children is perpetuated in several ways. When P.L. 94-142 was initially enacted in the mid 1970s, special educators, related services personnel, and administrators made substantial efforts to encourage regular education teachers to refer "suspected handicapped" students for psychoeducational assessments. In fact, many advocates came to view the increasing numbers in special education as indication of their effectiveness (Lipsky and Gartner, 1987). The intent was a noble one; prior to this time, many handicapped students were not being served appropriately. At the same time, however, a message was being given to regular teachers: "You cannot meet the needs of handicapped students in your classroom. These pupils must receive special education in order to succeed in school." In other words, although P.L. 94-142 did much to establish the rights of handicapped children, it also contributed to the perception that children experiencing difficulties need assistance that regular teachers cannot provide. (A similar message is being given today to these same regular teachers regarding gifted and talented students.)

The current educational system contributes to this belief through its continued emphasis on categorical services and labels for children; terms such as *LD* (learning disabled) begin to stand for the child, and they also implied internal causes for the difficulties. Tombari and Bergan (1978), for example, found that the use of "medical model" cues (verbalizations that infer internal causation) by consultants was associated with classroom teachers' lowered confidence in their ability to significantly help children and with an increased belief that the children would have to be referred for outside assistance. As a result, many classroom teachers and other school personnel look to special education as the only avenue for serving such children.

Because of legal mandates related to due process and multidisciplinary decision making, once questions arise about the education of a "suspected handicapped" student and a referral is filed, a comprehensive, multifaceted assessment must be completed. The resulting evaluation process more often than not focuses on compliance with special education eligibility criteria rather than on the functional assessment of performance and behavior. Instruments are chosen that provide scores used for comparison purposes but that contribute little information useful in clarifying problems or providing baselines for intervention purposes. Information obtained from these tests usually has little relevance to what the pupil is doing in the classroom.

The potential negative consequences of the current approach to services delivery for children with special needs are numerous but can be grouped into three major areas (Curtis, Zins, and Graden, 1987). First, referrals require an extensive, time-consuming, multidisciplinary psychoeducational assessment that is usually oriented toward determining eligibility for placement. Resources are heavily invested in efforts to name problems and categorize them. Furthermore, because of the tendency to inappropriately refer problems that might be resolved in the regular classroom, resources are often used unnecessarily in this way.

Second, the current system leads to an overidentification of students for special education (Reynolds, Wang, and Walberg, 1987). Special classes are often used inappropriately to meet the needs of students who might be served effectively in the regular classroom (Wang and Birch, 1984). Consequently, students are removed partially or entirely from regular classrooms, an action that can be contrary to the legal requirement for education in the least restrictive environment. Furthermore, the inappropriate placement of students who could be educated effectively in the

regular classroom exhausts resources intended to serve students with
severe handicaps.

Third, present practices do not result in the development of
effective intervention services for many children. Assessment results
that are focused on placement are often not instructionally relevant
or helpful to teachers (Thurlow and Ysseldyke, 1982). As a result,
special education teachers often must conduct additional evaluations in order to develop meaningful programs, which appears to
be an unnecessary duplication of effort. And, when students who
have been referred are found ineligible for special education,
"teachers often are left without any useful suggestions, and students
often do not receive alternative classroom interventions" (Graden,
Casey, and Christenson, 1985, p. 378). In other words, even though
these pupils are experiencing problems, their special needs are
likely to be unmet.

Thus, both regular education students with special needs and
special education students are not being served as effectively as they
might be. Clearly, educators must reconceptualize the delivery of
special services to effectively serve all students who experience
difficulty. In the next section, we present one alternative framework
for addressing this widespread problem.

Consultation as the Framework

We believe that all school-based special services to students
and support for teachers should be organized and delivered within
a consultative framework. Through such an approach, options can
be expanded for students within the least restrictive educational
setting. The term *consultation* refers essentially to a problem-
solving process that involves the collaborative efforts of two or more
persons to benefit another person (for example, a student) for whom
they bear some responsibility (Gutkin and Curtis, 1982). A
thorough description of the conceptual framework for the consultation model is presented in Chapter Three.

Consultation is essential if special services are to be delivered
effectively. Without consultation, a special services professional
would have to observe, assess, and remediate a student-related
problem in total isolation. For legal, ethical, and pragmatic

reasons, that practice should not occur in schools. Infrequently, special circumstances do dictate isolated service. For example, the services of a high school counselor might be requested by a student who has reached the age of majority and might be delivered without the involvement of a third party. But, except for this example of short-term counseling, extended services necessitate the involvement of others, including parents and other school personnel, in order to be effective.

At this time consultation is a limited aspect of the professional practices of most special services personnel (West and Idol, 1987), in spite of the emphasis that it has received since the mid 1960s. To some degree, its limited utilization reflects the fact that many professionals have received little formal training and supervised experience in consultation. Furthermore, when consultation is employed, it usually is linked solely to the special education decision-making process (for example, as part of psychoeducational assessment procedures) rather than serving as the foundation for the entire services system.

Overview and Definition

As consultation as an alternative framework begins to emerge in the literature and in practice, a number of terms are being used to refer to the process and to those who use it. They include *prereferral intervention, preevaluation activities, intervention assistance teams,* and *teacher assistance* or *support teams.* We have chosen to use the term *intervention assistance program* as the others do not capture the essence of the entire system to which we are referring (for example, prereferral evaluation implies that a referral and assessment eventually will take place). In the intervention assistance approach, consultation is the problem-solving process through which intervention assistance is provided. This approach, however, represents a renewed interest in consultation rather than a new type of service (Zins and Ponti, 1987). We define the intervention assistance process as follows:

> a systemwide consultation-based model of services delivery intended to meet the special needs of individ-

ual students through the systematic and collaborative provision, evaluation, and documentation of problem-solving strategies in the least restrictive setting prior to referral for consideration of a more restrictive placement.

The intervention assistance process should be available to all students, school personnel, and parents. Although our focus throughout the book is on regular education teachers and settings, parents can also initiate a request for assistance, and home/school partnerships can be effective (Zins, Graden, and Ponti, in press). Similarly, these services can be beneficial to special education teachers; for example, students receiving LD services can be helped to maintain their level of functioning in the mainstream classroom so that long periods of time in an LD resource room are not necessary. In other words, although this model works most efficiently with students who are experiencing mild educational difficulties, consultative assistance should also be available to teachers responsible for students with moderate, severe, and profound handicaps. Indeed, the system is all-encompassing and all-inclusive, potentially applicable to all students and all problems. Our intent in limiting most of our discussion to regular education teachers and settings is not to shortchange special educators or parents but rather to facilitate communication of our ideas. We are certain that readers can readily apply the various concepts to their own unique situations.

In the special services system currently employed in many schools, the referral for testing initiates special education decision-making procedures. The intervention assistance process, however, makes support readily available before the referral for testing. These two approaches are contrasted in Figure 1. We acknowledge that not all districts provide special services in the manner depicted in the figure as current practices. However, based on reviews of the published literature and our extensive experiences consulting throughout the country, we believe that such practices are prevalent in many districts. If they were not, the problems reported previously in this chapter would not exist.

Figure 1. Current and Intervention Assistance Approaches to the Delivery of Special Services

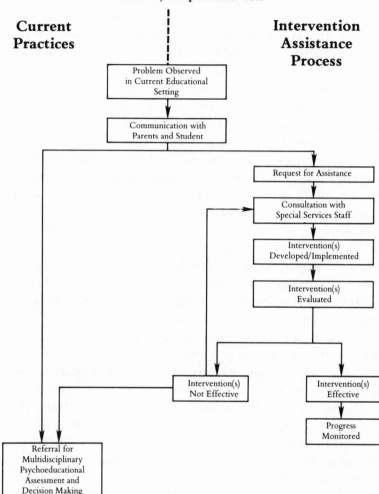

Current Practices

Intervention Assistance Process

Problem Observed in Current Educational Setting

Communication with Parents and Student

Request for Assistance

Consultation with Special Services Staff

Intervention(s) Developed/Implemented

Intervention(s) Evaluated

Intervention(s) Not Effective

Intervention(s) Effective

Progress Monitored

Referral for Multidisciplinary Psychoeducational Assessment and Decision Making

Source: Based on Ponti, Zins, and Graden, 1988; and Zins, Graden, and Ponti, in press.

On rare occasions an immediate psychoeducational evaluation may seem to be needed—for instance, when a student with an obvious handicap (for example, Down syndrome) moves into a district but for some reason the pupil's records are not available. It may be clear that the student has special educational needs, but even in these cases an evaluation should not be undertaken without first consulting with the student's parents and current teachers. It cannot automatically be assumed that a previous special education placement was appropriate, and few professionals can make placement decisions without additional information. Moreover, knowledge about attempts to alter instructional procedures and to implement various interventions may be helpful in the assessment process (if the child remains in the regular classroom for any length of time). Thus, even in instances such as this one, the intervention assistance process is applicable and desirable.

It is important to understand, however, that intervention assistance programs are most appropriate for helping students with mild learning or behavior problems who, with support, can function effectively in regular classrooms. It should not be used or misconstrued as intended to divert, or even delay, services for students with handicaps who can best be served through special education (Curtis, Zins, and Graden, 1987). Although this model usually focuses on intervention in the regular classroom, special classes remain a viable and effective means for serving some handicapped children. Moreover, as noted, the emphasis on interventions specific to each child's unique needs can be equally beneficial to those students who are served through special education. Thus, we strongly advocate adoption of a noncategorical approach to services as an effective system for meeting all students' needs (see Stainback and Stainback, 1984, 1987; Will, 1986). Unfortunately, at the present time categorical funding (and thus services) remains a reality. This book therefore presents a system that is consistent with our beliefs yet workable given current realities in education.

Intervention assistance programs are characterized by an emphasis on the provision of consultation services to teachers in an attempt to intervene effectively in the least restrictive setting. Accordingly, it is an indirect method of delivering services because children are helped through assistance to teachers (or parents). Thus, the process requires a major shift in the way special services personnel function. Rather than emphasizing assessment activities and placement decisions, these professionals act as consultants in the development, implementation, and evaluation of interventions. Thus, collaborative problem solving is their fundamental function.

The intervention assistance approach also necessitates a shift in the way problems are conceptualized. The placement emphasis of the current system reflects a fundamental belief that the causes for problems manifested by students are internal (Gerber and Semmel, 1984; Pugach, 1985). Medway (1979a) found that teachers overwhelmingly attribute student problems to causes either internal to the student or associated with the home. The most serious shortcoming of this notion is that it contributes to the belief that the locus of the problem is beyond the control of the teacher, who therefore can do little to bring about change. In the assumed absence of other alternatives, special education is often seen as the only solution.

In contrast, the intervention assistance process assumes that student performance is influenced by the interaction of a wide range of factors, including many external to the student. It stresses that many of these factors (classroom environment, instructional methods, curriculum, opportunities to learn) can be altered. Consequently, intervention development and implementation emphasize the identification and modification of these critical factors in order to enhance student performance and to enable students to succeed.

Another essential component of the intervention assistance process is its emphasis on the prevention and early detection of problems. Consultation services are provided primarily as a secondary prevention effort, aimed at prompt intervention for students with mild learning or adjustment problems (Zins and Ponti, 1987). Viewed as a preventive service (as illustrated in Figure 2), the intervention assistance process is potentially effective in terms of the numbers of students served and the dollar costs involved (see Zins and Ponti, 1985).

Potential Benefits

Intervention assistance programs have the potential to improve services delivery and to benefit students in a number of significant ways. First, it is one means of expanding educational

Figure 2. Cost per Student and Efficiency of Services.

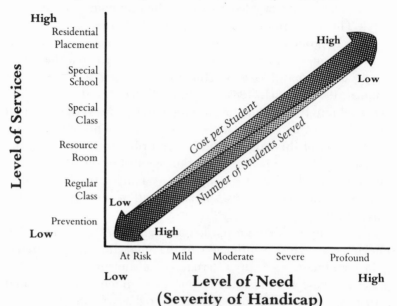

options for students experiencing difficulties. Through intervention assistance efforts, a variety of interventions can be developed during consultation and implemented by teachers in the classroom to meet individual student needs. Instructional techniques, the curriculum, or reinforcement procedures, for example, can be modified. (Chapters Five and Six discuss such interventions.)

Second, attention to student needs is immediate. This attention results as soon as the person initiating the process discusses the matter with the consultant. Many teachers and parents have found that the first ten or fifteen minutes of conversation with a consultant can be helpful in clarifying and understanding a problem. Often, progress is made toward resolving a situation without a formal assessment. Of course, complex problems may require a period of ongoing consultation.

Third, the emphasis on consultation is not intended to preclude the use of evaluation techniques, but such assessment activities are undertaken for the purpose of problem solving. Assessment is defined broadly as gathering data to answer a question about a student rather than as testing or as a method used to categorize a student. Thus, assessment is conceptualized as a key element in problem clarification, and is intended to be functional and relevant to the students' instructional needs.

Fourth, there also is a significant redirection of professional efforts and more efficient use of resources. Time and other resources that currently are used to determine eligibility for special education services are directed instead toward the development of interventions. Therefore, the likelihood is increased that students can succeed in their current classrooms and not have to be placed in more restrictive settings. Further, the system enables special services staff to serve more students because they do not spend as much time in unnecessary, time-consuming, placement-oriented assessment. Moreover, the process includes a built-in mechanism for systematically implementing interventions and for measuring their effectiveness; and communication among the various specialists is enhanced and duplication is reduced.

Fifth, classroom teachers are less likely than they are with current practices to believe that children in need of assistance can be served only through special education. Tombari and Bergan (1978) found that the use of behaviorally descriptive verbalizations was associated with teachers' increased confidence in their ability to resolve problems within the classroom setting. The emphasis of the intervention assistance approach on functional assessment and intervention development is likely to help teachers gain an in-depth understanding of various aspects of the problem and enhance their confidence. This increased confidence should in turn reduce reliance on referrals for special education.

Finally, as mentioned earlier, prevention is a key goal of the process. The system is directed toward preventing problems or resolving them in their early stages, and it also makes services accessible to all school personnel and parents so that they have assistance readily available when problems are first suspected.

As this discussion has suggested, a promising and growing body of empirical evidence shows that intervention assistance programs result in positive outcomes for students, teachers, and school systems (see Curtis, Zins, and Graden, 1987). Chapter Two reviews these outcomes and the theoretical foundations of the approach.

Need for Alternatives in Special Services Delivery

When attempting to implement a new or different way of providing services to students, it is important for those involved to understand both the rationale for considering changes in current practices and the basis for the new framework. A thorough knowledge of the reasons for change may increase the motivation to try alternatives, and resistance therefore may be decreased. Failure in implementation is often related to a lack of understanding and acceptance of the program, regardless of its merits (Sarason, 1982).

This chapter provides the reader with essential background information that establishes the context for intervention assistance programs. First, we examine the need for implementing alternative approaches to services delivery. We highlight practical and conceptual reasons why change should occur in the provision of services. Second, we provide an explanation of the underlying theoretical concepts of the intervention assistance approach. In addition to being critical for effective practice, this information may also be used by practitioners to influence educational decision makers, who are likely to want information about possible alternatives before adopting changes. Practitioners may share relevant ideas and refer to research from this chapter to facilitate such decisions. Additional ideas for using this information to effect change are contained in Chapters Eight and Nine.

The first section of this chapter includes reports of studies that highlight the most notable problems associated with current practices; a discussion of the assumptions inherent in the intervention assistance process, contrasted with those underlying practices currently employed in many schools; and a summary of trends that support adoption of an intervention assistance program. In the second part of the chapter, we delineate the theoretical foundations of the process, which lie in consultation, prevention, and social learning theory.

Need and Rationale for Alternative Systems

To the professionals involved in providing assistance to the many students experiencing difficulty in our schools, the problems and shortcomings of most current practices are obvious. Despite the vastly growing number of students being served in special education programs (Edgar and Hayden, 1984–1985), many additional students have special needs that continue to go unmet. Although gains have been made in making services available to the handicapped, it is becoming increasingly clear that special education cannot serve all students experiencing difficulty and that increased efforts to expand options in regular education are needed (Will, 1986).

In addition, many of the efforts to provide special services are not working effectively. There are significant problems with the categorical model, and the overall effects of special education have not been positive (Reynolds, Wang, and Walberg, 1987; Will, 1986). These problems are serious and will require extensive, long-term, systematic change efforts over many years.

Problems with Current Practices

What are the specific problems associated with current services delivery? What evidence indicates the need to adopt alternative approaches such as intervention assistance programs?

An extensive body of research documents the numerous problems with current practices of providing special services to students. The problems are wide-ranging; they include idiosyncratic and biased referral practices, inappropriate and sometimes educationally irrelevant assessments, and inconsistent and inadequate processes for making categorical placement decisions (see

Wang, Reynolds, and Walberg, 1987). To practitioners struggling to provide effective services to students, these problems are all too familiar. These professionals constantly experience frustration in trying to decide who is handicapped and who is not, who fits one category or another, and who gets services and who does not. In many cases, they know that a student who does not qualify for special education is unlikely to receive any special services whatsoever and, as a result, will continue to experience the same problems that stimulated the referral initially.

Growing Numbers in Special Education. One striking statistic indicative of the major problems inherent in many current services systems is the rapidly growing number of students placed in special education (Gerber, 1984). Each year, increasing numbers of students are placed; yet, the number of students seemingly in need of special services does not diminish. Special education cannot and perhaps should not ever expand sufficiently to accommodate all students in need of assistance, and there never will be enough categories to appropriately serve the special needs of all students. Moreover, the largest growth in numbers is found in the categories for children with mild handicaps (mild mental retardation, LD, emotional/behavioral disturbance, speech). However, these categories are also the most problematic in that categorical differentiation is not reliable (Reynolds, Wang, and Walberg, 1987).

Referral Procedures. Research suggests that initiating a referral to consider a student's eligibility for special education is the critical point in the decision-making process (Ysseldyke and others, 1983b). The question of whether a student is handicapped and eligible for special services does not arise unless a student is referred for a psychoeducational evaluation, usually by a classroom teacher or parent. And most students who are referred subsequently are placed in special education (Algozzine, Christenson, and Ysseldyke, 1982). A national survey of referral, testing, and placement rates revealed that (a) 3 to 5 percent of the school population is referred annually for consideration of special education; (b) of students referred, 92 percent are tested to determine special education eligibility; and (c) of students tested, 73 percent are placed in special education services (Algozzine, Christenson, and Ysseldyke, 1982).

It is thus easy to see how the numbers of students in special education have grown so dramatically and will continue to grow with current practices. What is needed to break this pattern is to view referral not as a signal to test for special education eligibility but as an indication that the student and the referring classroom teacher are in need of assistance.

Several additional problems are associated with viewing referral as the first stage in the process to determine special education eligibility rather than as an indicator of a need for assistance. The decision to refer is largely idiosyncratic, with different teachers using different criteria (Gerber and Semmel, 1984). A behavior that causes one teacher to refer a student may be considered acceptable by another. The decision to refer is thus influenced to a considerable degree by teachers' belief systems, their perceptions of students, and their tolerances for different kinds of behaviors (Shinn, Tindal, and Spira, 1987). A referral decision is inherently biased by these factors. Consequently, whether a student is referred probably will be determined by which teacher he or she has. Increasing evidence indicates that many students currently in special education are not handicapped and are not distinguishable from the large numbers of students experiencing academic and behavior problems who remain in regular classrooms.

What is problematic here is that referral almost seems to predetermine that something is wrong with the student. Consequently, subsequent efforts are intended primarily to determine precisely what is wrong with the student or to search for a handicap. In other words, the initial decision to refer is used to set in motion a search for pathology, to test for deficits, and to find and label a handicap according to a category (Sarason and Doris, 1979). As a result, little effort is devoted to identifying how the needs of the student can be met.

Numerous factors can lead to a referral for testing. The student's own performance (academic skills, classroom behavior) is typically the focus of referral concerns, as well as the less-investigated areas of teacher, administrator, and parent perceptions and tolerances of students' behaviors, and the availability of alternatives. How these factors operate to affect the decision to refer is not fully understood. However, it is clear that teachers should not bear sole responsibility for problems in the referral process. As noted in Chapter One, teachers are given the message that they should refer students who are special or who have special needs. Furthermore, teachers often have not received adequate preparation in alternative instructional and classroom-management techniques. Moreover, administrators, many of whom have not been prepared to understand and respond to the diverse needs of students, have encouraged referrals without supporting prior efforts at intervention. They (as well as others) also put increasing pressure on teachers to be accountable for student achievement. Current funding mechanisms are another contributor to these problems as they reinforce referrals by making most support services available only after a student is declared eligible for special education.

Testing. For many years, psychoeducational testing has been the subject of controversy regarding what tests can and cannot do, their potential biases, the overreliance on test data in decision making, and the relevance of test results for educational planning (Ysseldyke, 1987). A certain mystique surrounding test data leads to greater faith in their ability to assist in decision making than is justified given their inherent limitations. For example, test results are used to determine who is handicapped, as well as to which category of exceptionality the handicapped individual belongs. In fact, test data are limited as a basis for such decisions (Ysseldyke, 1987). Unfortunately, the widespread overreliance and overconfidence in tests have been a major contributing factor to some of the problems in the decision-making process (Gallagan, 1985).

Although tests are limited as a basis for placement decisions, they are almost useless as a basis for instructional decisions. Traditional tests (intelligence tests, standardized achievement tests) used in assessing student eligibility for various programs often were not designed for instructional planning and therefore are of little use for deciding what or how to teach a student. Teachers, who are the primary consumers of test reports, often complain that they do not indicate how to intervene with students (Thurlow and Ysseldyke, 1982; Zins and Barnett, 1983). In any case, current funding procedures provide a strong impetus for the use of tests for categorical decision making rather than for instructional planning.

Contemporary efforts directed at improving assessment practices focus on using assessment strategies (not only tests) that are useful for intervention planning. There is growing interest and research support for curriculum-based assessment (Deno, 1986), behavioral assessment, instructional assessment, dynamic assessment, and other methods that can meaningfully assess students' needs and contribute to the development of interventions (Fuchs and Fuchs, 1986).

Categorical Placement Decisions. Probably the most confusing and difficult phase of the entire special education referral-to-placement process is that of making decisions regarding eligibility and placement in categorical programs. The categorical system has been the subject of much research highlighting its difficulties (Morsink, Thomas, and Smith-Davis, 1987) and the focus of public policy discussion regarding its weaknesses (Reynolds, Wang, and Walberg, 1987). The current framework has been described by Glass (1983) as "a mixture of politics, science fiction, medicine, social work, administrative convenience, and what not" (p. 65). For students categorized as mildly handicapped in particular, research has shown that distinctions between categories are not reliable (see Morsink, Thomas, and Smith-Davis, 1987). Furthermore, for the most rapidly growing category, LD, reliable differentiations cannot be made between so-called handicapped LD students and low-achieving nonhandicapped students (Ysseldyke and others, 1983b).

The implications of these findings for decision making are clear. We cannot practically, reliably, and consistently make placement decisions for large numbers of students experiencing mild learning or adjustment problems (or both). Whether a student is considered handicapped varies depending on state criteria, district policies and implementation criteria, resources available, the team making the decision, and the tests given to the student, among other factors (Ysseldyke and others, 1983b).

Other Problems. When efforts of special services providers are directed primarily, sometimes almost exclusively, toward identifying, labeling, and providing direct assistance only to pupils with handicaps, students who are experiencing difficulty but who are not eligible for special education frequently go unserved. These students often remain in the regular classroom without any interventions being attempted or other special assistance being provided. In other words, the teachers of these students often find that they must deal with the students without any further help being made available.

A related issue is that when special services providers invest most of their time in decision making and delivery of direct services, their availability to other students and teachers in the school is limited. The expertise of these specialists is thus vastly underutilized and unnecessarily restricted to only a small number of students (Stainback and Stainback, 1984; Zins, 1985).

Assumptions Underlying the Intervention
Assistance Approach

The assumptions inherent in different approaches to services delivery often are not recognized and consequently are not questioned or challenged. Therefore, it is important to examine the assumptions regarding students served, professionals involved, and services provided within an intervention assistance program. These assumptions follow:

- Educators are competent to provide services to all students.
- All students have ample opportunities to succeed in the least restrictive setting.
- There is a wide range of possible attributions for problems experienced by students.
- Regular and special education personnel share responsibility for all students.

The first assumption views regular educators as having the skills and knowledge to accommodate most students in the regular setting, particularly if they are provided with appropriate assistance and support. This assumption is in contrast to current assumptions that teachers do not have the ability to respond to the special needs of students and that students with such needs should be referred for psychoeducational assessment. In the approach advocated here, teachers are encouraged to intervene with all students and are provided with supportive assistance to do so.

The second assumption indicates that the first step following a request for assistance should not be to suspect a handicap (or the need for a restrictive placement) and begin to assess for it but rather to assume that the student can be helped in the current classroom. Thus, the reaction to problems is to seek intervention assistance and thereby to enhance student options for success.

The third assumption expands attributions for student problems to include environmental causes, rather than limiting the focus to presumed problems within the student. Student learning and behavior problems are associated with many factors, including the type of instruction they receive, the opportunities they have to learn, family situations, and individual characteristics. Therefore, intervention assistance efforts are intended to focus on changing relevant environmental factors in addition to student characteristics. In contrast, when the first response to referral is to assess a student's eligibility for special education, the assumption is that the student possesses the problem. This assumption leads primarily to efforts to diagnose the problem, label it, and provide services based on presumed handicaps.

The fourth assumption is that there is no clear-cut dividing line between regular and special students (Stainback and Stainback, 1984). In other words, all educators are responsible for all students; specialists are not responsible for only special students, and regular educators are not responsible for only regular students. In sharing responsibility, special services personnel are viewed as collaborators with other educational personnel, not as experts who impart special wisdom to them.

Trends Supporting Alternative Approaches

The changes over time that indicate the need for alternative approaches are concisely and convincingly reviewed by Reynolds, Wang, and Walberg (1987). They argue that the research base does not support current categorical approaches and that several occurrences mark the trend toward adopting alternatives. Among these major developments are Hobbs's (1975) report discussing problems with categorical labeling; the National Academy of Sciences panel (Heller, Holtzman, and Messick, 1982) that criticized current assessment and placement practices for the mentally retarded; advocacy efforts, such as Rights Without Labels (a copy can be obtained from the Advocacy Center for the Elderly and Disabled, 9001 Howard Avenue, Suite 300A, New Orleans, Louisiana 70113), that promote prereferral interventions in the regular classroom and alternative assessment approaches; the National Association of School Psychologists/National Coalition of Advocates for Students (1985) position statement regarding increasing educational alternatives for all students; and the U.S. Department of Education report on the need to develop regular education initiatives (Will, 1986). Together, these developments signal a clear need to explore alternative approaches, and all specifically promote expanded options for students. Indeed, several states (among them Iowa, Louisiana, New Jersey, Ohio, North Carolina, South Carolina) have encouraged or even mandated the adoption of an intervention assistance approach.

At this time, however, concern is also being expressed about potential problems with some of the alternative approaches being advocated (Council for Exceptional Children, 1986). These concerns relate to the need for assurance that procedural safeguards are met, that services for handicapped students do not become diluted, and that change not occur too quickly without a supportive empirical base and careful experimentation. Promoters of intervention assistance programs, however, believe that in fact services for the handicapped should be made more readily available rather than diminished. Also, there is growing empirical support for the intervention assistance approach from the literature on consultation effectiveness. A critical issue, however, is that of funding. Alternatives to funding that is tied directly to serving students categorically must be made available so that other means of providing effective support services can be developed.

Theoretical Foundations of Intervention Assistance Programs

The intervention assistance process is not an entirely new approach but is based firmly on an already existing and empirically demonstrated model of services delivery—consultation. The innovative aspect of intervention assistance programs is utilization of consultation on a systemic basis and as a means to deliver preventively oriented services. Social learning theory is a foundation for this consultation process. In addition, a number of other theories from the psychological behavior change literature have been applied to consultation as a means of explaining the complex interactions that occur. Among the theories included are those from social psychology, cognitive psychology, counseling, assessment methodology, behavioral technology, marketing, systems and ecological theories, program evaluation, and organizational psychology (see Conoley, 1986; Dustin and Blocher, 1984; and Zins, in press).

Support for Intervention Assistance Programs

A limited number of promising initial studies have directly evaluated the effects of implementing procedures that are similar to the intervention assistance process described in this book. These investigations suggest that such programs lead to fewer students being referred and tested for special education eligibility, expanded job functions for special services providers, and more students being served through consultative assistance (see Chalfant, Pysh, and Moultrie, 1979; Graden, Casey, and Bonstrom, 1985; Maher, in press; Ponti, Zins, and Graden, 1988; Zins, Graden, and Ponti, in press). While these studies are encouraging, further research is needed that examines the specific variables that influence the implementation and the outcomes of intervention assistance programs, as discussed in Chapter Thirteen. In addition, because consultation forms the foundation of intervention assistance programs, the research based on its efficacy must be carefully examined.

Empirical Support for Consultation

Numerous studies have demonstrated the effectiveness of consultation as a process for providing services. Comprehensive literature reviews by Gutkin and Curtis (1982), Mannino and Shore

(1975), and Medway (1979b, 1982), and a meta-analysis by Medway and Updyke (1985) provide clear support for the conclusion that consultation is an effective approach to services delivery at the client, consultee, and systems levels.

This substantial body of empirical support for consultation provides the basis for the intervention assistance process. Although there is still need for further research on consultation to understand the process and how its effectiveness can be maximized (see for example, West and Idol, 1987; Gresham and Kendell, 1987), it clearly represents a viable mechanism for providing services to students.

Delivery of Preventive Services

A fundamental aspect of consultation is that it is based on the principle of preventing problems from becoming serious or, preferably, preventing problems from ever occurring. Prevention is accomplished by enhancing the competence and knowledge of the individuals who come in daily contact with children and are in the best position to help them. Consultation is thus a means of delivering preventively oriented services rather than a preventive intervention in itself. There is a growing body of empirical research supporting the efficacy of prevention services (see, for example, Conyne, Zins, and Vedder-Dubocq, 1988; Edelstein and Michelson, 1986; and Roberts and Peterson, 1984), and these approaches are becoming increasingly popular in the schools.

Curtis and Meyers (1985) provide a review of research findings on the preventive benefits that can result from consultation. Among the results noted are improved professional skills for teachers (Gutkin, 1980; Zins, 1981), improved teacher attitudes regarding the seriousness of children's problems (Gutkin, Singer, and Brown, 1980), improved teacher information about and understanding of children's problems (Curtis and Watson, 1980), generalization of consultation benefits to other children in the same classroom (Jason and Ferone, 1978; Meyers, 1975), reductions in referral rates for psychoeducational evaluations (Ritter, 1978), improved long-term academic performance (Jackson, Cleveland,

and Merenda, 1975), and reduction of various behavioral difficulties (Spivack, Platt, and Shure, 1976).

One of the goals of the intervention assistance approach is to ameliorate problems in the regular classroom and thus to prevent unnecessary referrals to special education. Typically, schools (and many other agencies) do not provide services that are prevention oriented. Many services are not even available to students until they reach the point of failure. For example, requests for assistance are typically initiated only when students are already having severe difficulty in school. In fact, funding practices in education seem to provide incentives for programs that react to failure rather than for programs that prevent failure (Gutkin and Tieger, 1979). It is our view that many students would benefit from the provision of services intended to prevent problems when the services are needed (when problems first arise) and where they are needed (in the current classroom).

Social Learning Theory

Social learning theory (SLT) (Bandura, 1977) provides a conceptual foundation for the consultation process as well as for the types of interventions developed for students. SLT is based on the notion that an individual's behavior can be understood only by examining interactions among the individual, other persons in the environment, and key aspects of the environment itself. Similarly, interventions should reflect consideration of the person within an environmental context. Appropriate changes should be sought not only in the person but in her or his interactions with others or the environment (or both) as well as in significant elements of the environment.

Another key concept in SLT is reciprocal determinism, which suggests that individuals are influenced by their environment and, in turn, have an influence on the environment. When a student exhibits aggressive behavior, for example, environmental variables (the behavior of peers, the teacher's response) affect the child's aggression, but the child also elicits reactions in others that contribute to those behaviors (displays poor social skills, misinterprets others' acts as aggressive). The importance of intraperson variables (thoughts, perceptions, attributions) is also recognized. Individuals' behavioral histories affect their personal views of themselves, which reciprocally mediate how they behave. Thus, behavior results from interactive cycles of intrapersonal factors, behavioral actions, and reactions from others. Each of these is reciprocally connected to the others in complex ways. Therefore, no simple cause-and-effect relationship for behavior can be discerned.

One implication of reciprocal determinism for the development of interventions is that a problem situation can be changed by altering any of the three elements (intrapersonal factors, interactions with others, or environmental context). Thus, changing the environmental consequences for an action changes the child's behaviors and perceptions of himself or herself; similarly, changing a child's behaviors changes reactions of others to the child. The social learning perspective is thus helpful for understanding student-related problems and subsequently for designing individual interventions.

Social learning theory also provides a useful framework for understanding the interactive behaviors of the participants in the consultation process. For example, a teacher's perspective of a student must be considered within the context of environmental conditions (the number of children in the room, the organizational climate, the availability of support services) and of personal beliefs and attributions about the problem. Without a social learning perspective, it would be all too easy to blame the teacher for resistance exhibited during consultation. As is discussed in Chapter Nine, both participants influence one another as well as the outcomes of the process.

In summary, we believe that SLT offers a strong conceptual foundation on which to base the intervention assistance approach to services delivery for students. It also can be helpful as a framework for analyzing and guiding the consultative process. In addition, it is extremely useful in efforts to understand student-related problems and to develop effective interventions.

CHAPTER THREE

Using Consultation
to Provide Services
to All Students

A s we emphasized in the first two chapters, the most fundamental aspect of the intervention assistance process is its foundation in consultation. Consultation is the process through which services are delivered and problems are solved. The intervention techniques discussed in Chapters Five and Six are the content, or substance, of intervention assistance efforts. These techniques for intervening on behalf of children will remain only ideas, however, if they are never applied (Gutkin and Curtis, 1981). Therefore, consultation is important as the method through which needs are clarified and appropriate strategies for intervention are developed and implemented.

In this chapter and the following one, we discuss consultation as the process through which problems are addressed. This chapter explains the conceptual framework for consultation, while Chapter Four describes the application of consultation to the intervention assistance process.

Definition

Before we examine the major concepts in consultation, it may be helpful to discuss the confusion that has been created by the widespread overuse of the term *consultation*. Many special services personnel still do not have an adequate background in consultation, although there is increasing understanding about the term among those who have completed the necessary training (Curtis and Zins, 1981b; West and Idol, 1987). As a result, for many people consultation continues to mean almost any professional interaction between two people. Such ambiguity clearly does not facilitate consultation practice, and definitional issues must be resolved to clarify important aspects of this method.

Although a number of different consultation models have been described in the literature, three major approaches are most often used in the schools: the behavioral (Bergan, 1977), mental health (Caplan, 1970; Meyers, Parsons, and Martin, 1979), and organizational (Schmuck and Runkel, 1985) models. Although they differ somewhat in their theoretical bases, they also have numerous aspects in common. (For detailed discussions, see Gutkin and Curtis, 1982; Curtis and Meyers, 1985.)

Curtis and Meyers (1985) offer a definition of consultation that integrates the similarities of the various models within a systems/ecological framework. This definition is particularly appropriate for intervention assistance programs and covers a wide range of circumstances. They define consultation as "a collaborative problem-solving process in which two or more persons [consultant(s) and consultee(s)] engage in efforts to benefit one or more other persons [client(s)] for whom they bear some level of responsibility, within a context of reciprocal interactions" (p. 80). This definition reflects several major dimensions of effective consultation that are discussed next.

Key Aspects

Participants

Participants in a consultative relationship have distinct roles. The *consultant* is generally considered to be the person who provides support or assistance to another person (the *consultee*) who has primary responsibility for the student about whom there is some concern. In other words, the consultee is the person seeking assistance regarding a work-related problem, and the consultant is the person providing it. In our discussion, special services personnel most often are consultants, and classroom teachers or parents are consultees. However, consultation skills can also be used by teachers in working with parents or with one another.

The *client* is the beneficiary of consultative interventions and is the third primary participant. Although discussions of the consultation process focus on the professionals involved in the relationship, viewing the client as a participant emphasizes the point that helping the client is the reason the professionals engage in consultation. Consultation is a means through which help is provided to clients and not an end in itself. Although the relationships among professionals or between professionals and parents are important, we sometimes forget that our primary objective is to benefit the student.

In intervention assistance programs, the individual student most typically is the focus of intervention efforts and therefore is the client. However, an entire class can be the client if the purpose of consultation is to improve the professional performance of the teacher (so that the students ultimately benefit). Students who experience a common problem can also be clients if the goal of consultation is to help a teacher or group of teachers learn to effectively serve students with those special needs. An entire school system can also be the focus, as when an organization-development program is designed to improve school climate. Consequently, the client is defined as the person or persons who are intended to benefit from the problem-solving process. In this book, the client most often is an individual student.

Consultation as Indirect Assistance

Essential to the consultative framework for services delivery is the concept that the consultant serves the client indirectly. Direct assistance is provided to the person who bears primary responsibility for providing services to the student. For example, consultation may be provided to a teacher who then intervenes directly to help the student. In contrast to those who provide direct services, such as counseling, the consultant does not work face-to-face with the student.

Indirect consultative services complement direct services and are not separate from them. It is not uncommon for a consultant to engage in both types of services to help solve a particular student-related problem. The consultant, for example, can assist the teacher in developing a classroom intervention and simultaneously work with the student in a counseling relationship.

Consultant/Consultee Relationship

A genuinely collaborative professional relationship among those involved in consultative problem solving is fundamental. It is assumed that all involved possess the knowledge and skills relevant to and necessary for effective resolution of the presenting problem. The development and maintenance of an effective collaborative relationship depend on careful attention to the following considerations.

Collaboration. Collaborative consultation involves a non-hierarchical, egalitarian relationship in that both the consultant and the consultee engage in efforts to develop effective intervention techniques. In other words, the consultant and consultee are considered equal contributors to the problem-solving process as each brings different perspectives and areas of expertise to the situation.

Confusion sometimes arises about the term *collaboration,* which is often considered to be synonymous with nondirective communication. However, this is not the case. Although consultants should not unilaterally solve the problem and tell consultees which strategies to implement, both participants share responsibility for applying their expertise. Neither party should hold back ideas or interact predominantly in a nondirective manner. The purpose of collaboration is to establish an atmosphere that encourages all participants to contribute and share their expertise and resources (Tyler, Pargament, and Gatz, 1983; Zins, 1985) as collaboration can improve the flow of communication (Gutkin and Curtis, 1982) and facilitate creative problem solving (Sandoval, Lambert, and Davis, 1977). In fact, teachers have been found to prefer collaborative consultation to an expert approach; they perceive the collaborative consultant as being more attentive and the process as resulting in the development of more successful and relevant interventions (Wenger, 1979).

The egalitarian aspect of the relationship differentiates it from supervision. The term *supervision* means to direct, inspect, or oversee. The purposes of supervision are to control and evaluate other people and their performance. These purposes are clearly inconsistent with the notion of collaboration. Besides the power issues inherent in the hierarchical relationship in supervision, any consultant activities that involve evaluation of the consultee seriously inhibit the open and honest communication essential for effective problem solving. Although at times it is necessary and appropriate for the consultant to openly discuss specific aspects of ideas generated by the consultee from a critical perspective, the consultant should never evaluate the consultee as a professional or a person.

Thus, the success of this type of relationship depends on a genuine belief by the consultant in the equal status of those involved. Game playing is dangerous! Consultees quickly see through the efforts of consultants who still consider themselves the experts yet who go through the motions of trying to get consultees to come up with the "right" answers. If the consultant genuinely believes in the equal status of the consultee, there is no reason to think that ideas generated by the consultee are less meritorious than those of the consultant.

When the consultant believes that an idea generated by the consultee will not work or could be improved, it is not only acceptable but appropriate to openly discuss those aspects of the plan that are of concern. Such discussions should clearly focus on specific aspects of the plan and not on the abilities of the consultee (or be misinterpreted as evaluating those abilities). Once a strong positive relationship is established, such discussions are not likely to result in a negative response from the consultee. However, early in a relationship, each comment tends to sound critical to the consultee. Even if the consultant does not believe that a particular idea is the best alternative, it may be desirable to agree to having the consultee attempt that strategy anyway. An exception arises when the consultant believes that the strategy would be detrimental to the client. In such situations, the consultant is obligated to discuss relevant concerns with the consultee. In these cases, however, it is better to focus on the unintended detrimental implications for the client than on the consultee.

Consultee Involvement. Active consultee involvement in all aspects of consultation, including efforts to analyze the problem and develop viable problem-solving strategies, is a key ingredient for success. As noted previously, the consultee is assumed to possess valuable knowledge and insight regarding the situation. It is naive for a consultant to assume that adequate and accurate problem analysis can be completed without meaningful input from other persons who interact with a student on a regular basis.

Furthermore, active involvement in problem clarification makes it likely that the consultee will gain increased understanding of the problem being discussed. From the perspective of understanding and evaluating possible intervention strategies, as well as from that of being prepared to deal with similar problems when they arise in the future, it is important that consultees play integral roles in all problem-solving efforts. Not fully understanding the problem itself limits the consultee's comprehension of the relevance of and rationale for the intervention methods developed. It also reduces the likelihood of the consultee's being able to effectively implement the method selected. And, each time a similar problem arises, the consultee must again request assistance because little knowledge has been gained from the previous case.

In addition, a consultee's lack of participation in the problem-solving process is related to an absence of ownership of and commitment to the planned intervention. This lack of ownership also makes it unlikely that the plan will be carried out as intended (Reinking, Livesay, and Kohn, 1978).

Strategy Implementation. Because the consultee has to implement most strategies, it is pointless for the consultant to try to unilaterally impose a solution. Authority to force a consultee to try a strategy does not carry with it the power to ensure that every aspect of the plan is implemented as intended. Unless someone controls all the contingencies, little is gained in that type of power struggle. Most importantly, such relationships quickly lose sight of client welfare as the primary objective. With the consultant and consultee concentrating on their interpersonal conflict, the student is likely to lose.

Beyond the issue of power and authority, the consultee usually has the best sense of what will work within the environmental context in which the problem occurs, typically the classroom. Although it often is helpful to have an outsider (the consultant) observe a situation in order to gain a different perspective or new understanding, it seems unjustifiable and contrary to the notion of a collaborative relationship to begin with the assumption that the consultee's perception is flawed. Information generated during consultation sometimes suggests that a second opinion could be helpful in order to gain an increased understanding of the problem. However, the need for or contribution of such activities should be dealt with forthrightly within the context of a relationship that is characterized by mutual professional respect.

Voluntary Nature of Participation. Although it is not always possible or even appropriate, it is most desirable for consultation to be initiated by the consultee. Consultee initiation suggests that the consultee recognizes that a problem exists and may be motivated to do something about it. The problem that is eventually defined may be markedly different from that which prompted the consultee's original request for assistance. Nevertheless, initiation by the consultee reflects a concern regarding the client at some level.

Consultee initiation, however, suggests merely that the consultee wants something done. The consultee may believe that the change can be effected through consultative assistance, or the consultee may want someone else to take responsibility for the problem (for example, may want someone to transfer the student to another class).

Consultation that is not initiated by the consultee may be problematic. For example, a potential consultee may not even recognize the existence of a problem. The consultee may view a student's actions as falling well within the range of acceptable classroom behaviors, while the consultant may view the student's behavior as a significant problem. Interacting with a consultee in such a situation is a challenge for a consultant. Similarly, if a consultee recognizes that a problem exists but is unwilling to do anything about it, the consultant faces other difficulties. These are simply examples of possible circumstances. A consultee may have justifiable and appropriate reasons for not initiating consultation, some of which may be related to issues at the organizational level. For example, research by Kuehnel (1975) demonstrated that the climate of a school had a significant bearing on whether teachers sought consultative assistance. The influence of such variables on teacher requests for consultation is discussed in Chapters Seven, Eight, and Nine.

Confidentiality. In the establishment and maintenance of a positive working relationship, those involved must interact within a climate of trust. They should be confident that information shared in their relationship will remain accessible only to those involved. The belief that sensitive information shared during consultation will be available to others seriously limits the honest and open communication essential for effective problem solving.

Organizational policies and operational procedures, as well as legal mandates, require that information be shared with others outside the consultative relationship at certain times. In such instances, it is appropriate for the consultant to point out to the consultee the necessity to provide the information to others. For example, information may need to be shared with parents or other professionals if the student is suspected of being suicidal or of harming others. In addition, some school policies may require personnel to report student drug usage. If an occasion arises in which a consultee is required to share information with others outside the consultative relationship, the consultant can assist by discussing ways in which to do so.

It is helpful for those involved in consultation, as well as others with whom such information may have to be shared, to understand the ground rules before consultation is begun. In that way, everyone knows which information may and may not be shared. Familiarizing everyone with expectations helps to avoid the unanticipated or unintended disclosure of sensitive information. It also reduces the likelihood of embarrassment to someone outside the relationship who may otherwise unintentionally "violate" the rules and inquire about topics being discussed.

This discussion of confidentiality is intended to emphasize the importance of trust in the establishment of an honest and open professional relationship. Confidential communication from a legal perspective is a different matter altogether and is determined by the laws of each state. Discussion of this aspect is included in Chapter Twelve.

Responsibility for Client

The consultation literature has consistently suggested that the consultee is responsible for the student. That statement is true with regard to primary responsibility. However, legally and ethically, many other professionals, in addition to the teacher or parent, must assume some level of responsibility. Furthermore, demands for accountability, as well as a sense of professional propriety, require some assumption of responsibility for intervention outcomes. Idol, Paolucci-Whitcomb, and Levin (1986) argue that both the consultant and the consultee own the problem (p. 5) and that accountability for intervention success or failure is shared. This perspective has the advantage of minimizing the "blame" that consultees occasionally perceive when interventions are not successful. (See Chapter Ten for additional discussion of this point.)

Work-Related Focus

Another important aspect of consultation is its focus on the work-related concerns of the consultee. This dimension differentiates consultation from other similar professional functions such as counseling. Counseling is based on the hierarchical relationship of two participants, the counselor and the client. The primary purpose of their interactions is to bring about personal change in the client. Counseling is thus a direct service to the person seeking assistance.

In direct contrast, consultation does not focus on the personal feelings of the consultee. The consultant and the consultee collaborate in efforts to address work-related problems whose resolution will benefit the client. Although the primary focus of the consultative interaction is the client, the consultant should not ignore the feelings of the consultee. To do so would be counterproductive to efforts to establish and maintain an effective professional relationship. The consultant must remain sensitive and responsive to the work-related feelings of the consultee and contribute to a warm, supportive relationship through procedures such as empathy and active listening. The feelings of all participants are important in any human interaction and must be taken into account if the relationship is to remain sound and productive. In consultation, however, they should not be the focus of the interaction as this would alter the objective of the process.

This point also applies to the personal problems of the consultee. Simply put, they should never be dealt with during consultation. The roles of many helping professionals in the schools, including counselors, school psychologists, and social workers, do not necessarily carry either formal or informal sanction to provide personal therapeutic services to other school personnel. Although some have suggested that such services be included among the functions of special services personnel, these activities would likely significantly alter the collaborative nature of the consultative relationship. As a result, the ability of professionals to work together to develop and implement effective problem-solving strategies would be seriously diminished.

The likelihood of personal feelings or problems emerging as central issues during consultation is reduced by familiarizing all potential participants beforehand with the work-related focus of consultation. However, when such issues arise despite precautionary efforts, it is vital that the consultant strive to retain the integrity of the consultative relationship and not lapse into counseling.

Consultants occasionally encounter consultees whose levels of affect are quite high. For example, a classroom teacher may enter a session with strong feelings of frustration regarding the problems presented by a particular student. The response chosen by the consultant determines whether the remainder of the interaction is consultative or therapeutic in nature. If the consultant focuses on the teacher's feelings of frustration ("It sounds like you are very upset. . . ."), the session will probably become largely cathartic for the consultee. Such consultant responses often exacerbate the situation and escalate the feelings of the consultee.

Sessions of this nature have a number of potentially negative consequences. Although the consultee may temporarily feel better following catharsis, the student-related problem that caused the frustration initially will have gone unattended. Furthermore, the problem may continue to cause such feelings in the future. Moreover, the experience can be damaging to the long-term relationship between the two participants. For example, the consultee may be embarrassed about having expressed such feelings. Or the consultant may resent not having controlled the interaction effectively. The experience may also confuse the consultee about the appropriate role for the consultant.

Rather than reinforcing expressions of frustration, the consultant can acknowledge these feelings and then redirect the discussion to the work-related problem that led to the frustration in the first place. For instance, the consultant might respond, "That sounds very frustrating. Tell me what the children around him are doing just before he loses control." It may be necessary to employ this strategy several times in order to reframe the discussion. If the consultee persists in expressing personal feelings despite such efforts, the consultant can express empathy and then reschedule the session for a later time.

In those rare cases in which it becomes apparent that the consultee is genuinely in need of therapeutic assistance, the consultant can help the consultee recognize the need for that support and then identify places where it can be obtained. This advice should be given in a way that minimizes embarrassment to the consultee. Sensitivity to the needs of the consultee and to the long-term integrity of the consultative relationship should be guidelines for strategies employed.

Consultants sometimes become confused as to what constitutes a work-related concern when working with parents, as family or personal problems may be revealed in the course of the consultation sessions. In such cases, a helpful guideline is that these problems should be discussed and dealt with only in the context of how they affect the child. As should be clear at this point, parents' marital or personal problems are outside the realm of consultation.

Goals

Consultation has two primary purposes. Because it is a problem-solving process, the first goal is to resolve the presenting problem. Thus, the immediate objective is the development and implementation of effective interventions for student-related problems.

The second goal is a preventive one—to enhance the problem-solving skills of the consultee. This outcome may result from increased knowledge or skills regarding either a specific type of student problem or an instructional technique in general. Positive influence on consultee attitudinal variables, such as tolerance for certain types of student behaviors or self-confidence in the ability to handle problems of a specific nature, is a desirable outcome as well.

A small but important research base is emerging that demonstrates the benefits of consultation to consultees. For example, teachers who worked with high-skilled consultants significantly improved their problem-clarification skills and their understanding of children's problems (Curtis and Watson, 1980). They also expressed increased confidence in their ability to handle similar problems in the future (Ponti and Curtis, 1984; Tombari and Bergan, 1978).

Consultation also enables special services providers to share their skills with many consultees, thereby potentially helping many children. Through the intervention assistance process, problems can be identified and interventions can be designed for students early, thereby preventing serious problems from developing in the future. As was shown in Figure 2, not only can many students be affected but preventive consultation also is a cost-effective approach to services delivery.

Systems Perspective

As noted in the first two chapters, the intervention assistance process emphasizes a systems/ecological framework within which to consider student-related problems. The integration of systems theory into the definition of consultation advanced here is one of the aspects of this model that makes it particularly appropriate as a foundation for problem solving with students.

The systems perspective suggests that all parts of a system influence and are influenced by other parts. The character of any school is determined by the particular composition of all of its parts and their influence on one another or their reciprocal interaction. If the specific nature of an organization is determined by its exact composition at any given point in time, it follows that if any part changes, the total system will change as a result. Moreover, each of the other parts will be affected as well.

Systems theory offers a conceptual framework that is helpful for thinking about individual students. Within a classroom, a student is influenced to some extent by each of the other students, the teacher, and even the physical environment. At the same time, that particular student also influences, to some extent, each of the other students and the teacher and, to a lesser degree, possibly the physical environment. Each of those other variables can change on a daily basis and, as a result, can affect that student. It is easy to think of examples in which the mood or behavior of one person influences others. However, even the physical environment can vary. If the classroom happens to become uncomfortably warm, as on a sultry June afternoon, it is bound to have an impact on the behaviors of both the teacher and the students. Without doubt, the personality and physical characteristics of the teacher and the instructional methods used affect students differently. Yet, when a student experiences difficulty in the classroom, the common tendency is to look only at the student in order to understand the problem and to determine its cause.

From a systems or ecological perspective, however, it is necessary to consider the various factors in the student's learning environment, including the student, in order to adequately understand the problem. Furthermore, once the problem is understood, changes can likely be made to improve learning or behavior.

Affective and Cognitive Components

Although the early literature seemed to explain the consultation process somewhat unidimensionally, authors now advance the notion that consultation is made up of two components, the affective/interpersonal and the cognitive/problem solving (Curtis and Meyers, 1985; Raffaniello, 1981). As noted in Chapter Two, SLT provides the basis for understanding the events that occur during both these aspects of the consultative process. This multidimensional view has facilitated analysis of the consultation process and has added to our understanding of effective consultation.

Affective Component. The affective component is the interpersonal dimension of consultation. It includes how the consultant views the consultee, and it pertains largely to those issues discussed previously in this chapter regarding the consultant/consultee relationship.

In the interactional problem-solving process, this relationship is collaborative. However, the expert/authoritative style (commonly associated with the medical/clinical model of services delivery) is predominant in the literature and in practice. Although we will not discuss the expert/authoritative model in detail, it might be helpful to briefly compare it to the collaborative model. Table 1 presents this comparison along a number of important dimensions.

As described previously, the collaborative approach assumes an egalitarian, nonhierarchical relationship in which the expertise and skills of both the consultant and the consultee are utilized to address the student-related problem. The consultee retains primary responsibility for the client and can accept or reject the suggestions of the consultant.

The expert/authoritative approach is based on a set of different assumptions about both the consultant and the consultee. Essentially, the consultant diagnoses the problem (directly or indirectly) and then either personally carries out the program of remediation or prescribes the program for implementation by someone else, usually the consultee. This approach assumes that the problem can be thoroughly and accurately clarified without the active involvement of the consultee, the consultant can independently develop solutions to the problem that will be effective, and the consultee will willingly and effectively implement as intended

Table 1. Comparison of Collaborative and Expert/Authoritative Styles.

| | Relationship Style | |
Dimension	Collaborative	Expert/ Authoritative
Objectives/goals	Resolve presenting problem and improve consultee skills	Resolve presenting problem
Target of behavior change	Client and consultee	Client
Relationship	Equal partners	Superior/ subordinate
Person responsible for client for intervention development	Consultee Consultant and consultee	Consultee Consultant
Consultee involvement in problem solving	Extensive	Minimal
Amount of information generated about problem situation	Usually extensive	Minimal to extensive
Number of alternatives generated	Usually multiple	Often one
Assumption about consultee's involvement	Wants to be involved in problem solving	Wants consultant to solve problem
Time involved	Usually greater	Usually less
Person with problem-solving expertise	Consultant and consultee	Consultant

the strategies prescribed by the consultant without having been meaningfully involved in the problem-solving process. Such an approach has been suggested by several authors (for example, Chalfant, Pysh, and Moultrie, 1979; Graebner and Dobbs, 1984; McGlothlin, 1981).

For the reasons discussed throughout this book, we believe that the collaborative approach is far more effective than the expert/ authoritative one under most circumstances. One rare situation in which the expert/authoritative approach may be more effective, and even then only on an interim basis, is when the consultee is essentially in a state of crisis (Curtis and Anderson, 1977). When pressures have created a stress level so high that the consultee cannot participate in or benefit from involvement in problem solving, a collaborative approach is not likely to be effective. Under such circumstances, it might be desirable for the consultant to operate temporarily with expertise and authority. However, the purpose of employing the expert approach would be to immediately reduce the functional stress of the consultee to a moderate level. Consultee involvement then could be established or resumed. In other words, the expert approach would be used only on a temporary basis with the objective being movement toward a collaborative approach as soon as possible.

It also might be necessary to employ the expert/authoritative approach in a situation that is in direct contrast to that just described—that is, when the consultee has extremely little motivation to address a problem. Conceivably, inaction on the part of a consultee may also reflect lack of recognition that a problem exists. In either case, the purpose of the expert approach is to increase the motivation of the consultee to a moderate level so that a collaborative problem-solving process can be utilized effectively. Regardless of the specific circumstances surrounding any student-related problem, a collaborative approach to problem solving is the most appropriate and most effective in the long term.

Cognitive Component. The cognitive component of consultation is the problem-solving dimension. While the affective component refers to how the consultant views the consultee, the cognitive component refers to how the consultant views the problem. For example, although Bergan (1977) describes a behavioral orientation to problem solving and Caplan (1970) advocates a mental health orientation, both models usually reflect a generally collaborative approach.

The steps or stages in problem solving may vary in number, but the same general pattern of problem solving remains consistent across various approaches. Moreover, both individual consultants and intervention assistance teams use the same problem-solving process. A detailed discussion of the consultative problem-solving process is in Chapter Four.

Consultant Skills

In order to effectively engage in consultation, the consultant must have four areas of expertise: systems/ecological theory, a professional specialty, individual and group problem solving, and interpersonal influence.

Systems/ecological theory is described briefly in this as well as in other chapters. Those discussions convey a general framework within which to consider student problems. A thorough foundation in this area requires formal study of both systems theory and the ecological variables that influence student learning and behavior (Bandura, 1977, 1986).

Professional specialty is the particular body of knowledge and skills that each professional brings to the consultative relationship. For example, a school social worker can contribute special knowledge in such areas as family processes and community characteristics and resources. A classroom teacher has knowledge of curriculum development and instructional methodologies. Parents have knowledge of the long-term development and experiences of their children. Each of these people has the responsibility to share expertise during problem solving.

Individual and group problem solving is the cognitive component of consultation discussed previously. It includes the consultant's and consultee's perspectives of the problem and the steps that they follow in trying to solve it. Despite possessing extensive knowledge in a specialty, a sound foundation in the systems/ecological perspective, and effective interpersonal skills, a consultant or intervention assistance team will likely experience little success in responding to the special needs of students without expertise in problem solving. Chapter Four discusses the problem-solving process as it should be used by individuals as well as groups.

Interpersonal influence is the affective component of consultation. Because consultation is an interaction among two or more persons, the ways in which participants influence one another through their interpersonal behaviors are extremely important in determining the success of their efforts.

Moreover, consultants must understand those interpersonal variables that can influence the problem-solving process. Factors that play a role in interpersonal influence are discussed in several places in this book. In this chapter, collaboration, consultee involvement, strategy implementation, the voluntary nature of consultation, and confidentiality were examined as factors affecting the relationship between the consultant and the consultee. Chapter Nine includes a discussion of some of the barriers that may be encountered in attempts to implement an intervention assistance program, several of which are interpersonal in nature. However, other factors that affect interpersonal influence deserve special consideration.

Communication skills are a major influence in the consultant/consultee relationship. Although an expansive body of literature addresses the general topic of communication skills (Benjamin, 1969; Carkhuff and Berenson, 1967; Gordon, 1974; Okun, 1976), Gutkin and Curtis (1982) specifically discuss the use of reflective listening skills, empathy, paraphrasing, summarizing, confrontation, and nonpossessive warmth for effective consultation. They also emphasize the critical nature of genuineness in communication. "Those who sacrifice spontaneity of expression in return for a rigid application of recommended communication techniques typically impair their effectiveness as consultants by coming across as artificial and insincere" (p. 822).

Gutkin and Curtis (1982) note that sociocultural context should also be considered; different communication techniques may have to be implemented differently depending on the cultural background of the consultee. The consultant must therefore be particularly sensitive to the implications of cultural differences for interactions with the consultee.

Attributions are our beliefs about the causes of behaviors or events. How the consultee explains a student's behavior can have a significant bearing on the consultative process. For example, a teacher may infer that a student's acting-out behavior is caused primarily by factors internal to the student. Believing that the cause for the problem is within the student, the teacher is likely to feel little control over the situation and to look to others to solve the problem. One strategy for addressing inaccurate attributions is to pursue clarification of the problem in behaviorally descriptive terms. Doing so provides the consultee with a different perspective from which to consider the student-related concern and encourages consideration of environmental factors as possible contributors to the problem. As we have mentioned, Tombari and Bergan (1978) found that the use of behavioral verbal cues by consultants resulted in consultees' increased confidence in their ability to resolve student-related problems and less likelihood that the consultee would believe it necessary to refer the problem to someone else.

Therefore, the consultant should attempt to understand the consultee's perceptions of the cause of the problem under discussion. However, it also is important to consider the consultant's attributions for the problem as these determine the framework within which the problem is analyzed and the interventions are developed. Both the consultant and the consultee need to maintain perspectives that facilitate intervention development rather than labeling.

The consultant should also remain sensitive to how the consultee perceives the behaviors of the consultant. Consultee assumptions regarding the consultant's ulterior motives, attitude about the abilities of the consultee, and so forth, can prove troublesome to the relationship and therefore to efforts to work together. Similarly, consultant attributions regarding the behaviors of the consultee can have a significant influence on their interactions. Different assumptions about the consultee can lead to different attempts to influence the consultative process. For example, an assumption that the consultee is not committed to implementing an agreed-upon intervention would call for markedly different interactive strategies by the consultant than would an assumption that the consultee does not possess adequate knowledge or skills to implement the intervention effectively.

Besides attending to perceptions of causation, reframing a student-related problem so that it is viewed from a different perspective can be helpful (Watzlawick, Weakland, and Fisch, 1974). For instance, if faced with multiple sources of stress and concern, a teacher may tend to think of a particular child as always misbehaving, when in fact the disruptive behaviors do not occur that often. It would be appropriate to clarify the situation from an objective perspective. Moreover, during problem solving there may be a tendency to focus only on a student's problems and to overlook the student's strengths. Reframing a problem to reflect student strengths may help increase the consultee's expectations for successful resolution.

Expert power and referent power can be significant influences on the consultative process (Martin, 1978). Expert power is influence associated with the consultant based on the consultee's perceptions of the consultant's knowledge or skills. Referent power is influence associated with the consultant based on the consultee's perceptions of common feelings, attitudes, values, or behaviors. Both are necessary, but neither is sufficient in an effective consultative relationship. Expert power can be advanced by familiarizing the consultee with the consultant's advanced training, presentations to professional organizations, and relevant publications, while referent power is enhanced by identification with the consultee on a personal level.

Although it is important that the consultant is perceived as having special expertise, respect for the knowledge and skills of the consultee should also be a fundamental component of the interactive process. "Unequal power relationships do not facilitate effective problem solving" (Zins, 1985, p. 122).

Consultant self-efficacy is also likely to have substantial influence during the problem-solving process. If the consultant sounds tentative and unsure, the consultee may not be willing to invest a great deal of time and energy in implementing intervention strategies developed during their interactions.

The confidence of the consultee has a bearing on the outcomes of the consultative process as well. Bandura (1977) notes that willingness to invest time and energy in efforts to resolve a challenging problem is related to expectations for success. Consequently, the consultee who has self-doubts will probably be hesitant or unable to make the personal commitment that may be necessary to implement an intervention effectively. Both moral and technical support may be extremely important in such cases.

CHAPTER FOUR

Step-By-Step Process of Helping Teachers Help Their Students

I n Chapter Three, we noted that consultation consists of both affective and cognitive components. This chapter presents a detailed discussion of the cognitive dimension—that is, the sequential stages of problem solving. After discussion of the problem-solving process, special considerations in the use of group problem solving are examined.

Problem-Solving Process

The stages of the problem-solving process apply to individual consultants as well as to teams. They are illustrated in Figure 3 and are described here.

Communication with Parents and the Student

Whenever a teacher becomes concerned about a student's progress, a good practice is to communicate directly with the parents to obtain their ideas and support. Parental involvement is important from several perspectives. First, the child's school performance has an effect on home behavior, and school behavior is affected by factors in the home. Second, parents have a right to be informed about school-related concerns and to be included in intervention plans whenever possible. Parents should be included because of the contribution they can make to the problem-solving process and not simply because of the necessity of obtaining legal

Figure 3. Options for Solving Student-Related Problems.

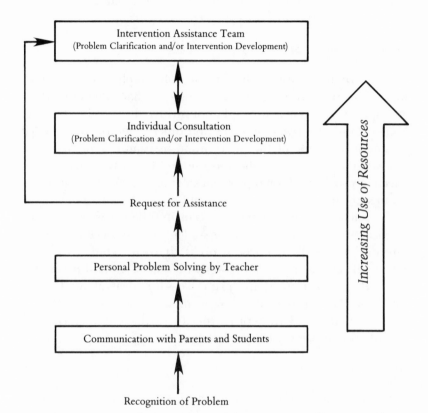

consent. Parents are often important participants and collaborators in problem clarification, treatment planning, and implementation of intervention strategies. The classroom teacher usually initiates the home contact by phone, by a note, or (preferably) through a meeting. The purpose is to communicate the nature of the concern, to elicit the parents' input, and to discuss plans to proceed.

Classroom teachers should also attempt to include the student in these early communications. Frequently, students are not told specifically about a teacher's concern and are not asked for their perspective on the problem. Students can participate, even at a young age, by explaining how they see the problem, offering suggestions for improvement, and choosing potential reinforcers that can be incorporated into intervention plans.

Personal Problem Solving by the Teacher

Certainly, most teachers try to solve problems before they initiate referrals, although research suggests that quite often these attempts are not systematic or do not involve the use of techniques known to be effective (Ysseldyke and others, 1983a). An intended long-term outcome of the intervention assistance approach is to increase the ability of teachers to use problem-solving techniques effectively so that informal problem solving is likely to occur before or, in some instances, even in place of formal consultation.

Such problem solving can occur in different ways. Usually, teachers first attempt to resolve the student-related concern by trying alternatives in the classroom on their own. They also often informally ask their colleagues—other teachers, support personnel, curriculum supervisors, the principal—for ideas about how to intervene. These problem-solving methods are less structured than the systematic and in-depth procedures that characterize the consultation process, which is described next.

Request for Assistance

The intervention assistance process is initiated when concern is expressed about some aspect of a student's performance or behavior and consultation assistance is requested to deal with the concern. To facilitate this process, the school must have clearly defined procedures (as will be discussed in Chapter Ten), which may include filling out a simple and easy-to-complete form on which problems can be outlined and attempts to resolve them described.

Individual Consultation

A request for assistance is usually discussed first during individual consultation. To help the person seeking assistance (most often a classroom teacher) identify a professional with expertise appropriate for the area of concern, districts should ensure that all personnel are familiar with the roles and responsibilities of other personnel, especially the providers of special services. When asked for consultative assistance, a prospective consultant can then if necessary direct the teacher to another professional better suited to respond to the specific request.

Data generated at this stage regarding clarification of the problem and interventions attempted should be recorded. Often-times, procedures such as CBA or behavioral assessment are appropriate as a means of gathering data and clarifying the problem. If the participants decide after problem clarification that the problem cannot be dealt with effectively at this level or if intervention efforts prove unsuccessful, the assistance of the building-level team (described in the next section) should be requested. Although requests for assistance typically begin with individual consultants, nothing should preclude initial contact with the intervention assistance team, particularly when a problem is especially difficult or serious.

Intervention Assistance Team

The intervention assistance team usually includes special services staff, an administrator, representative classroom teacher(s), and the teacher requesting assistance. (Additional discussion of the structure and operation of these teams can be found in the last section of this chapter.) A team approach is most appropriate when a case is particularly complex and it is important to draw upon the expertise of many team members, to coordinate their efforts, and to facilitate communication among them. When considering use of a team, the time costs associated with involving so many profession-als on a single case must be weighed against the potential advantages.

There are three alternative procedures to consider when an intervention assistance team is used. First, the team may be used to review and clarify the problem and assist in deciding further actions. With this approach, it is often necessary to end the first meeting with the decision to collect additional data that will help clarify the problem and then to schedule another session. Usually, once the problem has been clarified, it is most efficient to assign an individual team member to serve as the primary consultant to engage in problem solving with the person seeking help. The assignment of the primary consultant is made by matching expertise, skill, and time available with the specific features of the identified case. This approach may be most appropriate when a number of team members have knowledge about the student and therefore can assist in problem clarification.

A second option is for the special services staff member who was approached by the teacher to first engage in individual consultation to define and clarify the problem and collect needed data before the teacher meets with the entire team. Both of these professionals then would present the case to the team. This method allows the expertise of the multidisciplinary team members to be focused on brainstorming and problem-solving activities. It is particularly useful with complex, multifaceted problems in which the expertise of a number of disciplines is needed. While gaining access to the expertise of the team is a clear advantage of this approach, care must be taken to ensure that all details of potential solutions are addressed. Too often, we have observed team meetings to result in superficial intervention development.

As another option, the whole team can engage in the entire problem-solving process. All of the advantages cited in the other two options are then available. However, given the complexity of group dynamics, the extensive costs, and the amount of work that would result if the team pursued all cases in depth, this format can be unwieldy and ineffective. Consequently, it is desirable to limit the use of this approach.

Problem-Solving Steps

The eight steps constituting the problem-solving sequence are discussed in detail here. These steps are used in informal problem solving, by individual consultants, and by teams.

Step 1: Clarifying the Problem

The first step in problem solving is to clarify, or clearly define, the problem or concern. It seems obvious that a problem cannot be solved until it is defined in detail. In fact, research on the consultation process has shown that this initial step is critical to achieving problem solution. According to Bergan and Tombari (1976), once the problem is identified, a solution for the problem almost always follows. In order to clarify the problem, several actions need to be taken; these include exploring the many possible factors that may be affecting the problem from a systems/ecological perspective, determining the appropriate organizational level on which to focus interventions, identifying the real problem, and defining the problem in specific, behavioral language.

Systems Framework. Attempts to define a problem must include careful exploration of the wide range of factors that can be contributing to the problem or, more importantly, that can be critical for the development of interventions. The way in which a problem is defined determines the interventions that are considered. For example, if a student's difficulty with reading is defined as a reading disability (a condition presumed to be due to some processing problem), resulting actions might include the administration of tests to diagnose the disability and consideration of special-class placement. Alternately, if the reading difficulty is defined as the student's not having acquired needed phonic skills because of limited exposure to them, intervention efforts could include altering classroom instructional methods and increasing practice through peer tutoring.

How a problem is defined reveals underlying attributions for the source of the problem (for example, whether it is perceived as a "child" problem, a "home" problem, an "instructional" problem). The attribution assigned also has implications for expectations about intervention outcomes. If attributions for a problem are internal to the child (a learning disability, laziness, immaturity), positive expectations for teacher interventions are unlikely. However, if attributions are external to the child (has not had sufficient opportunity to learn the material, has not been adequately reinforced), then expectations for solving the problem are markedly increased. Research on teacher attributions for student problems (Christenson and others, 1983; Medway, 1979a) has shown that teachers tend to attribute causes to the child or to the home rather than to classroom or instructional variables. Thus, some teachers define problems in ways that make intervention efforts difficult.

Various systems-level issues that can influence student learning are listed in Table 2. These range from factors affecting a large number of individuals at the school or district level to factors internal to the individual student.

At the school or district level, factors that influence student learning include the curriculum, policies and procedures regarding special services, and intervention options. For example, a given curriculum may be better suited to students who learn quickly than to students who have difficulty learning. If the district requires the same curriculum for all students, the result for many may be failure.

At the classroom level, research has shown that several features consistently characterize effective classrooms. These variables can be manipulated so that they result in significant gains in student achievement and behavior. This category is one of the most important yet frequently overlooked contributors to student performance.

Peer, family, and student variables also need to be considered. Peer relationships are particularly important when there are concerns about behavior or social skills. Family and home factors also are important for understanding how family members may be involved in intervention designs. Finally, student factors, including skills and behaviors, need to be examined and targeted for intervention.

Determining the Appropriate Organizational Level for Intervention. Using a systems approach, the consultant and consultee determine possible contributors to the problem and decide which organizational level to target for intervention efforts. In general, the higher the level targeted, the greater the number of students affected. When a district, school, or classroom variable, rather than a student variable, is significant, intervening generally benefits more students. For example, in a district in which one of us worked, it was determined that the reading problem of a referred student was related to a districtwide policy regarding reading instruction and choice of curriculum. Intervention efforts focused simultaneously on modification of the district policy and on changes in the instructional approach for the student. As another

Table 2. Factors Influencing Students' School Performance.

School/District

Curriculum
Special services available
Program options
Policies and procedures

Classroom

Instruction (presentation, pacing, monitoring, reinforcement, motivational strategies)
Curriculum
Opportunity to learn (engaged time)
Physical environment (grouping, arrangement, distractions)
Classroom environment (climate)
Teacher variables (expectations, tolerances)

Peers

Interactions
Stressors/support systems

Family

Parenting
Stressors/support systems
Interactions

Student

Academic skills
Social behaviors
Task-related behaviors (study skills)
Motivation

example, consider a student who has problems with behavior because of behavior-management techniques that the teacher applies to the entire classroom. In this case, it would be desirable for consultation to focus on changing the classroom organization and behavior-management strategies rather than on developing an intervention program for the individual student.

Identifying the Real Problem. A potential pitfall is failure to identify and solve the real problem. Reaching premature definition of a problem or failing to clarify it adequately can preclude effective problem solving.

All of us have probably had the experience of developing a solution to an apparently simple problem only to learn later that the problem we solved was superficial and that the real problem was much more complex. A teacher, for example, may express concern about a child's task completion, but when attempts to get the child to complete work are successful, a "new" problem crops up—the child calls out instead of raising his hand or bothers other children, or does not listen to instructions. Sometimes, when new problems continually surface, the underlying issue may be quite different from the one being discussed. Efforts to clarify all aspects of the problem, including the consultee's perspective of it, make it more likely the real problem will be identified.

Defining Problems in Behavioral Terms. Once the real problem has been identified, it must be clearly and specifically defined before it can be solved. Allowing a problem definition to be vague and unspecified ("she's behind in reading") can lead to failure in consultation. If the specifics of a problem are unclear, the criteria for success will also be vague. As a result, it will be difficult to select an appropriate intervention strategy or to determine whether intervention efforts are effective. The possibility of solving problems defined in specific, behavioral terms is markedly greater.

Two aspects of performance must be clarified—the current performance level that is problematical and the desired performance level that would be considered acceptable. Once the problem is defined in clear, behavioral terms, the goal is described in similar terms, and the discrepancy between the student's current level and where he or she needs to be is determined. Interventions are targeted to reduce this discrepancy.

As an example, a teacher describes a student as "lazy and never getting his work done." Because these problems are not adequately defined, the consultant needs to elicit information about the specific behaviors that demonstrate laziness: Exactly how much work does he accomplish in each subject? Under what circumstances (for example, reading assignments, written reports, days of the week)? How does his completion rate compare with the teacher's expectations for him and for the class? Through this process, the consultant can determine that over the last two weeks the student completed only one of ten reading assignments, and only two of ten in each of language, math, science, and social studies, while the class average was over nine of ten in each area. Additionally, the completed assignments were handed in on Fridays, the day students receive free time if they turn in their work. This added information provides a clear definition of the problem and a basis for setting a goal as well as for determining whether progress has been made.

As demonstrated in this example, questioning is used to elicit information about specific behaviors, the contexts in which they occur, and the determinants of their occurrence. Additional data-gathering methods, such as having the teacher, student, or parent collect baseline data on behaviors of concern, can be employed. Baseline data include both specific measures of occurrences of behavior and existing permanent products (grade book, work samples), and can be relatively simple to collect. Observation by an independent observer (for example, the consultant) can be used to define specific behavioral occurrences and their contexts and to note pertinent classroom variables. Examples of these methods are highlighted in Chapters Five and Six.

Step 2: Analyzing Components of the Problem

After the problem is identified and defined behaviorally, the various components that may be contributing to the situation are analyzed, again utilizing a systems framework. All possible factors that may influence or maintain the problem are considered. The goal of this step is to determine antecedent and consequent events and the environmental contexts in which the specific behavior occurs. Information that might be helpful would include where and when the problem behavior occurs, the behaviors of others before or in response to the behavior, and conditions under which desired behaviors occur. For example, a behavioral analysis of a girl's antagonism toward peers may reveal that (a) she initiates negative behaviors that provoke peers to react negatively toward her; (b) when peers react negatively, she escalates her own antagonistic behaviors; and (c) this happens only between classes and during recess with two specific peers. Such a problem analysis can be used to identify specific targets for intervention. In this example, the student's behavior, peer reaction to the behavior, and the environ-mental context of her behavior are all viable targets. In some cases intervening in one area may be sufficient (for example, increasing supervision during recess or classroom changes). At other times, it may be necessary to target all identified areas for intervention in order to resolve the problem.

Step 3: Exploring Intervention Options

After a target or targets are selected, brainstorming for intervention options takes place. In this process, as many ideas as possible are generated without first evaluating them. It is crucial to refrain from evaluating ideas until the brainstorming process is completed in order not to stifle production and creativity. Next, alternative approaches, along with their feasibility, acceptability, utility, costs, and anticipated effectiveness, are considered.

Being aware of a broad range of intervention options is important. There are many sources of intervention ideas—the consultant and the consultee, other teachers and school resource personnel, the referred student and parents, and the professional literature. Many procedures that have been demonstrated to be effective in remediating a number of commonly occurring problems are summarized in Chapters Five and Six.

Alternative interventions may also be generated by a building-level intervention assistance team. Sharing intervention ideas among school professionals is one of the benefits of such interdisciplinary groups. Also, the team may identify interventions that currently are not available schoolwide but that are believed to be needed (peer tutoring, parent volunteers, adapted instruction). As a result, needed changes at high levels of the organization may be identified.

Step 4: Selecting Interventions

After a broad range of potential interventions is considered, the interventions are evaluated, and then one or more are selected for implementation based on the likely reduction of the current/desired performance discrepancy identified in Step 1. The selection of an intervention must be left to the classroom teacher or parent who will have primary responsibility for carrying it out. If a strategy is imposed by someone else (for example, the consultant), it is unlikely that it will be implemented as intended (Curtis and Anderson, 1977). The intervention must be acceptable to the user in its focus, ease of use, impact on the entire classroom, intrusiveness, cost and time effectiveness, and so forth. Often, a teacher or parent likes a particular strategy but feels that it is too difficult or time consuming to implement. At this point, participants may work to modify the intervention so that it becomes manageable.

Step 5: Clarifying Implementation Procedures

Once an intervention is selected, the next step is to explicitly discuss and agree on how the intervention is to be implemented. During this discussion, several aspects of the implementation process must be clarified.

Who? What are the roles and responsibilities of the teacher, the parents, the student? What assistance will the consultant provide? How can the principal support the intervention? What is the role of support staff (locating curricular materials, helping collect evaluation data)? Are other students involved (as peer tutors, peer reinforcers)? The specific roles and responsibilities of participants must be made clear so that each understands and agrees to the procedure.

How? What specifically is to be done differently for this student? What techniques will be used? What reinforcers will be tried? Sufficient detail is necessary so that the intervention is clear to all persons involved.

When? When will the plan be implemented? For how long will it be tried before its effectiveness is evaluated? Does the intervention span the entire school day, or is it to be implemented only during specific periods (reading, all academic subjects)? Does the intervention occur daily (oral reading drill) or weekly (a social-skills group)?

In making these decisions, the consultant and consultee need to decide whether the intervention is to be applied specifically to one situation (for example, math lessons) or whether it should be globally applied (for example, an intervention to increase work completion in all subjects). Another factor to consider is generalization of effects to other times and settings. For example, if an intervention is implemented to increase appropriate peer interactions within the classroom, the possibility of extending the intervention to encourage appropriate interactions in the hall, the lunchroom, and the playground should be considered.

Where? In what setting will the intervention take place? Is it primarily school- or home-based? Will it take place in more than one setting? Are there provisions for backup reinforcement and generalization of intervention effects to other settings?

Record Keeping. As all of these items are clarified, records should be maintained that specify the intervention plan and procedures. The main purpose of the written intervention plan is to clarify the various aspects so that all participants understand them sufficiently to perform their assigned duties. A secondary purpose is to have a record for future use. Record keeping is discussed in Chapter Ten.

Step 6: Implementing the Intervention Strategy

The careful planning and collaborative decision making that have occurred in all previous steps should facilitate the implementation of the intervention. However, two additional factors can also increase the likelihood that the intervention will be appropriately implemented. First is close follow-up contact by the consultant to provide any needed technical support as well as to provide assistance and encouragement to the consultee. In other words, the process does not end once an intervention is undertaken. It is desirable for the consultant and consultee to plan regularly scheduled meetings (after three days, one week, two weeks) to consider the effectiveness of the intervention plan. However, this decision to meet again should usually rest with the consultee. Nevertheless, the consultant should remain available for follow-up services as needed and to help in collecting data on intervention effectiveness.

A second consideration is ensuring the integrity of the intervention—that is, implementing the specified plan as closely as possible to the original design. An intervention does not have integrity if essential components are omitted or if a person does not carry out his or her role as planned. In these instances, the erroneous conclusion can be reached that the intervention did not work when in fact the specified intervention was not given an adequate chance. Ongoing contact between the consultant and consultee can help assure that the plan is appropriately implemented. It is also important to allow sufficient time for the intervention to be fully implemented and for desired outcomes to be achieved.

Step 7: Evaluating Intervention Effectiveness

The next step in the problem-solving process is to evaluate the effectiveness of the intervention. Procedures for monitoring the intervention need to be clarified. To determine effectiveness, some form of data collection needs to occur. Many methods of data collection can be used for evaluation; they are often the same methods that were used to assess the problem. Data collection can be as simple as keeping a student's daily work samples (for example, to determine percentage completed or percentage correct) or having the teacher or student keep daily counts of target behaviors.

More desirable than these methods are single-subject and multiple-baseline designs (Barlow, Hayes, and Nelson, 1984; Kazdin, 1980). Although these techniques have some methodological and interpretive problems, they are useful in evaluating intervention effectiveness and have grown in popularity. The reversal design, employed most frequently, enables the practitioner to examine the effect of an intervention by presenting and withdrawing a treatment at different points in time. A single behavior is usually targeted for change. In a multiple-baseline design, several behaviors, individuals, or settings are targeted for change. This design is used to demonstrate the effect of an intervention through its introduction at various points in time. Thus, it is not necessary to withdraw the intervention, an action that may be ethically questionable or at least professionally objectionable.

Although these and other methods are available to determine

the outcomes of an intervention effort, busy practitioners often omit the evaluation step. However, only through such efforts is it possible to determine the efficacy of the intervention process.

Step 8: Determining Next Steps

After the evaluation of intervention effectiveness, several outcomes are possible. If the intervention was effective, it may be decided to continue with the plan, gradually phase out the plan, extend the intervention to other settings, or design a second intervention for another priority area. When an intervention proves effective, it is not necessary to report back to the entire team. Records for the individual consultation sessions should be available to document outcomes, taking into account the legal and ethical issues discussed in Chapter Twelve.

If the intervention was not effective, previous phases of the problem-solving process can be reviewed to determine whether the problem needs to be redefined, current intervention plans need to be modified or extended, alternative interventions need to be planned and implemented, or other steps need to be taken. In such cases, the consultant and consultee may meet with the intervention assistance team to review the results of the interventions and to obtain the group's assistance in devising next steps. This action may be warranted at this stage either to utilize the team's full expertise to design further interventions or to consider the possibility of moving toward a restrictive phase of decision making, such as a determination of eligibility for special education services.

The intervention assistance team applies the problem-solving steps just discussed. However, additional considerations related to group process must be taken into account. These variables are discussed in the next section.

Group Problem Solving

As noted, the steps to problem solving discussed here are the cognitive component in consultation and are utilized in both informal problem solving and in one-to-one and group consultation. Regardless of the number of people involved in providing intervention assistance, problem solving should follow the same sequential process in order to maximize effectiveness. It is as important for a group (for example, an intervention assistance team) to proceed through these stages sequentially as it is for an individual consultant or a teacher to do so.

However, the use of teams introduces a number of special issues related to the affective/interpersonal dimension of consultation; these issues must be addressed if groups are to engage in effective problem solving. Although the team provides an expanded repertoire of knowledge and skills, the increased number of participants adds to the complexity of the interactive process. Ulschak, Nathanson, and Gillan (1981) note that "perhaps the most neglected area of problem solving concerns human resources, the people who participate in the problem-solving group. It is not unusual for a leader to overemphasize the intellectual process of problem solving and overlook what is happening to the people who generate ideas" (p. 7).

Pfeiffer and Heffernan (1984) point out that multidisciplinary teams have a long history in children's services, dating back to at least 1909. However, despite this fact and the availability of an extensive body of relevant literature, many existing assistance teams seem to violate the most basic rules about group process and decision making.

In many cases, teams are created and go into operation within a short period of time. Although attention is given to the representation of various disciplines, other equally important considerations, such as knowledge of team strategies, interpersonal factors, and problem-solving skills, seem to be overlooked. In reality, extensive planning and preparation, as well as ongoing maintenance, are essential in the introduction and continuance of effective problem-solving groups.

We discuss issues and strategies associated with the implementation of intervention assistance programs in Chapters Seven through Ten. Issues specific to problem-solving groups that merit special consideration are discussed here.

Sanction and Support

Administration. District-level sanction and support are essential for the implementation of an intervention assistance model of services delivery. However, building-level support is directly relevant to the use and functioning of a team. Even though the establishment of teams may be mandated on a districtwide basis, the attitude of the building administrator has a significant bearing on the effectiveness of the group within a particular setting. For example, Kuehnel (1975) found that organizational climate (which is determined to a great extent by the principal) influenced the frequency of use of mental health resources by classroom teachers. Consequently, in a closed organizational climate in which teachers are expected to take care of their own problems, a team is likely to find itself with few requests for assistance. Moreover, because principals sometimes serve as members of building-level teams, personal support for or resistance to the team has a major impact on the functioning of the group. On a logistical level, administrators control variables such as release time and scheduling adjustments that facilitate the attendance of school personnel at group meetings (Yoshida, 1983). Consequently, building administrators must understand and support not only intervention assistance services in general but the purposes and uses of specific components such as the problem-solving team and consultation as well.

Staff. Administrative sanction and support are necessary but not sufficient for the effective use of building-level teams. One of the most common and serious problems encountered in efforts to introduce the intervention assistance concept has been the failure to meaningfully involve regular education personnel in both the planning and the implementation phases of the process. Because regular classroom teachers bear primary responsibility for nonhandicapped students and are the typical initiators of the referral process in many current delivery systems, the failure to gain their understanding and support for building-level teams precludes success from the outset.

Clarity of Purpose

Another problem that has, in part, resulted from the failure to involve regular education personnel has been confusion and misunderstanding regarding the purposes of building-level teams.

One frequent misconception is that the team is a new way to get students into special education. Although this particular misunderstanding is probably related largely to the role of multidisciplinary teams in the special education decision-making process, it also reflects a lack of attention to involving regular educators. All parties need to understand the purposes of problem-solving teams. In addition to regular educators and administrators, these people include all potential members of the team itself and parents.

As indicated throughout this book, the major purpose of such teams is problem solving in regard to students' needs. The primary vehicle for the problem-solving process and for the development and implementation of effective interventions is collaborative consultation. Although teams provide operational support to teachers or parents who bear primary responsibility for students, the ultimate objective remains responsiveness to the needs of students. It is critical that the team not be viewed as a vehicle for or obstacle to special education, but rather as a mechanism to assist in resolving student-related problems in the classroom.

Structure

Models. The types of teams used in schools vary. Although some systems employ ad hoc teams, most use standing teams. Ad hoc teams, as the name implies, are created in response to specific problems. When a unique situation arises, an ad hoc team may be most appropriate because it is created to serve a specific purpose. However, such teams may not be as effective as standing teams in the long run because membership varies, and as a result, it is difficult for those involved to develop an effective working relationship.

Standing teams remain basically intact. In accordance with general systems theory, the character and effectiveness of each system (in this case, the team) are determined by the unique composition and interaction of its component parts. When any of the parts change, the system as a whole also changes. In order to increase the success of the team, it may be desirable to keep group membership as consistent as possible.

Some districts use core teams, which retain certain persons across all cases but add others on an ad hoc basis in response to special circumstances. Because there are bound to be situations in which the unique needs of a student require the involvement of additional people, the core team may be most effective for many districts. It allows for the development of a relatively intact team, while responding to unique situational demands through the addition of a select number of others when needed.

Size and Membership. Decisions regarding the type of team to be used have a bearing on team size and composition. An ad hoc team tends to be relatively small because selection of members is based on specific circumstances pertaining to a given case. A standing team is somewhat larger than an ad hoc team because members need to be able to respond to a broad range of problems. A core team itself is somewhat small but is reinforced by additional people on occasion. Regardless of the model chosen, the optimal number of participants for problem-solving groups is generally between six and ten (Ulschak, Nathanson, and Gillan, 1981). In fact, some suggest that decision making is maximized when the number is seven or fewer (Ohio Department of Education, 1985).

Typically, members of intervention assistance teams include special services personnel (such as a school nurse, school psychologist, school social worker, guidance counselor, and speech and language therapist), a special education consultant or teacher, and a regular education teacher. It is also desirable to provide for grade-level representation, which can be accomplished by having teachers represent specific grades (if membership varies) or represent a general level such as the intermediate grades (when stable membership is desired) (Ohio Department of Education, 1985). Some suggest that parents be included in teams (Pfeiffer and Heffernan, 1984; Pfeiffer and Tittler, 1983). However, although we fully agree with the desire to involve parents in the educational process, our experience has been that a team can be somewhat overwhelming for some parents. Special strategies such as the designation of one team member as a family advocate sometimes are helpful in this regard. It may be effective from a variety of perspectives to involve some parents in problem-solving efforts that include a small number of other participants, such as the teacher and a special services consultant. Decisions regarding how to involve parents, not whether to involve them, should be based on the specific circumstances of each case.

Professional knowledge and expertise as well as the breadth of knowledge and skills represented in the group as a whole must be primary considerations in decisions regarding team membership. However, it is also important to consider the interpersonal and problem-solving skills of individuals. Ulschak, Nathanson, and Gillan (1981) suggest that "some members of the group should be invited specifically because they are idea generators; that is, they are creative and are willing to look at things in a new light" (p. 25).

As noted previously, building-level teams often include the principal or another administrator. Inclusion of an administrator has both positive and negative implications. The administrator lends credibility to the group, may be able to encourage a teacher to attempt additional interventions, and may be able to facilitate the availability of various types of support and resources to assist the group in its problem-solving efforts. However, some teachers may be reluctant to discuss concerns in the presence of the principal, who is also responsible for performance evaluations. The inconsistencies between supervision and consultation were discussed in Chapter Three and should be considered carefully in regard to the inclusion of administrators on problem-solving teams. If the merits of including administrators are to outweigh the drawbacks, administrators should remain cognizant of and sensitive to potential pitfalls and reduce the likelihood of their occurrence. Most importantly, they should be guided by the primary purpose of the team—providing problem-solving assistance to classroom teachers for the benefit of students.

Incentives for Participation. For many team members, participation may be an added professional responsibility, which can be a disincentive. It is appropriate and perhaps necessary to provide incentives to members for their efforts. Recognition is one means of encouragement. Other strategies include release time, such as an additional planning period; relief from other responsibilities; supplemental compensation; and special privileges (for example, district support for attendance at professional meetings) (Curtis, Zins, and Graden, 1987; Ohio Department of Education, 1985). Many strategies that serve as incentives for individual participants may also contribute to general recognition of and credibility for the assistance team and its functions.

Duration of Membership. Length of service on a team depends on situational variables and other factors such as team type. The service of some team members may be ongoing, as when a core team is employed. Ongoing membership is also desirable for the long-term development of an effective group, as noted previously. All groups go through a period of growth before achieving functional maturity, and this process requires considerable time (Hersey and Blanchard, 1977). Without a certain amount of stability in group membership, the group will not remain intact long enough to attain functional maturity.

Policy Clarification

All members of the assistance team and all potential users of the team must clearly understand policies and procedures associated with its operation and access to its services. Policies and procedures should be specified in writing and widely disseminated. One district's description is provided in Table 8 (Chapter Eight). Meetings with groups such as the PTA and teacher organizations are helpful in disseminating this information. Interactions with such groups should also occur during the planning stages in order to seek their input before policies and procedures are developed rather than after decisions have already been made. Included in written descriptions should be such information as (a) the purposes of the team and how the team relates to other aspects of services delivery, (b) how a request for assistance is made, (c) what activities may be required prior to a request for team assistance (for example, prior attempts at intervention), (d) what information and documentation should be provided to the team and the format in which a written report should be submitted, (e) meeting procedures, and (f) meeting schedule and location. In addition, these policies should be supportive of informal problem-solving and of individual consultation.

Member Skills

In Chapter Three, we indicated that effective consultants possess knowledge and skills in four different areas: systems theory, a professional specialty, individual and group problem solving, and interpersonal influence. The same four areas are necessary for members of an effective problem-solving group. The systems/ecological perspective is stressed throughout this book as the framework within which students' problems should be considered. One particular advantage of a team approach to problem solving is that, because of its multidisciplinary nature, the team is likely to have access to a variety of sources of information regarding students' problems. Nevertheless, a conscious commitment to a systems/ecological perspective is necessary to avoid assessments and interventions that reflect an internal-to-the-student orientation, and to be certain that a broad range of potentially influential factors are considered.

A special strength of the collaborative consultation model is that it emphasizes the coordination of knowledge and skills from different professional perspectives. The multidisciplinary composition of the intervention assistance team enables the different perspectives of the participants to be brought to bear in providing assistance to the classroom teacher.

The same concepts that were described in Chapter Three regarding the development and maintenance of effective consultative relationships between individuals are also applicable within a group. In addition to consultation skills (for example, questioning and summarization), the attributes that are included in what Gutkin and Curtis (1982) call the "technology of communication" are essential in both settings (genuineness, listening skills, paraphrasing skills, empathy, skills in confrontation).

However, the interactive aspects of a team are much more complex than are those of a dyad. The complex interaction of the many interpersonal forces at play determines the overall effectiveness of the group. Consequently, in addition to all the other knowledge and skills noted to this point, participation in a problem-solving group requires knowledge of group dynamics. Furthermore, the team leader must possess special skills in group facilitation and management.

Training

Verification of member skills in all the areas discussed should be incorporated into the planning process. It is relatively certain that all members will not possess adequate skills in each area. In fact, few members will probably have received formal training in systems theory, consultative problem solving, or group dynamics. Therefore, training in all areas needs to be provided to all participants before teams are established.

Furthermore, once the team is established, members must be trained in small-group problem solving with particular emphasis on the development of a functional, intact unit. Despite the skill levels of the individual members in the areas noted, special attention must be devoted to the development of each team because of the uniqueness of any combination of individuals. The maturation of a group as a highly effective problem-solving unit is likely to take considerable time. This fact is often not understood by group participants, with the result being periods of discouragement and frustration. To achieve team maturation, ongoing team development should take place over a sustained period of time.

Evaluation

Although evaluation is a central component in the intervention assistance system as a whole, it plays a particularly important role in the development and maintenance of the problem-solving team. Evaluation methods, such as those discussed at length in Maher and Bennett (1984), can be used to assess how well the group is functioning as a unit. Results can lead to changes such as additional training for members in identified skill areas or to changes in operation that enhance the effectiveness of the group.

Evaluation methods should also be used to assess the outcome effectiveness of the team. Although factors such as teacher and parent perceptions are important, ultimately the effectiveness of the intervention assistance team must be judged by the benefits realized by students.

CHAPTER FIVE

Intervention Techniques
to Modify Behavior
and Increase Social Competence

W e have been describing a system of providing intervention assistance to school personnel so that they can effectively resolve problems within the regular classroom before referring students for consideration of special education. Although consultants using the intervention assistance process must first and foremost be skilled problem solvers, knowledge of empirically based intervention strategies is also of great importance. Consequently, this chapter and the next provide information about intervention techniques that may be developed and implemented through the consultative process.

This chapter presents a number of empirically based intervention strategies that can help resolve some of the common social and behavioral difficulties experienced by students. Student difficulties in this domain fall into a number of categories including behavioral problems, stress-related difficulties, self-management problems, antisocial behaviors, and social-skills deficits. Chapter Six will focus on intervention strategies that can be used to remediate many commonly encountered academic problems.

Although many methods of intervening exist for each problem discussed, both chapters focus only on interventions that have a sound empirical base, can be implemented through the consultative process, are consistent with a systems view of classrooms and with a social learning view of behavior, are not overly intrusive or restrictive, and are acceptable to most users. A further intent of these chapters is to familiarize readers with the broad range of intervention technology that can be applied through the consultative process. Although it is beyond the scope of the book to provide great detail about any one intervention, sufficient references are provided to facilitate easy access to such information. The problem-solving steps described in Chapter Four should be utilized to design, implement, and evaluate any of the various interventions described in this chapter and the next.

Assessment of Target Behaviors

Requirements

Prior to intervention development, a thorough assessment of the presenting problem must be conducted. Assessment is a process of gathering data to answer specific questions about a problem and is not synonymous with testing, which is only one method of assessment. In conducting an assessment it is important to have a systems perspective, recognizing that problems result from a reciprocal interaction between the child and the instructional setting (see Bandura, 1977). Assessment information needs to be collected under the guiding principle that it be useful and necessary for intervention. For example, data gathered for intervention purposes might include a functional analysis of the problem behavior, an assessment of the various environments in which the problem exists, and descriptions of the attitudes, attributions, and expectations of both the student and significant others.

Methods

Assessment of the problem generally begins with the consultative interview, during which information is gathered. This information includes specific details about the problem(s) demonstrated by the student, the contingencies maintaining the behavior and the consequences of the behavior, and past attempts to resolve the difficulties (Kratochwill, 1985). The consultative interview alone is often an adequate method for assessing the problem for the purpose of developing interventions. However, in some cases multiple assessment strategies are advisable in order to gain a thorough and valid understanding of the different aspects of the problem. These other strategies may include the use of standardized and nonstandardized observations, behavior checklists, question-naires, rating scales, and self-monitoring devices or systems.

Assessment strategies should be selected only as they are needed to clarify a problem and to help in developing interventions. The least intrusive and most parsimonious assessment strategies should be employed first. A list of some of the commonly used assess-ment procedures is presented in Table 3. A thorough discussion of some of these procedures can be found in Gelfand and Hartmann (1984) and Shapiro (1987).

When choosing assessment techniques, it is important to keep in mind that the same problem can be assessed on various behavioral levels. For example, a teacher may consult about a girl who is exhibiting aggressive behaviors on the playground. One level of assessment would be to collect data on the child's overt behaviors by identifying the types of aggressive behaviors the child exhibits and taking frequency counts of their occurrence during playground activities. Given the evidence that aggressive children may appraise social situations differently from the way their nonaggressive peers do (Meichenbaum, 1986b), a second level of assessment would be to ask the child to monitor self-talk or thoughts just prior to engaging in an aggressive act to understand how she perceives the situation. Finally, the child's behavior will have an effect on how other children and adults interact with her. Consequently, observation of others' reactions to the aggressive acts and assessment of the willingness of these people to approach the child and initiate positive play may be warranted.

The assessment strategies used to identify and clarify problems can also be used to monitor student progress toward goals and determine intervention effectiveness. As assessment data are collected, the information is utilized to select appropriate target behaviors, establish a baseline of student performance, develop goals and objectives for the student, determine appropriate means of interven-ing, and evaluate the effectiveness of the chosen intervention.

Table 3. Common Methods of Assessing Problem Behaviors.

Method	Description
Behavior rating scales and checklists	A caregiver rates the student on a number of behavioral items. Students can also be asked to rate themselves on a similar set of items. Rating scales and checklists can assess a broad range of behaviors or be specific in their focus.
Direct observation	Target behaviors are defined and systematically assessed through use of an observation coding system. Different types of data may be collected such as frequency and duration counts, interval recordings, time samples, or records of antecedents and consequences.
Permanent-product analysis	An analysis is conducted of the products of the student's behavior. Academic work can be saved and assessed for accuracy, completeness, or error patterns, or the number of toys broken during a temper tantrum can be counted.
Self-monitoring	Students are asked to monitor their own behavior. They observe their behavior and then record it in a journal or on a chart. This method is excellent for assessing variables that are not directly observable (for example, covert thought processes).
Peer assessment	Students rate each other according to a predetermined set of behavioral characteristics or provide nominations or rankings of their peers. These techniques can be used to identify students at risk for social-skills deficits.
Role play	Specific situations are described to students, and they must then explain how they would react. Students may also be asked to role play their solutions to problems. These techniques can be helpful in evaluating a student's level of social competence.
Interviews	Structured questioning techniques are used to gather in-depth information relevant to problem clarification and analysis. These procedures can be used with students, teachers, or parents.

Behavioral Interventions

One of the most successful models for remediating problem behaviors in school and home settings is based on the principles of behavior therapy (or behavior modification) and SLT (Wielkiewicz, 1986). A number of effective and empirically sound techniques in this general category can be implemented within a consultative framework. In consultation, teachers and parents are generally responsible for carrying out the specific behavioral intervention. The advantages of having them as the behavioral change agents are that they have usually established a positive relationship with the child, have opportunities to observe the child's behavior and to conduct interventions over long periods of time and across settings, and already serve as important models (Gelfand and Hartmann, 1984). However, because these caretakers often do not have extensive knowledge of behavioral principles or cannot devote a great deal of time to monitoring procedures, it is desirable to keep interventions as uncomplicated and as short as possible.

Behavioral interventions can range from having the teacher increase the amount of praise given to a child for demonstrating appropriate behaviors to comprehensive programs such as contingency contracting, response-cost procedures, and the Good Behavior Game (Barrish, Saunders, and Wolf, 1969). We describe here some widely used and effective behavioral intervention techniques.

Reinforcement

Reinforcement procedures may be utilized in a number of ways to remediate many different behavioral, social, and educational difficulties. Reinforcement techniques generally are used to teach children new skills, eliminate deviant or undesirable behaviors, or motivate children to engage in positive behaviors that may already be in their repertoire but are not being performed at acceptable levels. These approaches assume that behaviors followed by positive consequences will be strengthened or will increase in frequency, while behaviors that are not followed by positive consequences will become weak and will eventually be extinguished (Karoly and Harris, 1986). A few of the reinforcement techniques that can be instituted easily in a school or home setting are described here briefly.

Positive Reinforcement Using an Individual Contingency. This strategy is used most often to teach children new skills or to increase low-frequency desirable behavior. Target behaviors are identified and if the child displays them at an acceptable level, the child is reinforced. If a child does not meet established behavioral goals, then no reinforcement is received.

Gelfand and Hartmann (1984) provide guidelines to follow when establishing a behavioral program and choosing the reinforcers to be utilized: (a) Select realistic and easily achievable behavioral goals, particularly in the beginning of the program. (b) Use a variety of reinforcers (for example, a reinforcement menu) to maintain the child's interest and motivation. A reinforcement menu presents a selection of potential reinforcers (selected with input from the child) on a card; the child can choose a reinforcer from it when goals are achieved. (c) Administer reinforcers frequently and in small amounts. (d) Initially, reinforce immediately after the occurrence of the desired behavior. As the behavior becomes increasingly firmly established, lengthen intervals between performance and reinforcement. (e) Choose reinforcers that are practical and compatible with the intervention plan. Whenever possible, use social reinforcers such as praise and attention or reinforcers that are already part of the child's environment. (f) Whenever possible, use generalized reinforcers such as points, tokens, or stickers that can be exchanged for privileges or other backup reinforcers. (g) Withdraw reinforcers slowly over long period of time and in a planned, systematic manner. Replace with social reinforcers whenever possible.

A program for increasing on-task behavior illustrates how an individual contingency can be implemented in the classroom. Baseline data (the number of papers completed daily during seatwork) revealed that the student currently was completing an average of two out of five papers during seatwork periods; a realistic initial goal was set—to increase to three papers completed daily. Each time the student completed a paper, a sticker was placed on a chart. Stickers were traded (either at school or at home) for privileges or other backup reinforcers. The student met the goal four out of five days during the first week; therefore, the goal was raised to four papers completed daily during the second week. Requirements continued to be increased as the child met the goals. Once the student achieved the final goal of completing all required work for a specified period of time, the reinforcers were faded out slowly. Figure 4 is a chart for monitoring student progress toward specified goals.

Positive Reinforcement Using Peer-Mediated Contingencies. Peers can exert a powerful influence on other children's behavior. Some reinforcement programs take advantage of this influence and involve the entire class in changing a student's disruptive behavior (Kerr and Nelson, 1983). These peer-mediated reinforcement programs are also excellent classroom-management procedures in and of themselves. One such procedure that has been successful in eliminating disruptive behavior is the Good Behavior Game (Barrish, Saunders, and Wolf, 1969). As originally conceived, the Good Behavior Game was a response-cost system (discussed later), but it can be easily modified so that it is based on positive reinforcement procedures. Many teachers with whom we have worked prefer rewarding their students for positive behaviors rather than issuing marks for the occurrence of inappropriate behavior.

In a modified version of the Good Behavior Game, behavioral goals are established for the class, and the children are divided into two or more teams. Disruptive students should be divided equally among the teams. Students' behavior is observed at specific intervals during the class period in which the intervention is in effect, with points awarded to those teams whose members are all working or behaving appropriately. Teams with members who do not meet the behavioral goals do not earn a point at that time. Each team must earn a specified number of points in order to win or receive a reward. Many teachers who use this procedure have the teams working for points for a week and present the reinforcing event on Friday afternoon. Figure 5 is a chart that could be used to monitor team performances on a weekly basis. The rules of the game must be presented clearly, and the children must understand exactly what they need to do to earn points. It is best to implement the program initially during only one class period and to extend the

Figure 4. Work Completion Chart.

Name: _____   Date: _____

Rule: I will do my work each day!

Number of
Work Sheets

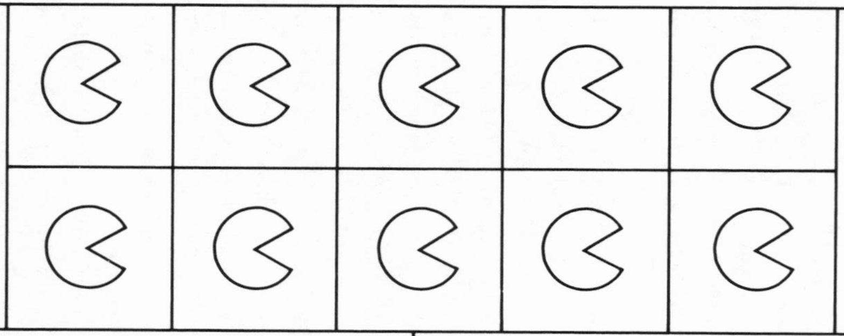

Total
Completed

Criterion

Teacher: _____

Parent: _____

Figure 5. Chart for Monitoring Team Performance When Using a Group Contingency.

Goals

_____

_____

_____

Reward

_____

_____

_____

	Monday	Tuesday	Wednesday	Thursday	Friday
Team 1					
Team 2					
Team 3					

intervention to other periods later if desired. An additional caveat is that such group activities as the Good Behavior Game may produce unintended negative outcomes for children whose behavior keeps the team from earning points. Consequently, the program must be implemented and monitored sensitively in order to circumvent this possibility.

Differential Reinforcement of Other or Incompatible Behavior. Differential reinforcement of other behavior (DRO) and of incompatible (appropriate) behavior (DRI) are used most often to eliminate undesirable behaviors through the strengthening of appropriate desirable behaviors. When using a DRI procedure, it is important to select for reinforcement an incompatible response that is already in the child's skill repertoire and that has a high probability of being maintained in the natural environment (Karoly and Harris, 1986). A slightly different approach, which involves reinforcing the child for exhibiting any behavior other than the problem behavior, DRO is sometimes used to reduce the frequency of self-injurious behavior.

The Principal Game, developed by Darch and Thorpe (1977), combines a DRI procedure with a group contingency. Darch and Thorpe reinforced students for exhibiting on-task behaviors that were incompatible with the disruptive behaviors previously exhibited in the classroom. Examples of on-task behaviors included raising one's hand to answer questions, waiting to be called on, looking at the paper while writing or at the book while reading, and keeping one's eyes on the teacher during presentation of instruction. Students were divided into teams, and a timer was set to go off six times during a class period. Whenever the timer sounded, the teacher awarded points to those teams that had all members working and following classroom rules. Teams that earned five or more points were allowed to spend time with the principal as a reward. This procedure could be used with other reinforcers as well. In evaluating the effectiveness of this procedure, Darch and Thorpe found that student on-task behavior increased from a mean of 26 percent to an overall mean of 86 percent. They point out that in addition to being time efficient and easy to implement, this intervention provides the principal with the opportunity to assume a role as a reinforcing agent rather than as just a disciplinarian.

Modeling

The modeling of behavior occurs naturally in many settings, particularly in the home and in school. As a result, modeling is an extremely viable and potent technique that parents, teachers, and special services personnel can use to change student behavior and facilitate learning. According to SLT, modeling influences learning or behavior change principally through its informative function; the modeled activities serve as guides for appropriate performances (Bandura, 1977). Bandura suggests that in order to learn from behavioral modeling students must attend to what the model is doing, process and remember what the model did, practice what the model did and receive corrective feedback, and begin to use what they have learned at appropriate times.

Modeling has been used successfully to teach children appropriate social skills and classroom behaviors, and to reduce children's fears of testing situations, medical procedures, and newly encountered school situations. Modeling is often an important component of commercially available structured training programs. For example, a program called Structured Learning (McGinnis and others, 1984; Goldstein and others, 1980) which teaches prosocial skills to students, combines modeling with other training techniques such as role play, performance feedback, and transfer of training. (This program is described later in this chapter.)

Parents and teachers have many opportunities to model appropriate behaviors for children through naturally occurring events in the classroom or at home. For example, if one child takes a toy away from another, the teacher or parent can model how to appropriately ask for a toy and then have the child practice similar behaviors. Kendall and Braswell (1985) point out that effective models talk out loud as they demonstrate behavior to show the child how to think through a problem. They also make mistakes and purposefully encounter obstacles so that they can demonstrate strategies for overcoming difficulties and for dealing with frustration and failure.

Modeling can also be incorporated into a classroom as a structured intervention. For example, Sarason and Sarason (1981) developed a program to teach high school students social and cognitive problem-solving skills; the program was incorporated into a regular classroom course. Students who viewed models of social and cognitive problem solving had lower rates of tardiness, school absence, and behavioral referrals than did students who received a different intervention or no intervention.

Peers can also be powerful models. Csapo (1972) taught students to model appropriate classroom behavior for classmates classified as emotionally disturbed. The emotionally disturbed children were told to watch the peer models and to do what they were doing. The peer models gave the target children tokens whenever they were exhibiting appropriate behavior. Inappropriate behaviors to be modified included speaking out of turn, thumb-sucking, and poking others. As a result of the intervention, the emotionally disturbed children exhibited fewer inappropriate behaviors and more appropriate behaviors than they had before.

Procedures to Change the Context of Behaviors

Interventions intended to alter conditions that affect the child's behavior (referred to as stimulus-control procedures) are easy to implement, economical, and in certain circumstances highly effective in promoting positive behavior change (Gelfand and Hartmann, 1984). Essentially, these techniques manipulate antecedent conditions (the factors that seem to influence display of the behavior).

Wurtle and Drabman (1984) introduced a game called Beat the Buzzer into a kindergarten class to help the teacher reduce the amount of time it took for the students to complete cleanup tasks. The teacher imposed a time limit by setting a timer and asking the children to clean the room before the buzzer rang. The buzzer was initially set for eight minutes and each day was set for one minute earlier until the children could clean up in four minutes. The teacher provided praise and encouragement for quick cleanup behavior. With this procedure, the teacher was able to reduce the average amount of time required for cleanup from 11.6 minutes to 4.3 minutes. We have used similar procedures successfully to increase the number of assignments completed by students within a specified period.

Certain teaching strategies have also been found to affect the amount of on- or off-task behavior displayed by students in the classroom. Scott and Bushell (1974) investigated how the amount of time a teacher spent with each child individually affected the off-task behavior of other children in the group. They found that when the length of the teacher's individual student contacts increased, off-task behavior in the other children also increased. Likewise, when the length of individual student contacts decreased, so did off-task behavior. Alternative management strategies (see Paine and others, 1983) can be used to keep children on task when a teacher must be engaged in individual instruction.

Carnine (1976) found that off-task behavior was also affected by the rate at which the teacher presented material. When teachers had a fast, consistent presentation rate, off-task behavior decreased and students' participation increased. Slow rates of presentation allowed delays between the students' response and the next task, which provided opportunities for misbehavior.

Contingency Contracting

An excellent way to increase the involvement of the student in the intervention process is through a contingency contract. The contract specifies what is required of the student and the amount and type of reinforcement the student will receive for meeting established goals (Gelfand and Hartmann, 1984). The contract is usually made between the student and the teacher or parents. Figure 6 is a sample contract. The ultimate objectives of the contract are to teach the student self-management skills and to have the student assume responsibility for behavior.

Several criteria should be met when contracts are drawn up. Contracts should stress student accomplishment and be equitable. The terms of the contract should be stated explicitly so that the student knows exactly what is expected. In addition, the amount

**Figure 6. Example of a Contingency Contract to Increase
Homework Completion.**

Flying High With Good Work !!

<u>CONTRACT</u>

I, _Nicole_ , AGREE TO COMPLETE THE
FOLLOWING RESPONSIBILITIES EACH DAY:

1. I WILL WRITE DOWN ALL HOMEWORK AND STUDY ASSIGNMENTS
   IN MY NOTEBOOK BY THE END OF EACH DAY AND ASK MY
   TEACHER TO SIGN IT.

2. I WILL COMPLETE ALL HOMEWORK, SHOW IT TO MY PARENTS,
   AND ASK THEM TO SIGN MY HOMEWORK NOTEBOOK AFTER
   THEY HAVE REVIEWED MY COMPLETED WORK.

3. ALL HOMEWORK AND CLASSWORK WILL BE TURNED IN ON
   TIME.

4. I WILL ATTAIN AT LEAST A PASSING GRADE ON ALL
   HOMEWORK AND CLASSWORK THAT I TURN IN.

IF I COMPLETE ALL OF THE ABOVE RESPONSIBILITIES FOR A
PERIOD OF ONE WEEK, I WILL RECEIVE THE FOLLOWING REWARD:

_I will be allowed to invite one friend
to spend the night over the weekend._

SIGNATURES:

Nicole
Student

Nov. 2
Date

Mrs. Smith
Teacher

Nov. 2
Date

and type of reinforcer should be commensurate with the responsibilities that the student has.

Homme and others (1970) outline a series of steps for transferring control of academic or behavioral goal setting and reinforcement from adult to student. During transition steps, the adult involves the child increasingly in the decision-making process until the child becomes accomplished in setting up his or her own goals and reinforcements. The objectives of this process are to teach children to use self-contracting, to monitor their own performance, to evaluate their performance, and to reinforce themselves when goals are met.

Response Cost

A response-cost procedure involves taking the reinforcer (frequently points or tokens) away from a child engaging in prohibited behaviors (Gelfand and Hartmann, 1984). Another easy method of monitoring the student's behavior is to place a tally sheet on the desk outlining behavioral goals. Each time the student misbehaves she or he must cross off a figure corresponding to the appropriate goal. The student must have a specified number of figures left on the sheet to receive a reward. Figure 7 is an example of a tally sheet. Response-cost procedures are effective in reducing aggressive and hyperactive behavior. They are often combined with reinforcement strategies to teach positive behaviors to replace the inappropriate ones.

Response-cost procedures can be easily instituted in the home to motivate children to complete their chores. For example, they may lose a portion of their allowance for each chore that is not completed within the specified time limit. Another way to institute the system is to allot each child a certain amount of points and require that the child maintain a certain percentage of points to earn a reinforcer.

Witt and Elliott (1982) evaluated the effectiveness of a response-cost lottery used in a fourth-grade classroom to increase on-task behavior and work accuracy during independent seatwork. Participating students were given slips of paper that were taken away each time a classroom rule was violated. At the end of the

Figure 7. Example of a Tally Sheet for a Response-Cost Monitoring System.

Behavioral Goals

I will leave my seat only with my teacher's permission.

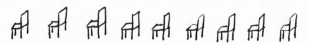

I will not talk to my peers during seatwork.

I will not hit other students.

Criterion: I must have at least 5 figures not crossed out to earn my reward.

Reward: Ten minutes of free time beginning at 3:00 P.M.

_____ teacher

_____ student

seatwork period, students placed their remaining slips of paper into a lottery box. The teacher held a drawing each Friday, and the winner selected something from a reward menu containing prizes such as extra recess or pencils. After institution of the response-cost lottery, the students' average level of on-task behavior increased from 10 percent to 73 percent, and work accuracy increased from an average of 27 percent correct to 90 percent correct.

The response-cost lottery is easy to implement and requires little teacher time. In addition, it does not interfere with regular classroom privileges, as inappropriate responding prevents students only from gaining access to extra privileges (Witt and Elliott, 1982). The lottery idea can also be successfully adapted to increase work completion, accuracy, or appropriate classroom behavior by giving all children who meet a certain criterion a chance in the lottery.

Cognitive Behavioral Interventions

Numerous intervention strategies can be categorized as cognitive behavior modification, including self-management procedures (Karoly and Kanfer, 1982), self-instructional training (Meichenbaum, 1977), and stress-inoculation training (Meichenbaum, 1986a). Although each technique is unique, Meichenbaum (1986a) has identified a number of commonalities underlying these approaches. Each is based on the assumption that emotional responses and behavioral outcomes are cognitively mediated. Therefore, it is important to help individuals become aware of their beliefs, their expectations, their attributions, their ways of thinking and feeling, and the impact of their behavior on others. Cognitive behavioral techniques teach people to think before they act—to interrupt their automatic acts, appraise the situation and their behavior, and influence the content and nature of their self-talk. These techniques also provide components for teaching a variety of behavioral, cognitive, affective, and interpersonal skills when needed.

Cognitive behavioral techniques have been used successfully with children to remediate a number of problems including hyperactivity, impulsivity, aggressive behavior, stress, and social withdrawal. They are used most frequently to teach self-control and self-management, to enhance academic performance, to reduce fears and stress, to teach anger control, and to help develop interpersonal skills. A few of the cognitive behavioral techniques commonly used with children are discussed here. They differ primarily in the specific strategies employed and the aspects of the individual's cognitive experience (self-statements, attributions, problem-solving style) that are chosen as targets for intervention (Meichenbaum, 1986a).

Self-Management Skills

The development of good self-management skills is crucial for effective interpersonal relationships and success in school. These skills include problem solving, anger and stress control, goal setting, and self-regulation. From a cognitive behavioral perspective, self-control or self-management skills are "part of the process in which individuals observe their own behavior, evaluate their performance against some standard, and provide consequences for their behavior in accord with their performance" (Mace, Brown, and West, 1987, p. 161). Self-management techniques can be used to effect self-directed or self-mediated behavior change in children. The self-regulation process has three stages—self-monitoring, self-evaluation, and self-reinforcement—and each can be targeted for intervention.

Self-Monitoring. Self-monitoring requires the individual to make observations about his or her own behavior and then to record these observations. The target behavior is clearly defined for the student, and then the child records specific dimensions of the behavior such as frequency of occurrence, duration, intensity, or latency using charts, observation record forms, mechanical counting devices (for example, wrist counters), stopwatches, or behavioral diaries (Mace, Brown, and West, 1987). Self-monitoring is a desirable technique to use in schools because it is less demanding of teacher time than are other observational methods. It can also give teachers, psychologists, and others access to behaviors (thoughts and other private events) that are not readily observable. A disadvantage is that children may not always produce accurate records of their behavior (Kendall and Williams, 1982). The probability of accurate self-recording may be increased by providing contingent reinforcers.

Self-monitoring can be used in assessment, or it can be an effective treatment procedure. Hallahan, Marshall, and Lloyd (1981) illustrated the effectiveness of self-monitoring as an intervention to increase on-task behavior during small-group instruction. After on- and off-task behavior were defined clearly for students, they were taught to monitor their own on-task behavior using a wrist counter. Self-recording led to increases in attention that were maintained after the self-monitoring intervention was withdrawn. Piersel and Kratochwill (1979) present four case studies that applied self-monitoring interventions to increase independent work completion and to decrease classroom disruptions. Self-charting was found to be an effective intervention for both behavioral (talking loudly, interrupting the teacher) and academic (percentage correct on assignments) targets.

Self-Evaluation. Self-evaluation occurs when students compare their behavior to a standard or imposed criterion (Mace, Brown, and West, 1987). Intervention in this area focuses on teaching children how to effectively evaluate their behavior and set realistic, achievable goals for themselves.

Children can be taught self-evaluation skills by comparing their self-ratings with ratings of others. In a study by Rhode, Morgan, and Young (1983), students classified as behaviorally handicapped were taught to rate their own classroom behavior every fifteen minutes on a six-point scale. The self-ratings were compared with teacher ratings for the same intervals. Each time the difference between the student's and the teacher's ratings was one point or less, the students earned a point that could be exchanged later for toys or snacks. Students increased appropriate behavior in the resource room and the classroom and also improved the accuracy of their self-evaluations. When working with depressed, anxious, or perfectionistic children, it is important to stress positive self-evaluation of less than perfect behavior.

Self-Reinforcement. Self-reinforcement is the process by which people enhance and maintain their own behavior by rewarding themselves when they attain set standards (Bandura, 1977). These intervention strategies shift the administration of reinforcement from the teacher or parent directly to the student. A variety of tangible reinforcers, points, or privileges, or verbal or symbolic reinforcement such as self-praise, can be used to help an individual acknowledge satisfaction with his or her performance. Self-reinforcement has proven effective in developing a number of positive behaviors in students, including weight reduction and improved dating skills. Self-reinforcement procedures are advantageous in that students can use them independently of teachers or parents, thereby increasing the probability that behavior change will be maintained over a long period of time (Kanfer and Gaelick, 1986).

In a study by Humphrey, Karoly, and Kirschenbaum (1978), self-reinforcement procedures were compared with a self-imposed response-cost system. The interventions were implemented in a second-grade reading class in which the teacher reported numerous behavior problems. Students were assigned to one of two groups. In the self-reward group, each child had a bank filled with chips and an empty cup placed on the desk during a seatwork period. They put chips in their cups when they completed papers and got answers correct. Chips could be exchanged for a variety of reinforcers such as additional recess, paints, clay, crayons, cookies, and card games. Children assigned to the response-cost group began the same period with an empty bank and with their cups filled with chips. They fined themselves (returned chips to the bank) for incomplete assignments and inaccurate work. Children in the self-reinforcement group demonstrated greater positive gains than did children in the response-cost group, although both interventions were effective in increasing work output and accuracy.

Self-Instructional Techniques

Self-instructional techniques help children overcome a broad range of nonacademic problems including hyperactivity, impulsivity, attentional difficulties, and stress-related disorders. This training procedure was initially developed by Meichenbaum and Goodman (1971) and was further refined by Meichenbaum (1977,

1986a). The typical training procedure includes these steps: cognitive modeling—an adult model performs a task while verbalizing strategies aloud; overt external guidance or coaching—the child performs the same task under the direction of the adult model; overt self-guidance—the child performs the task while instructing himself or herself aloud without prompts from the adult model; faded overt self-guidance—the child whispers the instructions while going through the task; and covert self-instruction—the child performs the task while guiding performance through private inner speech.

The purpose of this procedure is to change children's thoughts about how they are appraising situations and solving problems. The premise is that the statements the adult model teaches the child will lead to changes in the child's cognitions, which ultimately will lead to changes in how the child appraises situations and behaves (Mace, Brown, and West, 1987). Children should be involved in making up the self-instructions so as to increase the likelihood that they will use them. In addition, they need to be exposed to continual demonstrations by a model until the process becomes familiar and automatic (Kendall and Braswell, 1985).

Bornstein and Quevillon (1976) instituted a self-instructional intervention with three children in a preschool who were identified as experiencing difficulties with attention span, following directions, and aggressive behavior. The focus of the intervention was to train on-task behavior, defined as being attentive and silent during teacher instruction and performing the prescribed activity during the work period. The children were given self-instructional training for a two-hour period, in stages similar to Meichenbaum's. All three children experienced significant increases in on-task behavior in the classroom; these increases persisted for up to twenty-two weeks after baseline. The average rate of improvement in on-task behavior ranged from approximately 52 percent to 65 percent.

Covert Assertion

A technique to stop negative self-thoughts, called covert assertion, is a type of self-instructional strategy. It has been used effectively to treat childhood fears, thoughts of failure, chronic anger, and perfectionism (McKay, Davis, and Fanning, 1981). Essentially, the technique involves teaching the child how to interrupt distressing thoughts and then prepare statements to be verbalized (aloud or to oneself) before, at the beginning of, during, and after potentially disturbing situations. For example, a child who is fearful of getting sick in school can be taught to stop negative self-thoughts about getting sick with positive statements such as "I am going to feel fine. Take a deep breath, pause, and relax. I'm feeling fine. I did it! This is getting easier!"

Graziano and others (1979) taught relaxation strategies and covert assertions to children who had disruptive night fears. Self-monitoring and reinforcement were added to ensure that the children would practice their relaxation exercises and self-statements. Parental ratings after intervention indicated reductions in the number and intensity of their children's fears.

A combination of relaxation strategies and covert assertions was also used successfully by one of us to dispel a fifth-grade student's excessive fears of catching a disease or getting sick, both at home and in public places. These fears were interfering with school attendance and social performance. The student was taught to identify specific situations that triggered her fears and to monitor self-talk before, during, and after each occurrence by keeping a behavioral diary. She was then taught deep-breathing relaxation techniques, how to stop negative thoughts, and how to replace them with positive self-statements. Each time she feared getting sick, she engaged in deep-breathing exercises until she felt her discomfort subside, and then she began her positive self-statements. By the fifth week of intervention, the child was attending school regularly and reported approximately a 65 percent reduction in the occurrence of distressing thoughts.

Interventions to Increase Social Competence

An important part of children's overall adjustment is the ability to establish and enjoy satisfying peer relationships (Gesten and others, 1987). Schools provide numerous opportunities for children to interact and develop socially competent behaviors, but many children exhibit significant problems in this area. Increasingly, research has demonstrated that children who exhibit social difficulties, as compared with those who do not, perform at a lower level academically (Gresham, 1983), do not adjust as well in the classroom (Gresham, 1981), and may develop serious adjustment problems as they reach adulthood (Rinn and Markle, 1979).

Two important components of social competence are positive social skills and effective social problem-solving strategies. Although there is no generally accepted definition of social skills, in this chapter the term will refer to "highly specific patterns of learned, observable behavior, both verbal and nonverbal, through which we influence others and attempt to meet our needs" (Gesten and others, 1987, p. 27). Social-skills difficulties can be categorized depending on the child's ability to perform the skill and the presence or absence of an emotional response such as anger or anxiety. For example, Gresham (1985a) states that some children have difficulty with interpersonal relationships because they have never acquired the necessary skills or have not mastered a critical step in the performance of a skill. Others have the requisite skills in their repertoire but do not perform them at acceptable levels because of lack of motivation or lack of opportunity or because anxiety or anger interferes with their behavioral response.

The second component of social competence, social problem solving, is defined as a number of "interrelated skills used to resolve conflicts that require initiation of action or reaction to the responses of others" (Gesten and others, 1987, p. 27). Proponents of this approach believe that many children encounter interpersonal difficulties because they have not learned effective cognitive or problem-solving strategies to be used in social situations (Camp and Bash, 1981; Spivack and Shure, 1974).

Social Skills

Several intervention techniques enhance social skills and social problem solving in children and adolescents. Different techniques are helpful in remediating different aspects of the problem or different causes for the child's interpersonal difficulties. These techniques can be used individually but generally are combined into comprehensive training programs. In most situations, a combination of techniques is recommended.

One program that combines various strategies into a comprehensive approach to teach social skills to elementary-aged students and adolescents is Structured Learning (Goldstein and others, 1980; McGinnis and others, 1984). In this approach, social skills are broken down into specific behavioral steps that are taught to students through modeling, role play or behavioral rehearsal techniques, performance feedback, and reinforcement. In summarizing research regarding the efficacy of the Structured Learning program, Goldstein and others (1986) conclude that it improves prosocial skill development in areas such as empathy, negotiating, assertiveness, following instructions, self-control, and perspective taking. Examples of several commonly used techniques to teach social skills are described in detail here.

Modeling and Coaching. Modeling consists of having children observe models (live or videotaped) performing an entire behavioral sequence of a given social skill (Gresham, 1985a). Live modeling is often more practical than videotaped modeling because it can be carried out in natural settings (classroom, playground, lunchroom). Modeling effects can be enhanced by providing the child with multiple models similar in age and sex and by having them talk aloud as they perform the desired behaviors (Michelson and others, 1983). Modeling can be used alone or combined with coaching. Coaching involves three steps: providing the child with clear verbal instructions about how to perform the skill; having the child rehearse the skill; and providing feedback about performance to reinforce correct aspects of the child's response and further shape areas where improvements are needed (Gresham, 1985a; Michelson and others, 1983). These procedures are appropriate for children who do not yet have certain requisite social skills in their repertoire or who need to practice certain skills to build positive expectations about their ability to perform them.

Manipulation of Antecedent Events. If children possess the necessary social skills but are not performing them or if new skills have been taught to children with deficits, it may be necessary to structure opportunities in the environment to increase the probability that the skills will be performed at an acceptable level. This structuring can be accomplished in a variety of ways. Cooperative learning strategies, for example, promote positive social interaction among students (Madden and Slavin, 1983) by requiring them to work together to complete academic tasks and thereby providing opportunities for them to share, exhibit cooperative behavior, and assist in achieving a common goal.

Teachers and parents can set up structured situations that provide a child with opportunities to engage in positive or cooperative interaction with one or more peers. Strain, Shores, and Timm (1977) trained selected peers to appropriately initiate and maintain social interactions with withdrawn children. The rates of social interaction of the withdrawn children were significantly increased.

Manipulation of Consequences. Reinforcement procedures (manipulating consequences of actions) can also be used to increase the frequency of positive social behaviors or decrease the occurrence of negative behaviors. As with antecedent-event techniques, these procedures are useful when the child already possesses requisite social skills or needs reinforcement of newly learned skills in the natural environment. Numerous reinforcement procedures of the types previously described can be utilized. Either complete behaviors or approximations toward the final behavior to be developed can be reinforced (Michelson and others, 1983).

Social Problem Solving

When students' interpersonal difficulties are judged as resulting, at least in part, from the use of inappropriate cognitive strategies for dealing with social situations, social problem-solving (SPS) interventions may be helpful. These interventions focus on helping children gain an understanding of social situations and plan strategies for dealing with problematic situations they may encounter (Elias and Clabby, 1980). Children are taught a sequence of problem-solving steps that can be applied to interpersonal situations. The sequence generally includes the following components: identification of feelings, problem and goal identification, impulse-control strategies, brainstorming or alternative-solution generation, consequential thinking, solution selection, step-by-step solution planning, and planning for overcoming potential obstacles (Gesten and others, 1987). SPS skills can be taught to individual students or small groups of students, or they can be incorporated into the curriculum and taught by a teacher to the entire class.

Numerous published and unpublished SPS training programs have been designed for specific age or grade levels. Elias, Clabby, and their associates implemented and extensively evaluated a comprehensive project, Improving Social Awareness–Social Problem Solving, in a number of schools for nearly ten years (Elias and others, 1982). Their curriculum is designed for elementary school children and can be taught directly by teachers in regular classrooms. Children learn an eight-step problem-solving sequence, usually through a variety of techniques including a brief presentation of skills to be learned and situations in which they can be used, dialogues, role play, and the use of problem-solving charts and notebooks. Evaluations of the program have revealed many positive outcomes for students (Elias and others, 1986).

The Rochester Social Problem Solving Program (Weissberg and others, 1980) is appropriate for children ages seven to ten. The program is divided into five major units: recognizing feelings in ourselves and others, identifying problems, generating alternative solutions, considering consequences of actions and choosing the best solutions, and applying the problem-solving steps to real-life problems. A variety of teaching methods (discussion, role play, videotape modeling, workbooks, flashcards, and games) are used. The teachers' manual is comprehensive and provides a detailed explanation of how to teach each lesson as well as activities and materials to use. Encouraging results have been obtained (Gesten and others, 1987).

The Think Aloud program combines self-instructional techniques and SPS and is appropriate for use with elementary children (Camp and Bash, 1981). The training manual contains detailed lesson plans for approximately forty sessions. Children are taught a problem-solving sequence through the use of four questions: What is my problem? How can I solve it? Am I following my plan? How did I do? Students practice using several cognitive tasks such as puzzles or mazes. Social problems are then introduced, and pupils are taught to apply these problem-solving steps to resolve interpersonal difficulties (Camp and Ray, 1984). Research has demonstrated the effectiveness of the program (Camp and others, 1977).

Generalization of Behavior Change

For a behavior-change technique to be considered effective, students must exhibit newly learned behaviors over time, across settings, and with different people, and sometimes the change should spread to related behaviors. In other words, generalization of results must occur. Ensuring generalization has been a problematic area, and as Stokes and Baer (1977) point out, we need to actively program generalization rather than just train and hope that it is a natural outcome of the intervention.

Strokes and Baer (1977) and Meichenbaum (1986a) offer guidelines for enhancing the probability that generalization will occur: (a) Have students participate in all phases of intervention development. If students take part in developing interventions, they will probably actively participate in the resulting program and internalize newly learned skills. (b) Choose behaviors to teach that can be reinforced by natural contingencies present in children's environments. (c) When possible, train in a number of settings using multiple tasks and trainers. Have natural caretakers take part in the training and have it occur in children's everyday environments. (d) Anticipate and incorporate real failures into training procedures. Show children how to overcome possible failures and how to cope with the accompanying emotional response. (e) Make training tasks as similar to the criterion as possible. (f) Ensure that students understand the usefulness and relevance of the intervention or training procedure. (g) Use intermittent schedules of reinforcement whenever possible. Because of their unpredictability, they tend to maintain desired behaviors for longer periods of time than do regular schedules. (h) Include booster sessions and follow-up assessments in order to maintain positive behaviors.

CHAPTER SIX

Intervention Techniques
to Improve Academic Performance

The daily instructional routines of classrooms are appropriate for most children as they learn and progress through the curriculum at the expected pace. However, for many students the established educational structure and commonly used teaching procedures do not appear to be effective. Often, these children are brought through the intervention assistance process because systematic modification of instructional procedures may be needed to meet their educational needs.

In this chapter, descriptions of a broad range of intervention strategies for remediating commonly encountered academic problems are provided. Prior to describing the interventions, we present a model for assessing learning and academic-performance difficulties in the classroom. This assessment is directed toward helping select, design, and evaluate interventions.

Students can experience academic difficulties for a variety of reasons, including lack of mastery of prerequisite skills, motivational or performance problems, inadequate teaching, or failure to profit from commonly used teaching methods. Lentz and Shapiro (1985) propose that most academic problems result from a combination of student skills deficits and classroom variables. Consequently, the most effective intervention plans include direct teaching of skills and manipulation of certain classroom variables.

Based on this assumption, this chapter describes two major intervention categories. The first category focuses on remediating student skills deficits and enhancing ability to perform effectively with learning materials. These interventions include behavioral and cognitive behavioral techniques to enhance reading, math, or writing skills; teaching self-management and study skills; and use of peer-mediated programs. The second category of interventions alters instructional or environmental variables within the classroom to maximize academic achievement. Brief descriptions are also included of commercially available programs and curricula that focus on changing the instructional environment and that have empirically demonstrated success in improving achievement.

The criteria for the selection of academic and cognitive interventions in this chapter are the same as those in Chapter Five. The interventions have been empirically demonstrated to be effective; are practical, not overly intrusive, and acceptable to users; and are compatible with the consultative process.

Assessment of Student Academic Difficulties and Learning Environments

Requirements

As with problems of an affective or social nature, academic or learning problems are caused by the complex interactions of many variables. Consequently, all assessment activities should be conducted from an ecological standpoint. In addition, academic assessment that is direct and functional (for example, curriculum-based assessment) provides the most relevant information for intervention assistance planning (Fuchs and Fuchs, 1986). Several requirements underlie the assessment model proposed here: Because the primary goal of the assessment is remediation, assessment should provide functional data to be used in intervention planning; to provide a direct relationship between what is assessed and what is taught, the student should be assessed using the curriculum materials; instructional variables that have an empirically demonstrated relationship to achievement should be the ones assessed; and the assessment should be ongoing and should be able to be used

Figure 8. Flow Chart for Problem Analysis and Intervention Planning.

Problem Identification
- Define and clarify the problem through consultative interview
- Gather information regarding setting, instructional variables, and classroom procedures via interview

Assessment Activities

Direct Classroom Observation

Criterion-Referenced Diagnostic Tests

Curriculum-Based Assessment
- Design and utilize academic probes
- Determine where in curriculum student can succeed

Examination of Permanent Student Products
- Review student work sheets, unit or chapter tests, and other available work

Problem Analysis

Analysis of Resources Available
- Teachers
- Special services staff
- Peers
- Parents
- Materials
- Financial
- Community

Intervention Planning and Decision Making
- Areas of intervention
- Types of intervention
- Specific target behaviors
- Placement
- Details and logistics
- Responsibilities

Evaluation and Follow-Up

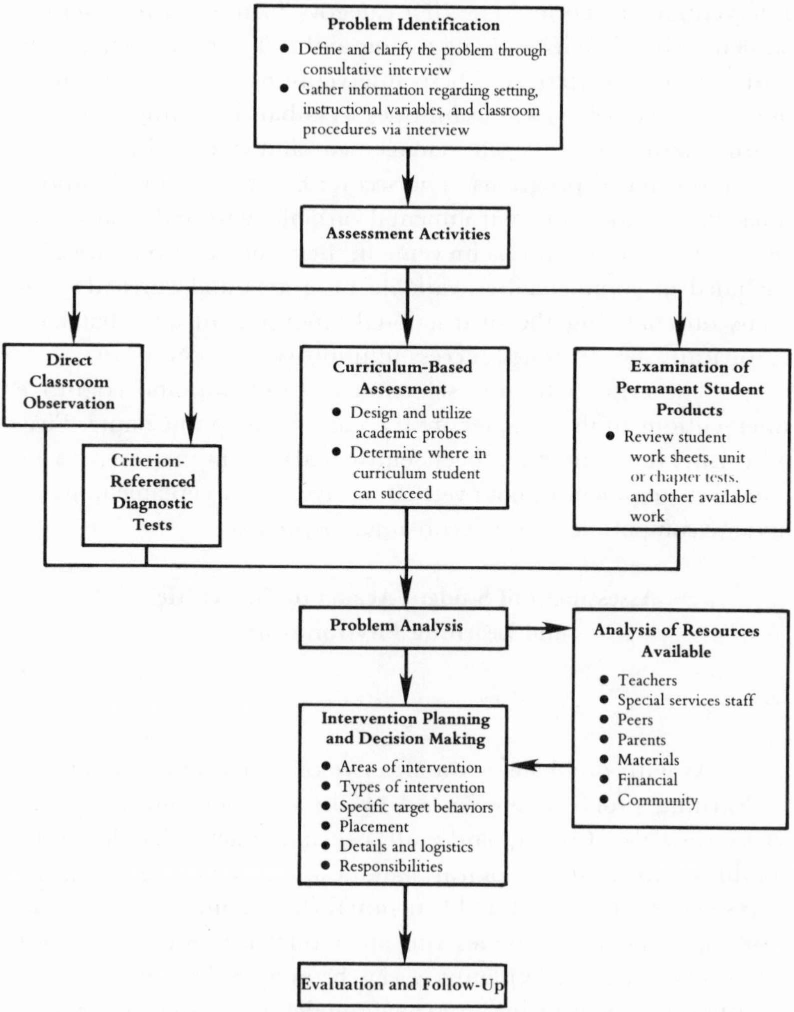

Source: Based on Lentz, 1987b.

repeatedly to evaluate student progress and intervention effectiveness. For further discussion of these requirements, see Fuchs and Fuchs (1986), Lentz and Shapiro (1986), and Shapiro (1987a, 1987b). Figure 8 is a flow chart of the assessment process adapted from the work of Lentz (1987b).

Methods

Numerous methods are available for evaluating student learning and performance difficulties, and many are discussed briefly in this chapter. In-depth discussions of the various procedures can also be found in Chapter Five of this book as well as in Gelfand and Hartmann (1984), Shapiro (1987b), and Fuchs and Fuchs (1986). All procedures do not have to be used for assessing every problem presented. The specific procedures used depend on the complexity of the problem and on the variables that need to be assessed to achieve adequate problem clarification. Lentz (1987b) compiled a list (Table 4) of common variables that may be assessed along with specific procedures that can be used to collect information pertaining to these variables.

Consultative Interview. An assessment should always begin with a consultative interview. Again, we emphasize that assessment is a data-gathering process and does not necessarily include formal measures such as tests. During this interview, information is gathered to provide a clear definition of the child's academic difficulties and of the classroom environment. Specific information that can be generated during consultative interviews includes the child's skill strengths and deficits, a description of the curriculum in which the child is working, teacher expectations for the class and for the individual student, type of instruction provided, contingencies for work completion and accuracy, type of teacher feedback and use of praise, and opportunities provided for the student to respond and practice skills in class. In some cases, all the information needed for intervention planning can be collected through consultative interviews. At other times, further clarification and additional information are needed, and other procedures must also be used.

Direct Observation. Observations of student behavior and classroom variables provide the consultant and consultee with important information about specific student skills and behaviors in natural settings and about areas in the instructional environment that could be changed to maximize student performance (Gelfand and Hartmann, 1984). Observation may also provide an opportu-

Table 4. Methods of Assessment for Academic and Instructional Variables.

Variable to Be Assessed	Method of Assessment
Placement of student in the curriculum	Curriculum-based probes Criterion-referenced tests
Expected placement of students	Teacher interview Analysis of permanent products
Opportunities to respond in class	Direct observation Analysis of permanent products
Time allotted to practice skills	Teacher interview Direct observation
Teacher's expectations of the student and placement procedures utilized by teacher	Teacher interview Analysis of permanent products
Student accuracy and progress	Teacher interview Analysis of permanent products
Immediate contingencies for completion or noncompletion of work, misbehavior, or correct responding	Direct observation
Competing behaviors exhibited by student	Direct observation Teacher interview
Student's orientation to materials and academic engaged time	Direct observation
Teacher feedback to student	Direct observation Teacher interview
Specific skill deficiencies	Curriculum-based probes Criterion-referenced tests Teacher interview Analysis of permanent products
Teacher planning	Teacher interview
Instructional presentation and provision of directions	Teacher interview Direct observation
Motivational strategies utilized by the teacher	Teacher interview Direct observation

Source: Based on Lentz, 1987b.

nity to clarify or verify information solicited during the teacher interviews. It is important to observe during at least one full period of the problem area (reading group, math instruction). Observations should be conducted in a systematic and purposeful fashion. Consistent with the goals of consultation, the purpose and scope of the observation, as well as all data gathered, should be shared with the teacher.

Many structured observation codes are available and appropriate for use in a classroom. Four commonly used observation techniques are event recording, duration recording, momentary time sampling, and interval recording (see Gelfand and Hartmann, 1984, for further descriptions). Choice of technique depends on the type of information the consultant and consultee are interested in collecting.

Other comprehensive observation systems are useful in analyzing not only student behavior but also classroom variables that may affect academic performance. One potentially useful standardized observation system is the State-Event Classroom Observation System (SECOS) developed by Saudargas and Creed (1980), which focuses on both student behavior and teacher behavior. Some of the areas assessed include student on- and off-task behavior, student behavior while receiving teacher attention, teacher approval and use of praise, teacher contact during seatwork, and teacher disapproval. The observation recording form for the SECOS is presented in Figure 9. Much useful information regarding student behavior and student/teacher interaction can be derived, but the code is limited in that it does not assess the qualitative nature of teacher instruction or the precise nature of the student's academic responses (Lentz and Shapiro, 1986).

Interviews and Observation. Because the purpose of the consultative model is to provide assistance to the teacher, in some instances an analysis of the qualitative aspects of the instructional environment can be helpful. The Instructional Environment Scale (TIES), developed by Ysseldyke and Christenson (1987), is intended to provide useful analysis of this area. According to the authors, the scale can be used to describe how student difficulties are related to classroom instructional variables and to define areas for instruc-

102 Helping Students Succeed in the Regular Classroom

Figure 9. The Observation Recording Form Used in the
Saudargas-Creed State-Event Classroom Observation System.

Sheet #: _____

| | (GR:) | | | M T W R F | Start: End: Total: |
| Student | | Date | | Day (circle) | Time |

1. ISW:TPsnt 3. SmGp:Tied
2. ISW:TSmGp 4. LgGp:Tied

School	Class Activity	
		Ac. Beh
Teacher	Observer	Referral Problem

STATES	1	2	3	4	5	6	7	8	9	10	11	12	13	14	15	16	17	18	19	20	Σ	%
SW																						
OS																						
LK																						
M																						
PLO																						
SIC																						
SIT																						
OACT																						

EVENTS	1	2	3	4	5	6	7	8	9	10	11	12	13	14	15	16	17	18	19	20	Σ	Rate
RH																						
CAL																						
OS																						
OAG																						
AC																						
OCA																						

TEACHER	1	2	3	4	5	6	7	8	9	10	11	12	13	14	15	16	17	18	19	20	Σ	Rate
TA/SW																						
TA/OTH																						
DIR-OPP																						
DIR-C+																						
APP																						
DIS																						

COMMENTS: _____

_____

_____

tional intervention. Twelve areas that have been demonstrated to be components of effective instructional environments can be analyzed. These include teacher expectations, student academic engaged time, opportunities for practice of skills, type of feedback and corrective procedures employed by the teacher, use of motivational strategies, use of adaptive instruction, instructional planning, and methods of monitoring student progress. Information for TIES is gathered through student interviews, teacher interviews, and classroom observations. Students are interviewed to assess their understanding of academic tasks and directions as well as their success rate on tasks. The teacher is interviewed to clarify data obtained through observations, to collect additional relevant information, and to understand the rationale for instructional decisions. Observations are usually conducted during instructional time and an individual seatwork period. Information obtained by all three methods is integrated to develop interventions.

Assessing Individual Student Skills. Students' academic skill levels can be assessed by a number of different methods including curriculum-based assessment, criterion-referenced tests, task analysis of skills, and analysis of cognitive strategies used for completing specific tasks. All methods provide information useful for intervention planning, and choice depends on the presenting problem. Three of these assessment methods—curriculum-based assessment, assessment of problem-solving strategies, and permanent-product analysis—are discussed in depth here.

Curriculum-based assessment (CBA) uses the student's curriculum as the source of assessment material (Shapiro, 1987b; Tucker, 1985). CBA is compatible with consultation because it has a direct link to instruction in the classroom and can be used to monitor the effects of the intervention over time (Shapiro, 1987b). In addition, CBA has a brief administration time, has been shown to be highly reliable (Deno, 1985), and overcomes some of the restricted sampling practices inherent in standardized tests (Gickling and Thompson, 1985). A comprehensive overview of CBA can be found in Tucker (1985).

Deno and Mirkin (1977) developed procedures for taking a series of brief, timed skill probes in the areas of reading, spelling, written language, and mathematics. For reading, one-minute samples of oral reading are taken from the student's basal reading series. The number of words read correctly per minute are graphed. Figure 10 is a sample graph of a child's reading performance. Other techniques include asking comprehension questions and developing probes of word lists or phonic sounds. In math, written computational problems are given to the student; the problems are based on the scope and sequence of skills to be taught. The number of correct digits computed per minute are graphed. For written language and spelling, the number of correct words (or letter sequences) written in a paragraph or from a spelling list in a specified time are used as the assessment measure. Detailed descriptions of how to construct and administer skill probes and how to graph and evaluate performance in these areas can be found in Deno (1985), Deno and Mirkin (1977), and Shapiro (1987b).

Assessment of students' problem-solving strategies is a new area, and many of the efforts to standardize this type of assessment are in experimental stages. Assessment focuses on determining the

Figure 10. Curriculum-Based Assessment of a Student's Reading.

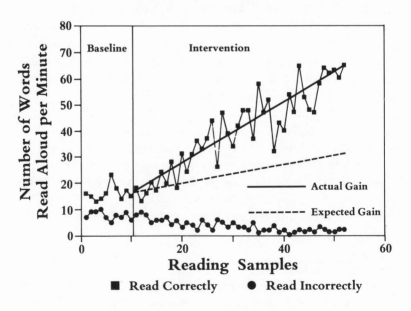

types of strategies students use to approach academic tasks or solve problems. Frequently, think-aloud techniques are used, which require students to verbalize their thoughts while working on an assigned task. The students' thought processes are analyzed to discover the strategies employed (Meyers, Palladino, and Devenpeck, 1987). For example, if a student has made a series of errors while computing subtraction problems, the student is asked to describe the process used to find the answer. By using this technique, the examiner can determine whether the student has a basic understanding of the subtraction process.

Meyers and Lytle (1986) describe a think-aloud protocol analysis that assesses strategies a student may be using for reading comprehension. The coding system contains twenty-one responses grouped into six categories: signaling, understanding, analyzing text features, elaborating on the text, judging the text, and reasoning. Research is currently being done to investigate the types of responses and strategies used by both elementary and secondary students (see Meyers, Palladino, and Devenpeck, 1987).

For permanent-product analysis, the teacher can be asked during initial consultations to collect students' daily work sheets, homework, tests, and special projects for review with the consultant. Analysis of these work samples provides diagnostic information regarding students' understanding of directions and demands, mastery of material, and patterns or types of errors. The consultant and teacher can then determine the particular skills that must be targeted for intervention and the type of intervention strategy needed.

Problem Analysis and Intervention Planning

Consultants and consultees must answer many important questions during the problem-analysis stage in order to plan appropriate interventions. The interventions chosen depend on how a problem is conceptualized. Most problems related to student characteristics can be conceptualized as a skills deficit, a fluency problem, a performance problem, or some combination of these (Lentz and Shapiro, 1986; Lentz, 1987a). If the student has a skills deficit, the problem analysis should reveal which skills to teach. If the student has a fluency problem, then problem analysis should determine how he or she can achieve an acceptable performance rate. If the child demonstrates the prerequisite skills and fluency but does not perform at acceptable levels, problem analysis should identify environmental variables that are hindering the child's performance.

Once the problem has been adequately analyzed, the next step is to decide exactly which variable should be targeted for change (accuracy, rate, environmental variables, problem-solving strategies). The choice of target behaviors is crucial because it dictates the type of intervention chosen as well as the measurement methods used for monitoring progress toward goals. Table 5 lists examples of targets for common problem areas as identified by Lentz (1987a).

Target behaviors must be consistent with the problem analysis and easily measured. For example, if a student is found to lack oral reading fluency, then improved oral passage reading can be chosen as a logical target. Oral passage reading lends itself to the establishment of clear goals and easy progress monitoring. If improved reading comprehension is the intervention focus, the percentage of comprehension questions answered correctly can be chosen as a target. If noncompletion of independent work is the identified problem, the focus of the intervention may be on changing environmental contingencies, but accurate completion of seatwork can be the measured target behavior.

Interventions That Focus on Student Behavior

Behavioral Strategies

Teachers have used behavioral techniques in the classroom for years. Many effective teaching practices, such as rewarding students for good behavior, clarifying classroom rules, and choosing tasks at an appropriate level, are based on sound behavioral principles. Many specific strategies have also been utilized successfully to improve performance in reading, mathematics, handwriting, and spelling. According to Sulzer-Azaroff and Mayer (1986), the most crucial factor is that the strategies be applied

Table 5. Targets for Academic Interventions.

Reading	Mathematics	Spelling
Oral passage reading	Math facts	Oral weekly spelling words
Oral sentence reading	Computation work sheets	Written weekly spelling words
Sight words	Computation strategies	Combination of oral and written weekly spelling words
Comprehension questions	Computer drill and practice	
Comprehension strategies	Word problems	Missed words from stories or essays
Word meanings	Daily classwork	Daily assignments
Phonic skills	Homework completion and/or accuracy	Weekly tests passed at a specified level
Basal-reading workbooks		
Homework completion and/or accuracy		

Source: Based on Lentz, 1987a.

in a systematic, thoughtful, and accountable manner. This process can be accomplished by following the problem-solving steps outlined in Chapter Four. A sampling of behavioral strategies for remediating academic problems is presented here.

Reinforcement

Altering the type or rate of reinforcement is an efficient and effective intervention method for academic problems as well as for behavioral or social problems. Systematic reinforcement can be used to teach academic skills to students, to increase fluency of skills, and to improve academic performance. The guidelines for choosing and using reinforcers outlined for behavioral and social problems in Chapter Five are applicable to academic difficulties. Examples are provided to demonstrate how reinforcement can be used to teach skills and to improve fluency, work completion, and accuracy.

Improving Sight-Word Vocabulary. Reinforcement procedures can be combined easily with daily or weekly sight-word drill using flashcards. After assessing the student's sight-word knowledge, the teacher divides the words into three groups: mastered words, words deciphered with extra time, and unknown words. Teaching begins with the words that the student can decode given extra time and proceeds to unknown words. Students receive rewards (such as points or stickers) for words successfully recognized within three seconds. The points or stickers are exchanged for secondary reinforcers such as free time, trinkets, supplies, or classroom privileges. Missed words are returned to the word bank for further drill, and all words are reviewed periodically.

Improving Computational Fluency. Many students who have learned basic computational skills still have difficulty in math because they lack the fluency to complete problems at an acceptable rate. In this case the intervention goal is to increase the rate of computing math facts. Lovitt and Esvelt (1970) found that, by reinforcing rate of performance rather than just accuracy, they were able to significantly increase a student's math productivity. The student was told that he would receive points for each additional problem solved correctly. Once the reinforcement schedule was changed, the student doubled the percentage of problems completed accurately.

The quick-draw math game, as reported in Sulzer-Azaroff and Mayer (1986), also reinforces fast rates of responding. This game has been used to increase fluency with multiplication facts but could also be used for addition, subtraction, or division. Numbers between zero and twelve are written on separate index cards. Two students are chosen to draw cards. When the teacher says "draw," the students face each other, show the numbers, and multiply the numbers mentally; the first student to respond with the correct answer remains in the game. Another child is then chosen to challenge the previous winner.

Completing Assigned Work. Individual seatwork is assigned to provide children with opportunities to practice newly learned skills; however, motivating students to complete assigned tasks is a frequently encountered problem. After it is determined that students have the skills to complete work independently, then accurate completion of homework or classwork can be chosen as a target. Students are told the number of assignments they are expected to complete within a specified period of time with a specified accuracy level. They can earn stickers or points for each assignment completed at the acceptable accuracy level before the timer rings. The stickers or points are traded for secondary reinforcers or privileges. As another example, Cowan, Jones, and Bellack (1979) used a group contingency to increase the number of reading assignments completed by a class. The teacher used a stop clock, which was activated when the students were working. When students achieved their goal of fifteen minutes of good work time, the group was allowed to select a reinforcing activity.

Self-Instruction

Self-instructional techniques have been found useful in teaching children academic skills and in improving classroom performance. Essentially, students are taught either a general problem-solving method or task-specific strategies that can be applied to particular subject areas or to maintaining on-task behavior. The more task-specific the strategy, the greater the likelihood that the student will benefit from its use (Lloyd, 1980). The self-statements or questions the students are taught organize information and help them decide on the next step to take (Hall, 1980). The training consists of modeling use of the strategies, self-verbalization, and strategy training (Lloyd, 1980). The use of modeling for self-instruction was described in Chapter Five. Self-instructional strategies that have been found to be effective for mathematics and reading comprehension are detailed here.

Mathematics. Self-instructional strategies can help students perform complex mathematical skills such as adding or subtracting with regrouping (Sulzer-Azaroff and Mayer, 1986). An example of a training sequence for teaching subtraction with regrouping is outlined in Table 6. The teacher demonstrates how to solve the subtraction problem and verbalizes the thought processes for each step. Then the child is taught the self-instructions and asked to verbalize the statements while computing each problem. Overt

**Table 6. A Self-Instructional Training Sequence for
Regrouping in Subtraction.**

---

1. What kind of problem is this?   62
                                     −35
                                     ———

2. I must look at the sign. It's a minus so I know that it is a subtraction problem.

3. The first thing I must do is look at the right column and see whether the top number is bigger than the bottom number.

4. If it is, then I can subtract the numbers in that column. Since it is not, then I must borrow from the left column and the 2 becomes a 12 and the 6 loses one and becomes a 5.

5. Now I subtract 5 from 12, and that equals 7. I put the 7 under the 5. Next I subtract 3 from 5, and that is 2. I put the 2 under the 3.

6. What is my answer?

7. It is 27.

8. I really did a great job on that problem!

---

verbalization should become covert once the student masters the self-instructions.

Reading Comprehension. Self-instructions have been used widely to enhance students' comprehension of written material. The training teaches students to maintain attention on what they are reading, to make self-statements or develop questions directed toward what they are reading for, and to make coping statements to deal with possible frustration and failure. Frequently, students learn self-statements that direct them to read for the main idea, important details, the order of events, and identification of the main characters and their motives (Lloyd, Kosiewicz, and Hallahan, 1982).

Study-Skills Training

Many students fail in school not because they lack basic skills but because they lack good study strategies. Yet study-skills training remains one of the most neglected areas of the curriculum (Barron and others, 1983). Study skills have been conceptualized in a variety of ways, and programs vary based on student needs. Wise, Genshaft, and Byrley (1987) identify two major areas that should be incorporated into a comprehensive study-skills curriculum: teaching study and test-taking strategies (extracting meaning from texts, processing and organizing information taught, recalling information for application to practical situations and tests) and teaching self-management skills to help students concentrate, set and achieve realistic goals, schedule and manage time, and control anxiety and self-doubts. We provide descriptions of strategies in a study-skills program here.

Study Strategies

A major component of good study skills is knowing how to extract meaning from textbooks in the various subject areas. Otto (1985) states that students must be taught to take an active role in reading their texts, understanding both their purpose for reading and the characteristics of the text being read. They also need to be able to monitor their own understanding of the text and know how to employ corrective strategies when they fail to understand. The following techniques have been taught to students to improve their skills in comprehending texts and organizing materials.

Self-Questioning. Self-questioning is a cognitive behavioral technique that helps students focus attention on relevant aspects of the story or text and organize or guide their thinking as they read (Nolte and Singer, 1985). For example, Cohen (1983) developed a program in which third-grade students were taught to generate questions while reading short stories. The children then read for the answers to their questions. Students who learned the self-questioning strategy improved from 74.5 percent correct to 88 percent correct on a comprehension test. Students who did not receive the training demonstrated no improvement.

In another program, Nolte and Singer (1985) taught self-questioning strategies through teacher modeling and student practice. The teacher discussed the importance of asking questions and modeled appropriate types of questions to ask. As students read silently, the teacher stopped them periodically to ask questions about the setting and the main character. Students were then required to ask their own questions about the remainder of the story. The teacher slowly phased out the modeling component over many days by prompting students to generate their own questions, having small groups of students work together with one student eliciting questions, having students practice questioning strategies in pairs, and finally by having students use the strategies independently. Students who received this training performed significantly better on comprehension tests than did students who did not receive the training.

Text Look-Backs. Many students do not know how to review previously read material to find specific information. They do not know where to begin to look or how to utilize key words and cues in the text to aid their search. Some students employ inefficient strategies such as trying to read the entire chapter from the beginning until they find the information they need. Reis and Leone (1985) developed a training method to help students retrieve material efficiently. The program teaches students why they should look back, when they should look back, and where they should look. Students are taught skimming techniques and how to locate key words and phrases in the text, and are also given practice in differentiating text-based questions from inferential or applied questions.

Note Taking and Underlining. Teachers can use many techniques to help students store information efficiently. McAndrew (1983) encouraged teachers to preunderline assignments for students before they read them, as preunderlined passages resulted in better comprehension than did student-underlined passages. Students often do not differentiate important from unimportant information when underlining; they must be taught to distinguish higher-order statements from details and to underline only higher-level sentences. To encourage efficient student note taking, McAndrew (1983) suggests that teachers insert questions or cues (verbal or nonverbal) when lecturing to highlight important points, write important information on the blackboard or on an overhead transparency to increase the probability that students will copy it, use handouts whenever possible (leaving space for student notes), and tell students what type of test to expect.

Test-Taking Strategies

Teaching students how to study for and take tests is another important component of a good study-skills program. Test-taking skills that can be readily taught include using time efficiently, anticipating test questions, informal guessing, error avoidance, and identifying and using cues (Millman, Bishop, and Ebel, 1965). Students can also be taught strategies for different test formats— essay, multiple choice, and short answer (Towle, 1982). For example, to be successful on essay tests, students must learn how to outline main points, write topic sentences, provide details (who, what, where, when, and how), use transitional phrases, and write summary statements. Success on multiple-choice tests, however, requires recognizing cue words in questions, using association, and using visual imagery. Students should also be taught to critically review questions missed on previous tests so that they can judge how well they mastered the content and can determine which skills need additional practice (Wise, Genshaft, and Byrley, 1987).

Motivation and Self-Management Strategies

Comprehensive study skills programs also address the affective components of academic achievement, which include student motivation, attributions for success and failure, and good self-management skills. Effective study habits require the ability to set realistic goals for oneself. Students can be taught how to set goals based on their current level of performance and the amount of effort that they are willing to expend to attain higher levels of achievement. Students also should be made aware of the internal (negative self-talk) and external (noise and confusion) distractors which could pull them away from their task. Strategies can be provided for helping them cope with such distractions. Finally, students should be taught how to realistically evaluate their performance and to reward themselves for achieving set goals. Bragstad and Stumpf

(1982) and Devine (1981) provide useful guides for conducting study skills programs for students.

Peer-Mediated Interventions

When developing interventions, school personnel continually face the problem of not having the resources needed for plan implementation. Too frequently, one of the most readily available and potentially useful resources—students—is completely overlooked. Students are an important source of control for classroom behavior, and they often produce stronger effects on their peers than teachers can (Gresham and Gresham, 1982). Peers are also reliable tutors for students experiencing academic difficulty; they can provide cost-efficient and effective individualization of instruction (Russell and Ford, 1983).

Peer-mediated academic interventions are "a variety of structured interactions between two or more students, designed or planned by a school staff member, " . . . to achieve academic (primary) and social-emotional (secondary) goals" (Miller and Peterson, 1987, p. 81). The most commonly used peer-mediated interventions are group-oriented contingency programs, peer and cross-age tutoring, and cooperative learning. Although each technique utilizes peers, their primary focuses are quite different. For example, cross-age and peer tutoring emphasize individual student learning, while cooperative learning emphasizes the simultaneous learning of students as they strive to achieve group goals or group rewards. Group contingencies provide consequences to group members based on group behavior, but they do not directly promote the goals inherent in cooperative learning, such as group collaboration (Bohlmeyer and Burke, 1987). In-depth descriptions of each of these peer-mediated interventions are presented here.

Group Contingencies

Group contingencies have been used successfully to modify academic and behavior problems in classrooms (Crouch, Gresham, and Wright, 1985; Gresham and Gresham, 1982; Shapiro and Goldberg, 1986). Their effectiveness is based on the premise that peer pressure is a powerful influence. Group contingencies are popular with teachers because they are an efficient use of teacher time; teachers can manage the behavior or performance of an entire classroom rather than of each student individually. They also provide a good alternative for teachers who object to behavioral interventions that single out individual students (Shapiro and Goldberg, 1986).

Group contingencies can be designed and implemented in three different ways depending on how goals are set and reinforcement is granted (Litow and Pumroy, 1975). Independent group contingencies require each student to meet the same criterion, but a child receives reinforcement solely on the basis of his or her own performance. For example, if all students are required to complete five out of six assignments, only those students who achieve this criterion receive the reinforcement. Interdependent group contingencies are based on the performance of the entire group. If the criterion of 90 percent accuracy is established by the teacher, all student scores are averaged, and everyone in the group gets reinforced if the group averages 90 percent, regardless of what each one's individual score on the test. Dependent group contingencies are based on the performance of one or more selected students. The entire class receives a reward if a certain identified student or students meet the goal. Shapiro and Goldberg (1986) report that because no evidence clearly indicates that one type of contingency is more effective than another, selection can be based on other variables such as acceptability of the intervention, ease of implementation, and the absence of possible unintended negative effects of the intervention.

Peer Tutoring

Peer tutoring provides opportunities for students to take an active role in the learning process by helping each other learn new skills or practice mastered ones (Jason, Ferone, and Soucy, 1979). Peer-tutoring interventions require the establishment of structured dyads (Miller and Peterson, 1987).

Dyads can be set up in a variety of ways, and there are mixed opinions regarding who makes an effective tutor. Several investigations have shown that academically oriented peer tutoring is most effective when the tutors are older than the students being tutored and are competent in the area in which they are providing instruction (Ehly, 1986). However, Harris and Sherman (1973) found positive academic outcomes resulted when fourth graders in dyads and triads helped each other solve arithmetic problems. Other studies have demonstrated the successful use of handicapped students as cross-age tutors (Maher, 1984; Scruggs and Osguthorpe, 1986). Overall, the research suggests that successful programs have been established using tutors of varying ages, abilities, and skill levels (Miller and Peterson, 1987).

Numerous studies have concluded that peer tutoring has positive effects on achievement and attitude toward learning of both tutors and tutees (Cohen, Kulik, and Kulik, 1982). Highly structured tutoring programs appear to produce the most positive outcomes. Jason, Ferone, and Soucy (1979) found that classwide tutoring programs also had positive effects on all students. The advantage of classwide peer tutoring is that all children are provided with the positive experiences of being both tutor and tutee.

Peer-tutoring programs have also been found to produce positive outcomes for handicapped students. Russell and Ford (1983) paired mildly handicapped students with cross-age tutors and found tutored students made greater gains in reading than did resource-room students who did not receive peer tutoring. Maher (1984) had handicapped adolescents tutor elementary-aged handicapped students, and reported positive outcomes for tutors and tutees in increased work completion, increased accuracy, and decreased disciplinary referrals.

When implementing peer tutoring, teachers should make decisions about the following components: supervision of the program; establishment of appropriate goals, lesson content, and instructional procedures; identification of the tutoring dyads or triads; training of tutors; and development of evaluation procedures (Ehly and Larsen, 1980; Miller and Peterson, 1987). Two of these components—establishing goals, lesson content, and instructional procedures, and training tutors—are briefly discussed here.

Tutoring programs can have both academic and behavioral goals. Ehly and Larsen (1980) suggest that goals should depend on the tutees' abilities and needs and should be incorporated into a contingency contract between the tutor and tutee. The goals and objectives for each session can be written into the contract, and both the tutor and tutee can be rewarded when these are achieved.

Although almost any material is adaptable to peer tutoring, highly structured academic tasks involving drill and practice may be most suitable (Lentz, 1987a). For example, tasks commonly used in peer tutoring are sight-word drills or reading-fluency exercises. Lessons to be taught and the materials to be used should be taken directly from the classroom curriculum to increase the likelihood that newly learned skills will generalize to other classroom tasks.

Students selected as tutors need training before being assigned to tutees. Training sessions for peer tutors should include teaching them how to maintain tutees' attention, organize and effectively use materials and understand the objectives of each session, provide clear directions, show the tutee how to respond to materials and how to verify answers, provide praise or rewards as appropriate, provide feedback for errors, use cues and prompts to encourage correct responses, assess mastery of a lesson, and identify areas in which they may need additional assistance from the teacher (Ehly and Larsen, 1980; Maher, 1984; Miller and Peterson, 1987).

Once tutoring has been implemented, Maher (1984) recommends that teachers conduct periodic support conferences with tutors to discuss problems, concerns, or questions; provide feedback and supervision; and highlight accomplishments.

Cooperative Learning

An exciting alternative to traditional instructional procedures emphasizing individual goals is the use of classroom peers in groups that have cooperative goals (Cosden, Pearl, and Bryan, 1985) and that use cooperative-learning methods. Cosden and colleagues describe groups with cooperative goals as involving structured student interactions with rewards dependent on the combined performance of all members. A variety of cooperative-learning techniques have been used successfully in classroom settings. These techniques vary according to the group tasks assigned, whether group competition is introduced, and the reward structure utilized

(Slavin, 1983). For example, in some techniques students work together on the same task to achieve a common goal, and in others students work on separate tasks and share information. Some cooperative-learning methods have reward structures based on individual performances, and others combine the performances of all group members to determine rewards. The most commonly used cooperative-learning techniques are presented in Table 7.

Research on the outcomes of cooperative learning has been promising. It has been found to enhance student achievement across subject areas (Johnson and others, 1981) and to promote self-esteem and improved interpersonal relationships among students (Blaney and others, 1977). These techniques have also been successful in promoting positive interactions between handicapped and non-handicapped students that generalized to other classroom and school situations (Johnson and others, 1986), thereby showing potential as a method to facilitate mainstreaming.

Before implementing cooperative learning in the classroom, teachers must consider several issues, including how to select the most appropriate method, how to determine group composition and size, and how to promote accountability and helping behaviors among students (Miller and Peterson, 1987). Bohlmeyer and Burke (1987) emphasize that the subject matter taught, the basis for dispensing rewards, practical implementation issues, personal teaching style, the goals and objectives established for students, and the age or grade level must guide the selection of techniques.

Cooperative learning has been used with students from preschool through college, and certain techniques seem to be more appropriate for different age levels as well as for different subjects (Miller and Peterson, 1987). For example, Miller and Peterson suggest that cooperative-learning methods that emphasize peer tutoring and focus on the acquisition of basic skills and information work with either younger or older students. Group study methods appear to work best with older students in content areas such as social studies or science. Johnson and Johnson (1978) recommend that group composition be as heterogeneous as possible and that group size remain small when working with young students.

Table 7. Summary of Cooperative Learning Methods.

Student Teams-Achievement Division (STAD) (Slavin, 1978)

Four to five students are assigned to heterogeneous learning teams. The teacher introduces the material to be learned and then provides study work sheets to team members. Students study the material with their team members until everyone understands the material. Next, students take individual quizzes, but the scores are used to compute a team score. The contribution each student can make to the team score is based on improvement as compared to past quiz averages. High-scoring teams and high-performing students are recognized in a weekly class newsletter.

Teams-Games-Tournaments (TGT) (DeVries and others, 1980)

This method of cooperative learning uses the same team structure and instructional format as in STAD. In addition, students play in weekly tournament games with students of comparable ability from other teams in the classroom. Assignments are changed every week with the high and low scorers of each table moved to the next highest or lowest table respectively in order to maintain fair competition. Students can contribute to their team score based on their performance in the weekly tournaments. Again, a class newsletter is used to recognize high-scoring teams and individual tournament winners.

Team Assisted Individualization (TAI) (Slavin, Leavy, and Madden, 1982)

In TAI, the focus is on mathematics instruction. Heterogeneous teams of four to five students are formed. Based on a diagnostic test, each student is given an individually prescribed set of materials. For each unit, students read an instruction sheet, complete skill sheets, take checkouts, and finally a test. Working in pairs, students check each other's work sheets and checkouts. When a checkout has been passed with a score of 80 percent or better, the student takes the test and the results are scored by a student monitor. Teams receive certificates for exceeding preset standards on the tests and for completing units.

Jigsaw (Aronson and others, 1978)

Students are assigned to six-member teams, and each team member is given one section of a five-part academic unit. Two students share a section as a precaution in case of absenteeism. Expert groups are composed of team members from different groups who share the same academic material. They meet to discuss their material before returning to teach it to their group. After being taught each section by the team members, students take individual quizzes and are graded on their performance on the quiz.

Table 7. Summary of Cooperative-Learning Methods, Cont'd.

Jigsaw II (Slavin, 1980)

In this modification of Jigsaw, students are formed into four-to-five member heterogeneous teams. Every student studies all of the material but is given a section in which to become an expert. As in the original Jigsaw, students meet in expert groups, teach their fellow team members, and take individual quizzes. However, individual scores are computed based on improvements, and these become a group score. A class newsletter is used to recognize high-scoring teams and individuals.

Learning Together (Johnson and Johnson, 1975)

Students work in four-to-five member heterogeneous teams on assignment sheets. A single product from the group is expected, and the group members may self-evaluate how well they worked together as a group at the end of the session. The teacher's role is to monitor the groups and praise the students when they demonstrate cooperative behavior. In some applications of this method there is an incentive system incorporated, such as group grades.

Group Investigation (Sharan and Sharan, 1976)

In this method, students self-select their cooperative group of two to six members. The group chooses a topic from a unit being studied by the class and then decides who will study and prepare information on subtopics of the unit for a final report. Students are encouraged to use a variety of materials, engage in discussion with each other, and seek information from many sources. The groups present their projects in the class, and evaluation of the group and/or individuals is completed.

Source: Adapted from Miller and Peterson, 1987.

One final issue for teachers to consider when implementing cooperative learning is the teacher's role in the instructional process. In cooperative learning, the teacher's task shifts from direct teaching to group facilitation and serving as a resource person. For example, rather than responding directly to students' requests for assistance, the teacher refers these requests back to the group and helps them to collaboratively solve the problem at hand. This behavior aids in developing an interdependent, helping relationship among students (Miller and Peterson, 1987).

Interventions That Focus on Instruction

As discussed previously, academic and learning problems usually result from the interaction of child characteristics and various environmental variables that affect the child in the classroom. Altering instructional variables that have an empirically demonstrated relationship to student achievement is as important to successful intervention as the remediation of specific skills deficits. Such changes are particularly necessary in consultation because a primary goal is to help the child function successfully in the least restrictive environment. The literature on teacher effectiveness, instructional effectiveness, and teacher planning and decision making identifies practices that have been empirically demonstrated to have a favorable effect on student achievement and learning (see Wittrock, 1986, for extensive review). The individual consultant or intervention assistance team can serve as a resource to teachers by sharing information on these practices. Together they can work to modify and improve instructional environments to meet student needs.

Instructional Factors Affecting Student Achievement

Close to 100 factors have been identified in the literature as affecting student achievement (Ysseldyke and Christenson, 1987). Factors that have the strongest empirical support and provide the basis for practical interventions are presented in this section.

Presentation. Instructional presentation includes lesson development and presentation, clarity of directions, and monitoring

of student understanding (Ysseldyke and Christenson, 1987). Ysseldyke and Christenson reviewed a number of the characteristics of effective instruction and concluded that children perform best when previous lessons are reviewed before teaching new concepts, an explanation is provided about how the material taught is relevant to their lives, and concept builders and advance organizers are provided. The frequent use of teacher modeling and guided instruction can improve the presentation of new concepts. A fast pace of teacher presentation has also been found to decrease off-task behavior and increase student participation and accuracy (Carnine, 1976). Finally, directions should be fully explained so that task demands are understood by students before they engage in individual seatwork.

Motivational Strategies. The importance of motivation in student learning and performance is well documented. Ysseldyke and Christenson (1987) emphasize the following strategies to increase student enthusiasm for learning: vary assignments as much as possible; have students set individual goals for learning and performance; assign tasks that are at the students' appropriate instructional level; have clearly defined contingencies for completing or not completing work; incorporate student interests into the lesson content as much as possible; and hold conferences regularly with students regarding performance.

Rewards and praise are also highly effective motivators for students. Paine and others (1983) discuss various types of praise that teachers can use effectively. One method is for the teacher to praise students nearby or across the room as the teacher circulates to assist students. When instructing small groups of students, teachers can periodically scan the room and praise students in other groups who are working appropriately. This method helps prevent off-task behavior (Scott and Bushell, 1974). Reinforcement programs and self-management techniques such as self-charting of progress, self-evaluation, and contingency contracting can also be effective motivators.

Opportunities for Practice. Increased opportunities to respond in class and to practice academic skills have been shown to improve students' academic performance (Greenwood, Delquadri, and Hall, 1984; Rosenshine and Berliner, 1978). For example, to improve oral-reading fluency and accuracy, one can increase the amount of time students spend reading aloud. Ysseldyke and Christenson (1987) highlight the following requirements for providing relevant practice opportunities: Assigned tasks for practice should be at an appropriate instructional level for each student; modifications in task requirements (length shortened, aids provided) must be made when necessary so that students can complete the work successfully; student performance should be monitored carefully and feedback provided frequently; error-correction procedures such as prompting, cueing, or modeling should be used when the student is unable to respond; and opportunities for practice should be provided for students until they make only infrequent mistakes.

Academic Engaged Time. Numerous studies have demonstrated that the greater the amount of time students spend engaged in academic tasks, the greater their achievement levels (for example, Greenwood, Delquadri, and Hall, 1984). Student engagement in academic tasks can be maintained in a variety of ways. For example, teachers can check students' understanding of tasks when they are observed to be off-task, scan the room and redirect student attention when necessary, provide frequent reminders to students who have a tendency to be off-task, and circulate around the room as much as possible when students are working (Ysseldyke and Christenson, 1987). Teachers can also increase on-task behavior by developing procedures for managing students' requests for assistance. Many children stop working and wait for the teacher to assist them, thereby losing valuable practice time. Paine and others (1983) describe a procedure involving student-made cards that said "Please help me" to alert the teacher. All students were also given folders with a supply of sure-fire work that the students could do independently but on which they could use additional practice. When students needed assistance with regularly assigned seatwork, they put the help card on their desks and worked on assignments from the sure-fire folder until the teacher could assist them. Other teachers have trained students in their class to be helpers who provide assistance to others when the teacher is engaged in small-group or individual instruction.

Informed Feedback. Students do best when their performance is monitored continuously and they are provided with reasonably immediate feedback about the accuracy of their answers or their behavior. Paine and others (1983) provide four strategies for providing quick corrective feedback to students. First, teachers can often correct papers as they circulate around the room. This procedure allows the teacher to provide immediate feedback to the student and to deal with problems students are having before long periods of time elapse. Immediate feedback can be reinforcing to students, and they may try harder if they know they are doing the work correctly.

Second, students can correct their own papers at times. The teacher sets up a checking station with correcting pens, teacher-prepared answer keys, and a box for completed and checked work. When students complete an assignment, they go to the checking station and circle any errors with a colored pen, return to their seats, correct the errors, and go back to the checking station to recheck their corrections. When they achieve 100 percent accuracy, they place their assignments in a box for completed work. Rewards are given for correct work and correct checking. Cheating costs the student points or privileges.

Third, group self-correction is a good way to provide immediate feedback at the end of a lesson or supervised practice activity. The teacher displays the correct answers on an overhead projector or on the blackboard, reviewing one problem at a time. Students are required to find their mistakes.

Finally, a feedback chart can be used to monitor student performance. Records can be made of behavior during transition periods, of whether directions are followed, of whether work is completed, and of warnings for misbehavior. A chart is posted where all students can see it, and students earn pluses for positive performance and minuses for not performing appropriately. Pluses earned for the day can be traded for privileges or other reinforcers.

Adaptive Instruction

Most classrooms have a diverse range of students, and entire-group instruction is not always effective for all learners. A number of programs have been developed that adapt the learning environment to individual student needs (Wang, Levine, and Reynolds, 1988). According to Wang and associates, these programs generally combine various instructional strategies such as mastery learning, prescriptive teaching, individual tutoring, and cooperative learning. Most programs monitor student progress regularly to determine the next set of skills to be taught. Two examples of adaptive instruction are presented here.

Direct Instruction. Direct Instruction (Becker and Carnine, 1981) has been shown to be effective in improving outcomes particularly for students with limited academic skills (Becker, 1977, 1978). Student achievement has been enhanced in reading, mathematics, and spelling. The program is based on three premises: All children can learn and be taught; children's learning failures should be viewed as teaching failures; and low-performing children need a highly structured program and need to be taught at a faster than average rate (Paine and others, 1983).

The program utilizes specific materials (for example, DISTAR for primary reading) and follows many fundamental behavioral learning principles. It focuses on academic goals and adheres to strict time schedules. Teachers and aides are trained to teach at a rapid pace and to provide numerous opportunities for student response. Feedback is provided immediately and systematically, opportunities are given for correcting errors, and reinforcement is provided for successful performance.

Adaptive Learning Environments Model. The Adaptive Learning Environments Model (ALEM) (Wang and Birch, 1984; Wang, Levine, and Reynolds, 1988) systematically applies empirically demonstrated principles of effective instruction to teach low-achieving and mildly handicapped students in the regular classroom.

The program has five critical design features. The first feature is early identification of learning problems through diagnostic/prescriptive monitoring. Teachers determine where to begin instruction with each student within a structured, hierarchical curriculum. Student progress is continually monitored so that new goals can be set or modifications made as needed. A second feature is noncategorical instruction. ALEM is designed to serve students in regular classrooms without the need to apply categorical labels. Instruction is provided according to diagnosed needs and is not based on labels. Individualized education programs are the third feature. These programs are provided through direct teacher-guided instruction, ongoing monitoring of student progress, provision of immediate feedback, and structuring of high levels of student time on task. The fourth design feature is the teaching of self-management skills to students. ALEM stresses the importance of teaching students to assume responsibility for their own learning. The acquisition of self-management skills is thought to have a positive impact on students' self-concepts, involvement in their own learning, and time spent on task. The final feature is that specialists provide consultation and support to regular education teachers. In ALEM, special services providers support teachers through consultation and team teaching. Specific training is given to teachers to enable them to provide instruction according to the model, and all work as a team to accommodate individual student differences.

Research conducted on the project has been promising. Positive outcomes have been demonstrated with regard to instructional processes, student attitudes toward learning, and student achievement in basic skill areas (Wang and Birch, 1984). However, external validation regarding program effectiveness is needed.

CHAPTER SEVEN

Assessing Organizational Need
and Readiness for Change

I ntervention assistance programs are appealing to most special
services practitioners and other school personnel. These professionals quickly recognize the potential benefits of these programs
once they understand their goals and operation. Moreover, most
personnel are cognizant of the shortcomings of current referral and
placement procedures. However, if some people are not convinced
of the need for and potential of the system, background information
presented in Chapter Two can be used to develop the rationale for
introducing this new approach into a school organization. This
chapter and the next address important issues in facilitating the
implementation of an intervention assistance approach to services
delivery. Specific suggestions for breaking down barriers to
implementation are offered in Chapter Nine.

Although mastery of the consultative problem-solving
process demands a great deal of knowledge and skill, additional
challenges are encountered in implementing intervention assistance
programs in schools. Indeed, the literature offers few descriptions
of successful program implementation. The scarcity of information
on this topic poses a significant obstacle to initiatives to change
current approaches to services delivery. Even the best program, "if
poorly implemented, may prove ineffective" (Maher and Illback,
1985, p. 81).

This chapter begins by discussing an essential element of effective implementation—understanding the school. We advocate a systems perspective as being helpful in understanding organizations, and we suggest a conceptual framework for examining various organizational dimensions. We then discuss specific areas of organizational functioning that may influence program implementation. As has been true throughout the book, our discussion assumes that most readers are school employees rather than external consultants. Nevertheless, most of our discussion is applicable to people external to the organization as well. The problem-solving framework discussed in Chapter Four and in Maher and Bennett (1984) is used to organize this chapter.

Understanding the School as a System

Substantial evidence indicates that organizational change is a slow process (Fullan, Miles, and Taylor, 1980). In fact, Derr (1976) notes that efforts to promote change rapidly within a system frequently meet with resistance and fail. Because implementation of an intervention assistance program involves complex organizational change, failure to heed cautions to plan for a long-term, sustained effort will doom this approach to services delivery.

As a problem-solving process, case consultation requires thorough attention to problem clarification before efforts are directed at problem solution. The same is true of organizational consultation. Organizational assessment (problem clarification) must precede efforts to bring about change in the system (problem solution). Prior to initiating any type of change in a school, one must gain an understanding of the organization, including its personnel, technologies, processes, and structures, and then assess its need and readiness for change. No planned organizational change should be instituted without a diagnosis of the system (Beer, 1980). Even when a practitioner has been associated with a school for a number of years, it is still essential to engage in a needs assessment.

This assessment should be part of a formal systematic planning process that clarifies the need for the program, describes program goals, determines required resources, and identifies appropriate evaluation procedures (Maher and Bennett, 1984). From this perspective, planning is ongoing, and assessment both affects and is affected by the other parts of the planning process. Not only do diagnostic procedures provide information about the school, but data collection itself has certain consequences (Goodstein, 1978). Moreover, goals for change must be linked to the identified needs of the organization.

Systems Perspective

As noted in previous chapters, many programs are not successful because issues are not considerd at a systems/organizational level by those involved in implementation. A systems perspective is particularly important for implementation of intervention assistance programs because implementation involves a systems-level change. School psychologists may become so overwhelmed by requests for individual psychoeducational assessments that they do not attend to the fact that the referral system promulgates requests for evaluation instead of requests for assistance. Or other special services staff may complain that they are unable to provide consultative assistance because "the administration will not allow us to do so" without ever attempting to work with administrators to modify job responsibilities.

A critical aspect of the systems perspective is reciprocal interaction. As mentioned previously, this concept refers to the tendency for change in one part of a system to cause change in other parts of the system. Some examples of variables that can influence consultative interactions are school climate (for example, open systems encourage the use of consultation services by prospective consultees), consultant and consultee characteristics (for example, consultants often prefer to work with consultees who are responsive to intervention efforts and sensitive to children), acceptability of the interventions developed (positive interventions are more acceptable than are negative interventions), and district policies (districts that explicitly emphasize meeting individual student needs may facilitate consultative interventions). The reciprocal influence of systems variables is also reflected in the fact that the school social/

emotional environment affects students, and students in turn affect the school environment.

The point of this discussion is that interventions to resolve student-related problems or systems-level difficulties cannot be developed in isolation; they must take into consideration district, school, and classroom variables in order to be effective (Curtis and Meyers, 1985; Curtis and Zins, 1986).

Framework for Understanding Schools as Organizations

Numerous strategies are available for considering schools from an organizational perspective (for example, Fullan, Miles, and Taylor, 1980; Sarason, 1982; Schmuck and Runkel, 1985). A framework that we have found to be particularly useful in examining any school unit (special services department, school district) was devised by Maher, Illback, and Zins (1984a). They delineate three important organizational domains and their related elements: structure, process, and behavior. These interrelated domains determine how successfully the organization operates and how it achieves its goals. Figure 11 is a graphic representation of these domains.

Organizational structure guides the operation and functioning of the organization. As noted in Figure 11, organizational structure includes the school's philosophy (ideals that it values and toward which it aspires), policies (written statements that inform others of the philosophy), and services and programs (including instructional, assessment, related, administrative, and personnel-development services) (Maher, Illback, and Zins, 1984a). For example, the school's philosophy could emphasize the need for individually guided instruction for all students, consultation procedures could be included in the written policies, and consultation services could be made available to all school personnel.

Organizational processes are defined by Maher, Illback, and Zins (1984a) as the means that enable the philosophy and policies to be enacted and the services to be delivered. These processes are planning and evaluating (designing new programs, modifying those already existing, and judging their worth), communicating

Figure 11. Framework for Viewing Schools as Organizations.

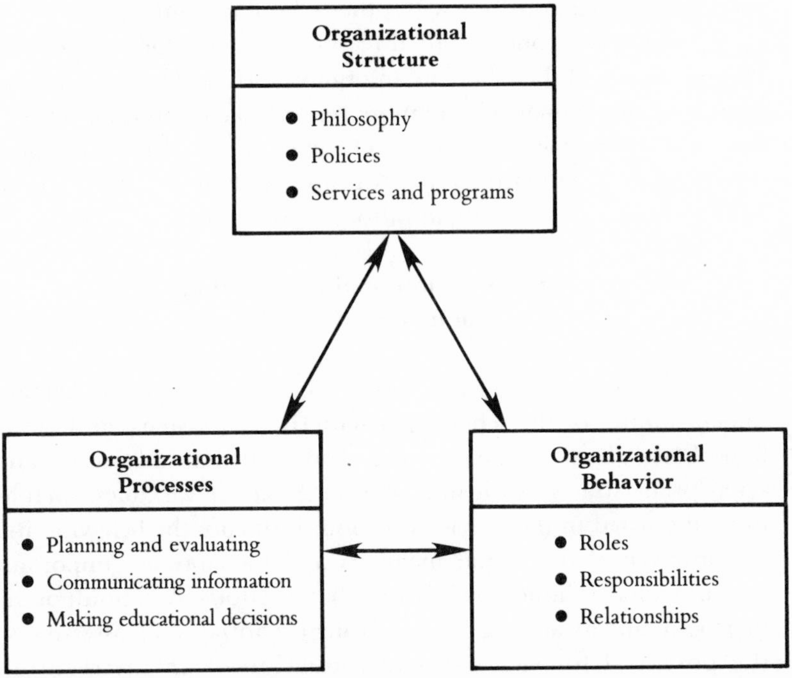

Source: From Maher, Illback, and Zins (eds.), *Organizational Psychology in the Schools*, 1984. Courtesy of Charles C. Thomas, Publisher, Springfield, Illinois.

information so that school and community members understand organizational intentions, and making educational decisions. In this area, schools need formal methods for implementing and evaluating the worth of the consultation program.

The third domain in Figure 11, organizational behavior, refers to the skills, activities, and motivations of organizational members involved in providing educational services. It consists of three important elements: roles, responsibilities, and relationships. Roles are the assignments of members (for example, science teacher), responsibilities are members' duties as defined in their job descriptions (for example, to teach seventh-grade science), and relationships are the connections members have to each other (for example, member of the science department) (Maher, Illback, and Zins, 1984a). For special services staff, consultation might be included in their job descriptions, and if it is, they would establish collaborative relationships with other school personnel.

One must consider all three domains in order to increase understanding of the school as an organization, realizing that some aspects of this framework are more central to consultation services than are others. Clearly, various elements can facilitate or hinder openness to a consultation program. Therefore, they are an important focus during organizational assessment.

Assessing Organizational Functioning and Readiness for Change

The goals of organizational assessment are to increase understanding of the school, particularly as a system; to develop hypotheses about its functioning; and to determine needed and appropriate strategies for intervention. Systemic variables, such as those discussed in the previous section, influence the behavior and performance of individual members and therefore are important determinants of the acceptability of change efforts. As a result of the increased understanding gained from organizational assessment, the potential for successful introduction of an intervention assistance program into the system is maximized.

Just as there are numerous methods for viewing schools as organizations, there are a variety of approaches for assessing organizational functioning (morale, efficiency of services delivery, long-term planning, cohesiveness) and desire for change. A collaborative approach that actively involves organizational members in the diagnostic process enhances participants' feelings of ownership of the resulting program and commitment to resolving problems that are identified.

Methods

In this section we provide examples of assessment techniques that can be helpful in developing hypotheses about organizational functioning. Each approach can be structured so that relevant information about an individual organization and its desire for change is obtained.

Schein (1969) emphasizes the importance of making participation in all data-gathering procedures voluntary. Those providing the information must be informed about their freedom to participate as well as about the uses that are to be made of the data. Moreover, the identity of individual respondents must remain confidential, and data collection should proceed in a manner that produces minimal reactivity among members. Without these safeguards, the quality and validity of the data obtained may be lessened significantly.

Organizational Flow Charts. A graphic representation of organizational structure and the formal chain of command can be helpful in understanding the school or in identifying the location of a particular problem. As one becomes familiar with the organization, one can add informal leaders and people with significant power in order to make the chart descriptive of actual organizational functioning.

Flow charts may likewise be developed to describe the activities involved in providing services within the school. Of particular interest here is the sequence of events involved in making requests for assistance or in making referrals for psychoeducational assessment (see Figure 1 for an example). It may be helpful to assess operational reality in this regard. All activities may occur within only one of the options listed on an official chart. For instance, although a flow chart may indicate that if regular classroom interventions prove effective, a referral for psychoeducational assessment is unnecessary, it might be found that nearly all cases are forwarded for assessment anyway. This information would suggest that some problems interfere with the process as described in the flow chart.

Records. Memoranda, minutes of school board meetings, statements of school philosophy and procedures, district financial records, student files, staff performance evaluations, staff and student attendance data, grievances filed, community newspapers, student handbooks, data on support for tax levies, and so forth provide important information about schools. These documents are readily accessible and contain information that may be highly relevant to the introduction of a program. For example, if the district has an extremely high percentage of its students in special education, there may be a recognized need to establish an intervention assistance program. If a review of the records of special education students indicates that a large number of those placed received relatively few educational interventions before being referred for psychoeducational assessment, one can assume that some or many of these students may be able to function in their current classrooms if provided with alternative instructional techniques and support.

Observations. Informal norms, lines of communication, procedures, leadership styles, gatekeepers (such as secretaries and informal leaders), patterns of behavior, and so forth can often be identified by observing the school in its day-to-day operation. Observations conducted while one is a participating member of an organization are particularly useful, although it is sometimes difficult to maintain objectivity.

Questionnaires and Surveys. These instruments are usually developed locally, although some questionnaires have been published (for example, the Organizational Climate Description Questionnaire by Halpin [1966]). Locally developed questionnaires have the clear advantage of addressing specific needs. For the purpose of considering an intervention assistance program, knowledge of teacher satisfaction with current referral procedures in the school may be relevant. Or one may wish to know whether teachers are aware of how to request various support services. Because questionnaires are usually administered to only a sample of organizational members rather than to each one, they can be a relatively efficient and inexpensive method of obtaining information.

Anonymous responses are usually preferred in order to increase quality and frankness, particularly concerning sensitive issues such as morale, values, leadership, organizational climate, and relationships. Assessing the staff's openness to an intervention program or their dissatisfaction with current referral procedures may also be easier to ascertain through administration of an anonymous rather than a signed questionnaire as some teachers may be concerned about making negative statements about current procedures and operations.

Interviews. A sample of members can be interviewed about their perceptions of organizational functioning and effectiveness. To gain an accurate picture of the situation, special efforts must be made to ensure representativeness. Questions can be based on results obtained through other techniques; interviews are thus usually follow-up procedures. However, interviews with a select number of key personnel beforehand can be helpful in the development of questionnaires and in deciding on the types of information to be gathered.

The advantage of interviews over questionnaires is that investigators have the opportunity to pursue respondents' answers to questions in depth. For example, if questionnaire results indicated that teachers did not know that they could request the consultative assistance of special services staff, this issue could be explored. Determining the resources that they perceive as available when they require additional assistance for problems outside their areas of expertise might be desirable. However, although the quality of the information obtained may be improved through the interview process, such procedures are costly, and some members may be reluctant to provide candid responses in a face-to-face situation.

Organizational Dimensions

Myriad organizational dimensions can be examined to assess organizational functioning, perceived need for change, and potential areas of change. Examples of several dimensions most relevant to intervention assistance programs are reviewed in this section. A variety of these dimensions can facilitate or impede the implementation of intervention assistance programs. Clearly, the characteristics of some school organizations make them more receptive to an intervention assistance program than do those of others.

We have stressed the importance of taking a systems perspective. Such an outlook continues to be important when attempting to gain an understanding of the way an organization functions. Schools should be viewed as existing within larger systems—districts, communities, cities, counties, states. Many forces external to the school can exert considerable influence on organizational functioning: district administration, teacher unions, parent groups, community support, advocacy groups, state and federal laws, and the economy. Some schools, for example, encountered a great deal of resistance to intervention assistance programs from advocacy groups who did not understand the intent of the programs. Their perception was that these programs were an attempt to delay the provision of needed services to handicapped students. Personnel contracts may likewise have an influence on the establishment of intervention assistance programs. Many schools hold assistance team meetings before or after school. However, some contracts specify work hours and thus may (even unintentionally) discourage teachers from meeting at these times.

Certain factors or forces internal to the school may also exert influence: formal and informal leaders, personnel and equipment resources, lines of communication, values, morale, staff cohesiveness, absenteeism, policies and philosophies, skills of staff, leadership style of principal, atmosphere, and parental involvement. For example, the staff may be task oriented and work well together on problem solving in one school, while staff may have few interactions in another. Schools also differ in the amount of autonomy given to staff. These contrasting social climates obviously have implications for intervention programs. Schools also differ in their attitudes toward meeting the individual needs of students. If there is support for such activities, teachers may be receptive to an intervention assistance approach.

Another dimension on which schools vary is what Conoley and Conoley (1982) refer to as the organization's health, or its operational effectiveness—how well it meets its goals and objectives. Major objectives for any school include student learning in areas such as reading, mathematics, and language arts, as well as in vocational education, health, and physical education. The school's future is based partially on how well it achieves these objectives (see Gallessich, 1973). If, for example, a school had a serious morale problem following the defeat of a tax levy that followed a significant decline in student test scores, the teachers and administrators are not going to be receptive to the introduction of intervention assistance or other programs that necessitate major organizational changes, particularly if such changes will take several years to become fully operational.

Sociological characteristics of the school such as its size, the neighborhood in which it exists, stability or turnover of students and staff, ethnic/cultural background of community members, and socioeconomic status of students can also exert influence. Students in smaller schools, for example, tend to participate in more extracurricular activities because these schools encourage more involvement than do larger schools (Barker, 1976). Relatedly, in a smaller school, it may be more difficult to arrange meetings with special services staff because they often have itinerant assignments. Thus, there may be less flexibility regarding times to hold consultation sessions.

In order to systematize assessment of these dimensions, Parsons and Meyers (1984) developed a checklist that includes the various elements of the system (personnel, physical plant, products), the structures and processes of the system (formal and informal roles of members, norms, communication patterns, decision-making styles, reward structures), and forces affecting the system (internal, external, organizational trajectory).

Program Design

Based on organizational assessment and the resulting increased understanding of the school, decisions must be made about the need for an intervention assistance program and about the specific type of program to implement. The program should be introduced because of clearly identified organizational needs rather than imposed because someone wishes to have consultation services available.

The purpose and goals of the intervention assistance program need to be clarified before deciding on a specific program design so that the attainment of goals can be evaluated. The intended recipients of the services (students and teachers) also must be identified. Will the program be implemented systemwide, will it be used on a trial basis in one school, or will it be used on a carefully selected case-by-case basis?

Once the purpose and objectives are defined, options for structuring an intervention assistance program must be evaluated, and the alternative that will best meet the needs of the organization must be selected. In addition, consideration should be given to how compatible an alternative is with existing programs. If significant changes are required in the organization, it may be difficult to implement a particular alternative, but some other alterations in the intervention assistance program may be relatively easy to accomplish. (See Ponti, Zins, and Graden, 1988, for an example.)

CHAPTER EIGHT

Practical Strategies
for Implementing the Program

I n the previous chapter, we outlined briefly some of the important conceptual and practical issues that affect program planning and implementation. The assessment activities described should be helpful in identifying the human, informational, technological, financial, and physical resources necessary for successful program operation. Efforts can then be directed toward assuring that these resources are available. In this chapter, we discuss specific strategies for implementation of an intervention assistance program.

We provide an explicit, detailed description of implementation activities because our experiences and those of others (for example, Lippitt, Langseth, and Mossop, 1986; Stolz, 1981, 1984) indicate that many authors fail to describe adequately the practical issues involved in implementing human services programs. Experimental design and outcomes may be reported clearly, but information about how events were arranged for implementation of the program usually is lacking or is sketchy. As a result, knowledge gleaned from effective programs is probably not used as widely as it might be. Our intent in this chapter therefore is to provide details about practical strategies. These strategies may be more effective when used in combination than in isolation.

Changing Consumer Perceptions and Expectations

For an intervention assistance program to operate successfully, consumers such as teachers and parents must make frequent and effective use of the service. However, people accustomed to a method of services delivery that differs significantly from the intervention assistance approach may have preconceived notions about the types of services that will be available and therefore may be resistant to the new program. Therefore, it may be necessary to deal with role perceptions and expectations of consumers on a proactive basis in order to minimize the development of resistance.

Three important factors exert considerable influence on consumer perceptions of the functioning of special services staff: history, title, and behavior (Curtis and Zins, 1986). Expectations are based on previous experiences with a special services professional, on the professional's job title, and on interactions with the professional. Because it may be impossible to alter past events or job title, the professional's current behavior is the major determinant of consumer expectations, and significant changes in their perceptions can be made in this regard. For these reasons, maintaining collaborative relationships in all interactions with consultees gives consumers a consistent message about their relationship with special services staff. In addition, it is important for the actions of special services personnel to be consistent with the underlying values and assumptions of the intervention assistance process. Through such actions special services personnel can begin to gain acceptance for the new approach to services delivery.

Consumers and decision makers must also understand what the special services professional *can* do before they decide what the person *will* do (Curtis and Zins, 1986). Thus, special services staff need to help others become adequately informed about consultation and intervention assistance. One method that we have found to be effective is use of an entry presentation, or in-service, to describe and discuss the intervention assistance program (Zins and Curtis, 1984). Specific details of such a presentation are discussed at length later in this chapter. Use of such an approach is based on evidence suggesting that an organization may be more receptive to the introduction of a new program that it understands than to one it does not (Reimers, Wacker, and Koeppl, 1987).

As we have noted elsewhere, there is also a tendency to confuse consumer desires with expectations (Zins and Curtis, 1981). Teachers and parents may not expect special services staff to function in a consultative role, but considerable data suggest that many of these consumers prefer (desire) that they do so (for example, Gutkin, 1980; Manley and Manley, 1978). Such preferences have been found to exist even when teachers are accustomed to nonconsultative approaches. These desires should be kept in mind by those implementing new programs for services delivery.

Integrating Special Services and Regular Education

The need for special services to become integrally related to regular education is discussed at the end of this chapter, but a brief mention of this issue is appropriate here. Stainback and Stainback (1984) call for a merger of special and regular education, in which mildly handicapped students would be integrated into the mainstream (see Chapter Two for additional discussion). Without the acceptance of such integration by school personnel, intervention assistance programs have little chance of success. School policies must reflect acceptance and tolerance of all students and include specific procedures for meeting individual needs. Even in this period of competency testing and renewed emphasis on the acquisition of basic skills, all students retain the right to an appropriate education within the least restrictive environment. Often, however, because few people cross over professional boundaries, the amount of interchange between regular and special education is limited. Ties between the groups may facilitate implementation of intervention assistance efforts by increasing interaction, cooperation, and the sharing of expertise.

Publicizing Services and Benefits

Other ways to encourage participation in the intervention assistance program are to publicize the availability of services and to emphasize their potential benefits. In many districts, teachers and parents have the mistaken notion that for students to receive special services, they must be referred for individual assessments. To counteract such assumptions, alternative means of obtaining these services must be made known to consumers. Essentially, increased efforts in knowledge diffusion, or marketing efforts, are needed in order to inform others of the new program. The program rationale provided in Chapter Two can be quite helpful in formulating a statement of need for the program as well as in presenting convincing evidence of the potential benefits.

The school staff must be sold on the benefits and the efficacy of the intervention assistance program. Although the administration might encourage them to utilize these services, long-term success depends on their becoming true advocates for the approach as well as regular consumers of the services. As teachers experience success with the process, their expectations may likewise increase. Moreover, there is a tendency for staff to share successful experiences with their colleagues, thus helping further to publicize the program and build positive expectations about it.

Because parents are frequently an important component of intervention assistance activities, efforts must be expended to market the program to them and to encourage their involvement as well. They can be approached through talks at PTA/PTO meetings, articles in school, church, and volunteer newsletters or community newspapers, and personal interactions. Involving parents in the process is also an excellent means of demonstrating the system to them.

Use of a personal approach with decision makers and potential consumers is another effective marketing approach. Face-to-face discussions of the proposed intervention assistance program are desirable; they may be supplemented with written descriptions, memos, copies of articles containing supportive data, and so forth. Stolz's (1981) analysis of the relevant literature suggests that personal interaction between the person promoting a program and the person who will make the decision to use it is the most important variable in implementation. During these initial discussions, the school's or the district's goals and objectives can be reviewed and problems with the current system discussed. The intervention assistance process can then be introduced as a program option, and its compatibility with the organization's goals and policies, utility to and acceptance by teachers, and benefits for students can be emphasized. Thus, a collaborative approach to discussions about the intervention assistance program is desirable. The special services provider's referent power may likewise be important for successful adoption.

Similarly, as will be noted in detail in Chapter Eleven, the benefits of consultation and the intervention assistance process (based on evaluation efforts) need to be demonstrated to decision makers so that they will maintain their active support for the program, particularly during the two to three years it typically takes for full implementation. Due to the complexity of organizational change, substantial results should not be anticipated sooner (see Fullan, Miles, and Taylor, 1980). All potential constituents (teachers, administrators, citizens, parents) should be recipients of evaluation data as their support is critical for success. The satisfaction of the community with the entire educational system is obviously important; the intervention assistance program can be publicized as an innovative and effective service provided within the district.

Obtaining Sanction and Support

During the organizational-assessment phase, the appropriate level (district or individual school) for introducing the intervention assistance program should have been determined. In all cases, sanction for implementation must be obtained at both administrative and staff levels (Meyers, Parsons, and Martin, 1979; Zins and Curtis, 1984) as sanction at one level does not imply approval at the other. Administrative support is absolutely essential. If a principal allows teachers to bypass the intervention assistance process and does not encourage them to engage in consultation with special services staff, requests for psychoeducational evaluations can easily become the predominant focus of special services delivery.

Our discussion of sanctions is organized by levels: district, building, and individual practitioner. In practice, the three levels are interrelated and influence one another.

District

As already noted, a major aspect of program implementation and operation is obtaining administrative sanction and support. Administrators can be instrumental in facilitating change at a district level through the development of policies, procedures, incentives, and staff-development activities conducive to intervention assistance efforts.

A number of school districts have adopted a philosophy and enacted policies supportive of intervention assistance programs. These documents may emphasize, for example, the individuality of each student and of his or her learning style, the importance of meeting the needs of every student, early intervention in problem situations, and the advantages of education in the least restrictive environment. The intervention assistance program may not be mentioned by name, but the philosophy and policies are consistent with the approach.

Some districts also communicate the availability of the intervention assistance program to potential consumers. Simply doing so and hoping that the program will be used, however, is not sufficient for successful implementation (Stolz, 1984). Appropriate procedures supporting the district philosophy and policies are also needed. These might stipulate, for example, that interventions must be developed, implemented, evaluated, and documented in the classroom prior to a referral for psychoeducational evaluation. Table 8 is one district's specific procedures for referring students who are experiencing difficulties.

After developing relevant policies and procedures, the district administration can also provide training sessions and incentives for staff involvement in the intervention assistance process. Such activities may be coordinated by the central administration or by individual schools depending on local circumstances and preferences.

Building

Many activities are necessary for implementation in individual schools. A description of them follows.

**Table 8. Procedures for Referring a Student
for Psychoeducational Assessment.**

1. The Intervention Assistance Team receives referrals from teachers, parents, and/or directors of private agencies who have identified children who are experiencing learning and/or behavioral difficulties in the classroom.
2. The Intervention Assistance Team (Director of Special Education, special education teacher(s), student's teacher(s), school psychologists, building principal, and/or parents) will meet at a designated time and place to develop intervention strategies to help the student achieve in the classroom. Communication with the parent(s) will be initiated as necessary by the referring teacher.
3. Information from outside the school (from physicians, agencies, and/or parents) is collected concerning the student to assist in developing intervention strategies as necessary and appropriate.
4. The teacher implements and documents appropriate intervention strategies in the regular classroom (estimated period of time is four to six weeks). Modification of the initial plan will be made as necessary by the Intervention Assistance Team and teacher.
5. The teacher and the Intervention Assistance Team evaluate the success of the intervention strategies as documented by work samples, behavior logs, parent reports, behavioral observations, and/or other means.
6. If at the end of the intervention period the student is progressing satisfactorily, the intervention strategies are continued as appropriate, and the student's progress is monitored.
7. Should a student continue to experience problems at the end of the intervention period, the student's teacher(s) shall request that the Intervention Assistance Team reconvene to determine whether a formal request for additional assistance should be made.
8. Emergency, priority (as determined by the Director of Special Education and the school psychologist), and three-year reevaluations are exempted from the above process. In addition, these procedures are not meant to preclude other consultations that occur among teachers and special services staff.

Source: Beechwood (Kentucky) Independent Schools, 1986.

Administrative Support. Building administrators are crucial elements in the successful implementation and operation of an intervention assistance program. They must understand the rationale for the approach, the process of organizational change, and the need to provide the necessary resources and support.

The following example demonstrates the importance of administrative understanding for the program. One of us worked with a principal who was new to his position. He told the school psychologist that he strongly believed in prevention, and he expressed a great deal of support for the school's intervention assistance program, which had been established during the tenure of the previous principal. To demonstrate his support, he scheduled appointments for every teacher in the school with the intervention assistance team, but he did not ask teachers whether they felt a need for such meetings or were interested in attending. Members of the team explained to him that teacher participation was most effective when it was voluntary, but he insisted that he wanted to show his support to the superintendent. The team found itself in an awkward position. Members did not want to offend the "supportive" principal, but, even more, they did not wish to impose meetings on teachers because this manner of operating had the clear potential for sabotaging the entire program. Therefore, the team decided a compromise was in order. To meet the requirements imposed by the principal, they met for a short time with small groups of teachers and provided additional explanation of the intervention assistance process (an explanation had been briefly presented at a previous faculty meeting). They felt that the time would be spent productively and teachers would not be put in uncomfortable positions. Although most of the teachers followed through and expressed at least some interest in the discussion, several were quite overt in their hostile reactions. One even sat with his back to the team during the entire discussion!

This example demonstrates that principals must thoroughly understand the entire intervention assistance process and its rationale as well as issues related to systems change in order to provide appropriate support. This requirement cannot be over-stated. One of the factors contributing to the problems in this example was that the psychologist assumed that the principal understood more about the approach and systems change than he did. Furthermore, as a person new to the position, the principal had a need to be accepted by the superintendent—a need the psychologist may also have underestimated.

Initial Staff Acceptance and Understanding. Once administrative sanction has been given, staff acceptance must be obtained

and their concerns addressed. Individual teachers may need to have
the intervention assistance system explained to them several times
or may need to participate in the process before they develop an
adequate understanding. In addition, misunderstandings or
problems that arise at various times will need to be resolved. At this
level, for example, one of the most frequent issues is when to hold
individual consultation or intervention assistance team meetings.

Failure to address staff concerns may result in long-term
ineffectiveness or in a lack of participation by some members. Ultimately, students may be adversely affected. Therefore, clarification
of the intervention assistance process and resolution of any
misunderstandings that arise must take place on a continual basis
over a long period of time. A detailed discussion of common barriers
and strategies for overcoming them is contained in Chapter Nine.

We have found an entry presentation, mentioned previously,
to be extremely helpful in facilitating staff understanding and
acceptance of a consultative approach. This presentation, made by
special services staff (either individually or collectively) to the entire
school faculty, including the principal, takes place after administrative sanction has been obtained for the intervention assistance
program. In most instances, the presentation is made at the
beginning of the school year, and it informs staff of the services
available, particularly consultation and intervention assistance.

Among the topics discussed, three are essential. The first is
a discussion of rationale, goals, and intended outcomes. These
include providing early intervention, enhancing instructional
options for all students, making assistance readily and immediately
available, extending the skills of special services staff to teachers and
students, and decreasing unnecessary psychoeducational assessments. The second topic is a step-by-step description of procedures.
This description is often accompanied by a graphic illustration of
the process similar to Figure 1. An explanation is given of how and
when teachers can use the system, the specific information they
should have available to facilitate the consultative process during
the meetings, and the various stages in the process. The roles of all
participants (teachers, parents, special services providers) are also
delineated.

The third topic is an explanation of the consultation process:
the core characteristics of consultation and the specific problem-

solving steps. In particular, issues such as responsibility and confidentiality are emphasized. Thus, teachers are informed that they are to retain responsibility for the students whom they discuss during consultation and that both they and the special services staff are responsible for developing interventions. Confidentiality issues to be emphasized include the fact that topics discussed during these meetings are considered confidential as far as the consultant is concerned, although teachers may discuss these issues outside the meetings if they so desire (within a professional context, of course).

In one case, for example, a teacher who was consulting with a school counselor expressed feelings of inadequacy as an instructor because of his difficulties in dealing with some student problems. After revealing these feelings, the teacher was fearful that the counselor would share this information with the principal. The counselor reassured the teacher of the confidential nature of the session and then focused on activities to improve the teacher's skills in dealing with problem situations.

As a result of the entry presentation, teachers develop an understanding of the intervention assistance process and of how to use it effectively. We noted previously that an organization's understanding of an intervention may affect its acceptability. Evidence also suggests that acceptability may be increased through education (Reimers, Wacker, and Koeppl, 1987). The entry presentation also provides an opportunity for teachers to raise any concerns they may have about the new program and to participate in the final program design. However, entry of staff into the system is not an isolated or single event; it takes place over an extended period of time (Zins and Curtis, 1981), and it can be facilitated by the numerous activities suggested in this chapter in addition to the entry presentation.

Similar but usually less detailed presentations can be made to parents through the PTA/PTO or other school-related groups as well as to the board of education. These activities promote and publicize the intervention assistance program, with the intent of encouraging staff and parental participation.

Another tactic that has been advocated is to implement an intervention assistance program on a pilot basis—that is, to implement "sufficient exemplars" (Stolz, 1984). Several cases can be selected, based on their adaptability to the process and their potential for success, to go through the consultation system. As a result, difficulties in the operation of the system can be resolved before introducing it to the entire staff, chances for successful implementation can be maximized, and positive expectations by other teachers regarding the effectiveness of the system can be created. An assumption is that use by others will be increased if good examples of program effectiveness are provided. Furthermore, evidence suggests that principals who "volunteer" their schools as settings in which to experiment with this new approach are likely to eventually adopt an intervention assistance program (Stolz, 1981). Although there are certain potential advantages to initiating the system on a limited basis, we usually recommend schoolwide or districtwide implementation if sanction can be obtained for doing so because the process operates best on a systemic basis.

A final tactic is either to have decision makers (and special services staff) visit a few well-chosen programs to see how they operate or to inform them of successful programs that have been implemented in other schools (for example, Graden, Casey, and Bonstrom, 1985; Maher, in press; Ponti, Zins, and Graden, 1988; Zins, Graden, and Ponti, in press). In this manner, positive expectations can be developed; such beliefs are important to program success.

Reinforcement. Reinforcers are often used with students; however, many educators rarely receive reinforcement for their efforts, even when attempting to implement new programs or to make changes to improve job functioning (Ponti, Zins, and Graden, 1988). Reinforcement should be provided to both special services providers and to teachers for involvement in the consultation program and intervention assistance efforts.

Booster Sessions. As noted previously, entry is not a unitary event; efforts to gain program acceptance and use must continue over time. In this regard, booster sessions to foster staff enthusiasm and increase skills may be useful. Peer support groups are one means of fostering the development of new skills (Zins and others,

1988). In essence, a peer support group "is a small group of professionals with a common area of interest who meet periodically to learn together and to support one another in their ongoing professional development" (Kirshenbaum and Glasser, 1978, p. 3). In such a group, special services providers can receive support and encouragement for implementation, concrete suggestions regarding the system, and technical assistance for resolving any problems that might arise (Zins and others, 1988).

Adoption of an intervention assistance program usually necessitates introduction of a mechanism whereby team members can receive ongoing assistance in developing their skills in consultation and their teaming strategies. Clinical supervision is one such mechanism, as are peer support groups. Another means that we have utilized is a multilevel training approach, through which all group members receive training in relevant skills. Those who have had previous experience and training in these areas and who possess a special interest in them receive additional, in-depth training as well as instruction in guiding others in the development of these skills. These people, referred to as learning facilitators, assist others through peer review activities, case presentations, discussions, and reading the professional literature. Because there are two levels of training in the organization, the need for outside consultants is decreased; this is an efficient way of providing necessary staff development.

Adaptation. Finally, at all levels, there is a need to review and possibly adapt the intervention assistance program based on information received through evaluation procedures. Unexpected problems can lead to significant difficulties in program implementation. For instance, in one school in which we were involved, initial plans called for the creation of a team to provide intervention assistance in order to utilize the skills of all the special services staff. However, it was not possible to schedule meetings because all the special services staff were assigned to several schools and were not in any one school at the same time. Furthermore, only the school psychologist had training in consultation and teaming strategies; thus, other special services staff did not have the necessary technical skills to provide intervention assistance. As a result, the school psychologist assumed primary responsibility for consultation, although efforts were made to gradually involve other special services staff (Ponti, Zins, and Graden, 1988). This example demonstrates the necessity of adapting a program to meet local needs in order to achieve success.

There is, however, a caveat in regard to program adaptation. Program adaptation has the potential advantage of making it likely that the program will be used, but because the procedures differ from those in the original model, the new program may omit an essential ingredient and therefore not be as effective. Unfortunately, at this time we do not have sufficient research data to determine all the components necessary for success.

Individual Practitioner

Several requirements for individual special services providers can promote implementation of an intervention assistance approach. First, although we acknowledge the importance of administrative support and sanction in program implementation, "there is little doubt that the primary variable in determining whether consultation services actually become available and are implemented will be the *desire* of the individual practitioner to bring about change. . . . The 'bottom line' may well be the desire of each individual practitioner to incorporate consultation into his/her repertoire of skills and services. Without that desire, change will not occur" (Zins and Curtis, 1984, p. 239). Practitioners must actively search for ways to implement alternative services delivery approaches rather than passively accept barriers that they inevitably encounter. The most productive efforts are directed at addressing problems and not simply at discussing them.

Second, a key reason for practitioner resistance is lack of adequate preparation. Many special services providers have not received preservice training in consultation, problem solving, teaming strategies, behavioral observation and assessment, and intervention development. Clearly, university-based training programs must emphasize the development of these skills in the future. However, to meet current needs, in-service training should be provided for special services personnel. The state of Iowa, as an illustration of this point, obtained a federal grant that has enabled them to train vast numbers of special services personnel in consultative and intervention assistance skills (J. Grimes, personal communication, September 1986). Such an effort is commendable, although it is likely that in most states responsibility for funding will rest with individual school districts. Districts will have to determine the training needs of special services staff and also ensure that building administrators have a thorough understanding of the intervention assistance process and of how to meet individual student needs.

Third, practitioner job descriptions should include consultation and prevention services. Once these responsibilities are formalized, they become legitimate and expected. However, many special services providers either do not have job descriptions or have descriptions so vague they are essentially meaningless. By including consultation and related activities in job descriptions, the school district formally acknowledges the importance of these services and makes a commitment to their provision. Furthermore, such statements make practitioners accountable for delivering these services, and they also imply that the district will provide the necessary resources for implementation.

Practitioners should expect to expend great amounts of effort and energy in order to implement an intervention assistance program successfully. There is no quick, easy method of introducing change. In order to avoid the discouragement that frequently accompanies unrealistic expectations, practitioners need to realize from the beginning that change takes time, patience, perseverance, and energy.

Coordinating Services Delivery

When consultation was introduced in the educational and psychological literature in the late 1960s and early 1970s, much emphasis was placed on describing essential characteristics of the consultative process, with little attention devoted to consultation as an integral component of the entire services delivery system. Because consultation was a new concept, it was necessary that it be discussed in its "pure" form, separate from other services. Unfortunately, this early description has led to some confusion among practitioners and trainers. Many have incorrectly assumed that one either consults or provides other services. In fact, however, there are few people in schools whose jobs involve only consultation. Most special services staff provide consultation as part of the many services that they deliver, such as assessment and counseling. Educational diagnosticians, for example, should consult with teachers and parents every time they evaluate a student, both before they undertake the evaluation, in order to determine relevant concerns and to specifically understand the referral questions to be answered, and following the evaluation to discuss results and implications.

Similarly, an intervention assistance program should not be viewed as separate from other services provided by a school. Special services providers in a consultative capacity can be viewed as integral adjuncts to classroom teachers and the instructional process. Responsibility for student learning does not rest solely with teachers; the entire educational system must be designed to provide an appropriate education for each student. Furthermore, consultation can provide data useful in the assessment process with regard to the types of interventions that have been successful or unsuccessful.

What emerges from this approach is integration of the entire educational system rather than separate special and general education units. The result is the effective and efficient utilization of resources and personnel.

Program Evaluation

Program evaluation is an essential aspect of the implementation process. Consideration should be given to appropriate assessment activities during initial program planning. Accountability and program evaluation methods are the focus of Chapter Eleven.

CHAPTER NINE

Resolving Resistances
to Program Implementation

Throughout the book we have emphasized that implementation of an intervention assistance program is a complex and usually challenging process. The suggestions and ideas discussed at length in Chapters Seven and Eight should prove helpful in efforts to implement such programs. As should be clear by now, establishing, demonstrating, and monitoring collaboration is the cornerstone of successful program implementation as well as of effective consultation services. However, no matter how well planned and skillfully executed the implementation process is, barriers frequently must be overcome. This chapter discusses various sources of resistance that may hinder the implementation of intervention assistance programs, and it offers practical suggestions about how to alleviate difficulties encountered.

Understanding Resistance

A critical ingredient for successful program implementation and effective individual consultation is the ability to deal with resistance. Resistance is not an entirely negative phenomenon. In fact, it can be a normal and even positive reaction that is necessary for system maintenance and as a means for dealing with change (Brown, Pryzwansky, and Schulte, 1987).

In almost all endeavors, resistance is a natural reaction to change; individuals, groups, and organizations develop habitual ways of functioning (Brown, Pryzwansky, and Schulte, 1987) and strive to maintain the status quo. Change is approached with caution because of its uncertainty, its unpredictability, its newness. We do not know, for example, all the ramifications that instituting an intervention assistance program may have for a school district.

Moreover, although people may be ready for change because of notable problems with the current system, they may still resist efforts to alleviate those problems. For instance, even if a school district clearly seems to be experiencing a great deal of distress or difficulty (low morale, inefficient services delivery, frequent staff turnover, overt complaining), resistance to change among school personnel should not be unexpected. Although this point may appear self-evident, it is often lost once we become personally involved in the change process.

Furthermore, consultants committed to the new program may take resistance to change or consultee desire for system maintenance as a personal affront. And consultants sometimes forget that consultees may be upset by the suggestion that the system of which they are a part is badly in need of change.

Consultants need to recognize therefore that change takes time, no matter what its focus. As with any organizational change effort, an intervention assistance program often requires two to three years to implement (see Fullan, Miles, and Taylor, 1980; Ponti, Zins, and Graden, 1988). We may overlook this point when involved in a change effort because of a natural tendency to want immediate results for our efforts.

Finally, system-level change will cause multiple responses as a result of reciprocal interactions among different parts of the system. Change in one area of the school organization will result in changes in other areas as well. Failure to anticipate such reciprocal interactions and reactions is likely to result in implementation problems.

Resistance to change is discussed from several perspectives in the following sections. Although this discussion focuses primarily on consultees and organizations, many of the ideas are equally applicable to consultants.

The perspectives discussed may be helpful in increasing our understanding of resistance, but it should be noted that hesitation or reluctance to change may not be a reflection of resistance per se. Rather, these behaviors indicate a choice or decision about not implementing a specific intervention or the intervention assistance program. The benefits of intervening may be perceived as not warranting the risks involved. Therefore, if it is obvious that a consultee or an organization has made a decision regarding change, the consultant should consider the perceived costs or benefits associated with that decision.

Behavioral Perspective

A behavioral/cognitive behavioral framework has been found to be helpful in examining resistance or conflict (Abidin, 1975; Piersel and Gutkin, 1983; Zins, 1985). From this perspective, resistance may result when change efforts do not lead to reinforcement or if they are associated with insufficient reinforcement, punishment, or both. Therefore, readiness and willingness to change may be related to the perceptions of consultees and organizations of the costs involved (especially those related to failure) and the distress experienced (Goodstein, 1978). However, there are consequences to changing as well as to not changing; thus, the decision to change or not change may be related to consultee considerations of which action results in more reinforcement or less punishment. By trying to understand consultee perceptions of the immediate consequences of suggested changes, consultants may be able to deal with and overcome sources of resistance.

All participants in the intervention assistance process, from administrators to special services staff to teachers, need to be rewarded and reinforced for their efforts in implementing the program and in carrying out interventions. Because initial efforts directed toward change frequently meet with strong resistance, this type of support may be particularly important when first introducing an overall program or specific interventions for individual students. An often-neglected benefit of accountability procedures is that participants are provided with specific feedback regarding their professional performance and program outcomes—results that one hopes are reinforcing! However, the suggestion to collect such data must be made cautiously and early in the change process as it may prove too threatening to consultees who are already wary of the implications of the new program.

The anticipation of potentially negative consequences by the consultee requires special sensitivity. Piersel and Gutkin (1983) suggest that during consultation there is usually some focus on consultee "failure" because previously unsuccessful efforts of the consultee to resolve the problem must be reviewed. Admitting that one's efforts have not been successful, although necessary, is not reinforcing. Likewise, although interventions should be developed collaboratively by the consultant and consultee, primary responsibility for carrying out the intervention plan generally rests with the consultee. As a result, it might be inferred that an intervention was unsuccessful because the consultee did not execute the plan as it was designed (even though another factor may have been the cause of the failure). Again, the outcome may be negative for the consultee, and the experience may lead to resistance in the future (Piersel and Gutkin, 1983).

Attribution Theory

Individuals often make markedly different attributions about the causes of the same behaviors. According to attribution theory, we tend to attribute our own behaviors to external causes (for example, environmental conditions), while attributing others' behaviors to internal characteristics (for example, their lack of ability) (Jones and Nisbett, 1972). These tendencies are referred to as "the fundamental attribution error" (Ross, 1977) and are due to differences in the information available to actors and observers as well as in the focus of their attention.

Consultants and consultees may differ in their perceptions of events because of their different roles (teachers as performers and consultants as observers), and these different perceptions can lead to conflict (Kelley, 1979). Although performers tend to perceive their behavior as being influenced by situational or external variables (policies of the school, student ability), observers may view the same behavior as being caused by the actor's personal characteristics (effort expended in carrying out teaching responsibilities, for example).

As a result of differences in causal attributions, people working together on implementation may not agree about the causes of environmental events, and these different explanations may result in resistance to the program (Zins, 1985). Several brief examples follow.

Some school psychologists complain that they want to provide comprehensive psychological services (for example, National Association of School Psychologists, 1984) but that they are unable to offer services other than traditional testing because administrators will not allow them to do so. As a result, these psychologists believe they have a valid reason for not even attempting to change the services delivery system or their individual practices.

Similarly, some counselors tend to attribute blame for ineffective interventions that are developed during consultation to acts or characteristics of the consultee or to external aspects of the situation rather than to their own skills (Martin and Curtis, 1981). In fact, they may not even examine their own behaviors to see whether they contributed to the failure of the intervention. Gutkin and Clark (1984) found that the consultants in their study believed that the primary determinant of consultation outcome was the consultees rather than their own skills or the organizational contexts within which they worked.

As another example, a special services provider may attribute an administrator's resistance to change to the administrator's need for system maintenance and for avoiding disruption of the organization's equilibrium (an internal attribution). In fact, the administrator's reluctance might be linked to a lack of understanding about how to bring about change. Conversely, an administrator might attribute the resistance of special services staff to the introduction of an intervention assistance program to lack of motivation and unwillingness to deliver new services (an internal attribution). The actual cause might be that the special services staff have an unusually high caseload, and few have had training in consultation and teaming strategies. They might also believe that they receive little support from the administration for changing their situation so that they could devote the necessary time and energy to implementing the new program.

Consultants and teachers may also differ in their attributions for student-related problems, particularly if the consultant has an ecological orientation and the consultee believes the problems are caused by factors internal to the students. In such cases, the teacher may attribute student failure to a lack of effort or ability, while the consultant may consider additional variables such as teaching style and classroom organization and management as contributing factors.

These examples demonstrate how differences in the attributions of participants in consultation can lead to conflict. Consultants need to be aware of these potential differences and must be ready to address them should they arise.

Intervention Acceptability

An important influence on whether a recommended intervention will be successful is its acceptability, which is "based upon unique interactions between the target behavior, proposed treatment, and change agent" (Reimers, Wacker, and Koeppl, 1987, p. 212). Intervention acceptability can be related to resistance in that school personnel may not implement interventions if they do not like or are not satisfied with them (Witt and Elliott, 1985; Wolf, 1978). In other words, consultees must view a treatment in a positive manner before they will implement it. Moreover, acceptability may determine the integrity with which the treatment is implemented (Reimers, Wacker, and Koeppl, 1987). Therefore, consultants must understand the aspects of interventions that make them acceptable or unacceptable to consultees.

Two extensive summaries of the research on factors influencing the acceptability of interventions have been published (Reimers, Wacker, and Koeppl, 1987; Witt and Elliott, 1985). Several of the factors for which the most support was found are summarized here, although it should be noted that treatments cannot be identified categorically as acceptable or not acceptable. The setting, resources required, client characteristics, goals of treatment, problem focus, and so forth are important contextual variables affecting acceptability.

We list here major factors that influence acceptability and an example of each: effectiveness of the treatment (for example, those that are more effective or perceived as more effective are usually more acceptable), type of intervention (positive reinforcement is usually preferred over punishment), resources required (excessive time often makes an intervention unacceptable), person responsible for carrying out the intervention (preference for teachers or other professionals varies under different conditions), theoretical orientation of the intervention (a behaviorally specific intervention is likely to be more acceptable than one based on vague internal attributions), ecological intrusiveness (if implementation of an intervention interferes with established procedures, it may not be acceptable), and side effects (negative side effects of the treatment may outweigh the benefits) (Reimers, Wacker, and Koeppl, 1987; Witt, 1986; Witt and Elliott, 1985). Linn and Zaltman (1973) also suggest that more complex interventions may meet with more resistance or be less acceptable than less complex interventions.

Although all these factors are important to consider when developing treatments, intervention acceptability remains a rather complex and not well understood area (Witt and Elliott, 1985). Moreover, most of the research in this area is based on analogue studies. There is a need to validate these findings with pre- and post-study measurements in situations in which the interventions are actually carried out.

Resistance to Change at Various Organizational Levels

In this section, sources of resistance at various organizational levels—district (and building), consultee, and special services staff—are examined selectively from the perspectives presented previously. Each barrier is followed by suggestions for its removal. These levels are admittedly somewhat arbitrary, as the three are overlapping and interactive. Nevertheless, this breakdown facilitates discussion of the topic. Furthermore, one of the few empirical investigations in this area found that consultants perceived these same three dimensions to be the primary variables that affected resistance (Gutkin and Clark, 1984).

District and Building

The following review of resistance at the district and building level is not intended to be exhaustive but to provide examples of common barriers that may be encountered.

Perceived Evaluation. One cause of resistance (usually difficult to detect) is that introduction of an intervention assistance program may imply that administrators have been ineffective managers of services delivery. They may justifiably ask, "If the system was functioning adequately, why is it necessary to introduce such a major change?" People associated with the district special education program, in particular, may have adverse reactions because a proposal for an intervention assistance program will cause them to carefully examine the special education system. They may have to face the fact that current referral and placement procedures are not satisfactory. Such an admission is clearly not reinforcing.

For these reasons, it is important to ascertain who has instituted efforts to implement the intervention assistance system and why. If an outside consultant, a school board member, or a special services professional suggests a new program, the administrator in charge of student services may resist the project, particularly if she or he is not ready to change. There may also be a loss of status in not being the one responsible for introducing the program, which may also cause the administrator responsible to be resistant. Therefore, it is important that the program be introduced as a way of improving the overall quality of services to children and that no blame for possible ineffectiveness be attributed to personal performance or be attached to introduction of the change.

Internal Pressures. Another concern relates to the overall performance of the school organization. "Low-functioning" or inefficient schools, although most in need of change, may be least able to institute interventions and most resistant to a new program. In these settings, tension associated with a fear of failure or with devoting significant efforts to merely meet minimal levels of performance may make it difficult for members to consider alternative services delivery; the change would only increase the level of tension. Severe organizational problems in the school may also hamper its ability to even recognize its needs or to discuss them freely. In such cases it may be necessary to work either toward addressing those aspects of organizational functioning most in need of change or toward overall organizational improvement (of which the intervention assistance program may be part) (see Maher, Illback, and Zins, 1984b; Schmuck and Runkel, 1985). The goal is to help the organization develop the capacity to initiate the change.

External Pressures. A number of forces beyond the school exert tremendous influence on services delivery. These include legislation, court decisions, funding, standards of professional organizations, societal and community norms, technology, training, and continuing education (Curtis and Zins, 1986). Several of these issues warrant elaboration here. Additional detailed discussion about external forces that can influence services delivery can be found in other sources (for example, Conoley and Conoley, 1982; Curtis and Zins, 1986).

Particularly noteworthy is legislation such as P.L. 94-142, which exerts significant, direct influence. This law guarantees a free, appropriate public education for all handicapped students in the environment that is least restrictive for each child. Because a major goal of intervention assistance programs is to facilitate the functioning of students in the regular classroom (which is the least restrictive of all school environments for most students), this approach is highly consistent with P.L. 94-142. However, because the law also places considerable emphasis on the identification of children suspected of being handicapped and provides special funding for those so identified (Gutkin and Tieger, 1979), many practitioners have experienced tremendous pressures to engage in diagnostic and labeling activities that lead to an increase in the number of handicapped students identified. For these and associated reasons, as discussed in Chapter Two, special education has come under attack for overidentifying students as handicapped.

Another external force is community groups. On several occasions we have encountered student advocates who have argued that intervention assistance programs are merely a means through which schools will deny special education services to children who need them. Although these advocates are well intentioned, they do not have a thorough understanding of intervention assistance programs and their goals.

Another external force that is a frequent concern of administrators (as well as of special educators) is the loss of funding that may result from an effective intervention assistance program. Because a primary goal of this approach is to decrease the number of students in special education programs who potentially can succeed in regular classrooms, there could be a decrease in funding of special education units from state or federal sources (or both). Relatedly, in-service training to prepare special services providers to engage in consultation and teaming strategies can temporarily increase the costs of implementing these programs.

Although we are not aware of any districts in which there have been significant decreases in funding, we continue to advocate alternative funding mechanisms for intervention assistance programs. State departments of education, as well as the federal government, should be encouraged to provide financial support for program implementation. Primarily, alternative means of computing reimbursable services are needed so that districts are funded for consultative support services. Funding should also be made available for in-service training and staff development to assist personnel in preparing for expanded roles. However, regardless of developments at the state and federal levels, local districts still must make critical decisions about using available funds. They may decide that it is in their best interest to maintain a low enrollment in special education classes for the mildly handicapped in order to enable special education teachers to provide assistance to regular classroom teachers and parents. Therefore, local funds may be used to supplement those received from the state in order to keep the unit operational.

Educational Philosophy. The educational philosophy of a school can influence the operation of an intervention assistance program. Philosophy plays an important part in determining the organizational climate, which in turn influences organizational characteristics such as communication; values; relationships among staff, students, and parents; and cohesiveness of staff (Curtis and Zins, 1986). Kuehnel (1975) also found a significant relationship between organizational climate and the use of mental health resources in elementary schools.

In order for an intervention assistance program to operate successfully, it is necessary for the school to emphasize meeting the needs of individual students and not to expect every one of them to progress at the same rate. It may be necessary for the school's educational philosophy to be carefully analyzed before the new program is introduced.

Lack of Understanding. Sometimes an administration pays lip service to intervention assistance programs but then does not support implementation of such systems with the necessary resources—human, financial, and technological. Usually this discrepancy between words and actions occurs because administrators do not have a clear understanding of the intervention assistance process and its implications for the entire educational services system, or they have different conceptualizations of and expectations for service delivery. Thus, administrators and other decision makers must clearly understand program goals and must view the program as an acceptable organizational-level change. The development of a complete understanding of the program among key personnel requires consistent and systematic efforts over an extended period of time and, therefore, efforts to instill familiarization with the program must be ongoing.

Lack of Ownership. Those implementing intervention assistance programs sometimes also find that administrators desire system maintenance or attempt to protect their turf. To counter such attempts, administrators must develop a sense of ownership of the intervention assistance program, particularly if they themselves did not initiate its adoption. Eventually, the entire organization must come to own the program if it is to become part of the district's routine operation. To promote ownership, all levels of the organization must be involved in all aspects of program planning and development.

Lack of Measurable Outcomes. Administrators may be hesitant to support a new approach if they are not convinced of the efficacy of the program or at least of its potential effectiveness (which is related to intervention acceptability). When their expectations for efficacy are not high, they may unwittingly transmit less than positive expectations about the program to school staff, parents, and the community. This source of resistance is compounded by the fact that some outcomes of intervention assistance programs are difficult to measure. Although we can straightforwardly count how many teachers participated in consultation sessions, we have difficulty in determining how many students were not placed in restrictive programs as a result of intervention assistance or in ascertaining related improvements in student behavior. Furthermore, although differences between numbers of special class placements before and after implementation can be readily determined, it is usually not possible to establish cause-and-effect relationships. It is also difficult to measure changes in individual student behaviors subsequent to the development and implementation of interventions.

To counter this source of resistance, it is helpful to share the outcome data from intervention assistance programs established in other districts or the data reported in the literature. Likewise, visits to observe successfully implemented programs in operation may be helpful. Use of single-subject designs, as described in Chapter Four, is certainly relevant in this regard, and adoption of a comprehensive evaluation plan (see Chapter Eleven) can also be reassuring and helpful. Administrators often need some assurance that the program will be evaluated periodically to determine whether it is meeting district needs.

Consultee

Caplan (1970) suggests that the major sources of resistance are consultee psychological deficits, and our discussion expands on his conceptualization. Caplan identifies "four common reasons for the work difficulties [that consultees may have] that underlie the need for consultation. These are: (a) lack of knowledge, (b) lack of skill, (c) lack of self-confidence, and (d) lack of professional objectivity" (p. 127). Although each may be a reason why consultees "need" consultation, each can also be linked to resistance. For example, lack of confidence may be associated with a teacher's failure to carry out an intervention developed during consultation. Building consultee confidence through support and assistance may be necessary in this instance. As another example, lack of knowledge may cause a teacher to see an intervention as unacceptable. It may then be necessary for the consultant to ensure that the consultee clearly knows how to implement the treatment and why it needs to be implemented. Additional sources of resistance related to consultees follow.

Lack of Involvement. Resistance may result from the school staff's lack of involvement in the development and adoption of the intervention assistance program and their resulting feeling that the system has been forced on them. The potential usefulness of the process may not even be a consideration in such cases. In addition, people providing consultation services may be perceived as outsiders, particularly if they are external consultants, new to the school, or operate on an itinerant basis. Resistance to the program or to an individual consultant may be the result of such perceptions.

Active involvement at all levels of the organization is an effective means of reducing the threat associated with change. Moreover, involvement in the change process itself can lead to increased commitment to the success of the program. In any case, failure to involve members of the organization is inconsistent with a collaborative approach and may reflect broad problems that need to be examined.

Perceived Evaluation. Resistance may develop because of the perceived criticism of consultee competence that consultation implies (Gross, 1980). Such resistance may be evidenced in several ways during interactions between the consultant and consultee. Often, the consultant will feel uncomfortable, bored, indifferent, irritated, or disinterested (Block, 1981). These feelings may result from verbal or nonverbal messages conveyed by consultees. They should be a warning or red flag to the consultant that something is amiss and that clarification of the resistance is needed.

The consultant must attempt to seek understanding with the consultee. It is not necessary for consultants and consultees to always agree, but because resistance may be a form of not expressing concerns directly, a minimal level of understanding of these concerns should be attained (Block, 1981).

Special Services Personnel

Like consultees, special services providers may not accept an intervention assistance approach and therefore may be resistant to it. Special services staff who possess such attitudes may view the addition of consultation to their jobs as punishment and may resist efforts to have them go beyond providing direct services. This reaction may be a result of several factors. First, special services personnel may not be adequately prepared to be consultants. We are not suggesting that special services staff who have not completed training in consultation and intervention assistance methods engage in the process. On the contrary, as discussed in Chapter Twelve, such actions may be unethical. Rather, these people need to seek out and obtain appropriate training.

Second, another realistic reason for special services staff not to engage in intervention assistance activities is related to provider-to-student ratios. An extremely large caseload makes the provision of consultation services exceedingly difficult (Zins and Curtis, 1987). In fact, Smith (1984) found that the roles of school psychologists expanded as the ratio of psychologists to students became smaller.

Third, special services providers may want to continue in their familiar role as experts. It is not uncommon therefore for a special services staff member to invest considerable energy on system maintenance rather than on change. Dealing with change is frequently an emotional rather than a rational or intellectual process (Block, 1981). In these cases, consultants must examine and be aware of their own vested interests and values. They should be cautious to avoid creating unnecessary attitudinal barriers in themselves that may result in ineffective behaviors. As we have stated elsewhere, a significant requirement for providers of consultative services is the desire to engage in these activities (Zins and Curtis, 1981, 1984).

Fourth, special services staff members may be concerned that if the intervention assistance program is successful, their positions will be eliminated because of reduction in both the number of special education students and associated funding. The funding issues need to be addressed primarily at state and federal levels, although professional and parent organizations can also and perhaps should initiate efforts to bring about changes in the ways services are reimbursed. Nevertheless, we are unaware of any special services personnel whose jobs have been eliminated as a result of funding cuts associated with this approach. Job security may in fact be improved when job descriptions are expanded to involve special services staff in classroom-based assistance.

A related issue is that funding of special education services by the federal government is likely to be reduced in the future. Thus, there may be a strong impetus for special educators to expand their services because fewer staff will be available to meet student needs. A consultative approach is an efficient and effective means of providing assistance to many students. In addition, if special education personnel are perceived as delivering only direct services to students in resource and self-contained classrooms, their value may be diminished. Those who can offer a broad range of services will become more attractive than those who cannot. For all these reasons, it is highly desirable for special services staff to take a proactive stance in demonstrating their importance to the overall educational system, which can be done through marketing and accountability techniques.

If special services staff are encouraged to adopt a consultative approach, they should be reinforced and supported for their efforts in order to reduce the threat that may be associated with changes in job responsibilities. Leaders can provide the support necessary to minimize consultee feelings of ambiguity, lack of self-confidence, and so forth that may accompany the change.

Methods of Preventing and Overcoming Resistance

The skill of the special services provider in preventing and resolving resistance may be a major factor in determining whether the intervention assistance program is implemented and maintained successfully. Many strategies for dealing with resistance have already been discussed. This section elaborates some of these ideas. In many instances, the strategies are used in combination rather than alone.

Identifying Resistance

Before one attempts to overcome resistance, it is necessary to recognize that it exists or that it may arise. As the saying goes, "It's the shell you don't hear that gets you." One way of identifying resistance is through an organizational assessment. Using this approach may make it possible to prevent resistance or to deal with it before it becomes widespread or deeply embedded in the organization.

Resistance can take many forms, from the subtle to the overt, and it can occur during initial implementation or even after the intervention assistance system has been operational for some time. A fifth-grade teacher may frequently say "Yes, but . . ." to suggestions made by the consultant. A principal may provide verbal support for the program but then neglect to find ways and times for teachers to participate in the process. A parent may ask for help but then consistently fail to carry out the interventions developed during consultation. A state department of education may promote the concept of intervention assistance but then not explore or provide alternative means of funding, or continue to require services inconsistent with the new approach.

Maintenance of Collaborative Relationships

In order to reduce the likelihood that various barriers to intervention assistance programs will arise, developing collaborative relationships is essential. "Maintaining a collaborative approach can be one of the most important strategies in resolving or avoiding conflicts in . . . professional relationships" (Zins, 1985, p. 118). Not only are such relationships necessary for effective consultation with individual teachers, but they are also helpful in bringing about organizational-level change (which also involves individual consultation). We elaborate on collaborative relationships here by discussing how to establish them, consultant power, a possible benefit of collaboration, and consultee responsibilities; additional discussion is contained in Parsons and Meyers (1984) and Zins (1985).

Specific suggestions for establishing collaborative relationships in consultation were made in Chapter Three. To summarize, the process essentially involves showing respect and positive regard for consultees, their expertise and knowledge, contributions they may make to the problem-solving process, and the problems they are experiencing. Listening in a nonjudgmental manner and understanding concerns are also important, as are sincerity and genuineness. Both consultants and consultees should feel free to contribute their ideas to both problem identification and problem solution.

Consultants have expert, referent, and informational power available to them (French and Raven, 1959), and they need to make use of all three types in collaborative relationships rather than relying primarily on one to the exclusion of others (Zins and Curtis, 1984). A consultant who focuses only on expertise, for example, is implying that she or he does not value the potential contributions of the consultee. Consultants must be cognizant of the fact that unequal power relationships do not facilitate effective problem solving (Zins, 1985). Acknowledging the contributions of consultees to the problem-solving process may help to equalize power within the relationship (Parsons and Meyers, 1984). A consultant who relies only on referent power will not offer suggestions for resolving the problem.

Although seldom discussed, collaboration may be one antidote to burnout or professional alienation (Tyler, Pargament, and Gratz, 1983). By working closely with other professionals in problem resolution, one may gain camaraderie and support.

Consultees also bear responsibility for the maintenance of collaborative relationships. For example, consultees must learn to form realistic expectations about the skills and responsibilities of consultants and the consultation process (Sandoval, Lambert, and Davis, 1977). Consultants do not possess all the "answers," and most problem situations do not have simple, quick solutions (Zins, 1985). Consultees also need to understand the role of the consultant

(Sandoval, Lambert, and Davis, 1977). Consultants cannot provide direct service to every student who needs assistance, nor would such assistance be appropriate. Therefore, the provision of indirect service, with the consultee as the provider of the treatment, is necessary in most cases. In addition, consultees must describe problems accurately (Sandoval, Lambert, and Davis, 1977). Although the consultant facilitates this process through questioning and other problem-clarification strategies, efficiency can be increased when consultees are able to describe clearly and succinctly the antecedents, consequences, and other relevant details of a problem (Zins, 1985). Finally, consultees should realize that consultants may not be familiar with many aspects of consultees' jobs (Sandoval, Lambert, and Davis, 1977). Initially, consultants will be unfamiliar with teachers' norms, policies, and procedures, and with other contextual variables. Therefore, consultees need to provide this information to consultants.

Attribution Management

Resistance to a new program can be lowered when negative, divergent, and faulty attributions are recognized and altered. Attitudes of consultants toward consultees can influence the attributions developed about them. If we like other people, we may attribute their negative behavior to situational causes or at least acknowledge their good intentions. However, if we do not like them, we are likely to perceive their negative behavior as confirming our previous beliefs (Strong and Claiborn, 1982) and as reflecting their personal characteristics (Zins, 1985). Furthermore, consultants tend to work with consultees whom they find likable (and thus about whom they make positive attributions) and who are responsive to intervention efforts (Alpert, Ludwig, and Weiner, 1979). Such tendencies mean that many consultees who need assistance are avoided by consultants because they are not likable or are resistant. Consultants must be sensitive to how their feelings about consultees affect expectations and their willingness to work with them.

Empathy has been shown to be effective in reducing differences in causal attributions (Gould and Sigall, 1977; Regan and Totten, 1975; Storms, 1973). By using empathy to see a problem situation from the consultee's point of view, consultants can curb the tendency to blame the consultee for unsuccessful sessions. (It may be found, for example, that the reason a teacher did not implement an academic intervention was not because of a lack of concern but because the teacher was experiencing an unusually high level of stress at the time.) In addition, consultants can try to increase consultees' empathy for clients.

Consultants need to be aware that they may attribute failure in consultation to consultees and may neglect to examine their own role in the process (Martin and Curtis, 1981). Recognition of one's own tendency to make faulty attributions may facilitate the problem-solving process and facilitate control of this tendency (Martin, 1983; Ponti, 1983).

Improving Problem Identification

Many of the efforts designed to improve problem identification are closely related to attribution management. Improving problem identification reduces resistance by encouraging consultees to define problems in a manner in which they can be more readily solved.

A technique that is helpful here is to elicit from consultees during problem identification information about specific student behaviors (Tombari and Bergan, 1978). Changing observable behaviors is usually considered more possible than altering characteristics internal to the child. Similarly, if consultees perceive problems as global and ambiguous (Johnny *never* sits still), they feel little control over the situation. Gathering objective, behavioral data helps teachers to view problems realistically and to see them as manageable (Martin, 1983; Tombari and Bergan, 1978). Thus, reframing the situation can change its significance and meaningfulness. Reframing is taking "the conceptual and/or emotional setting or viewpoint in relation to which the situation is experienced and [placing] it in another frame which fits the facts of the same concrete situation equally well or even better and thereby changes its entire meaning" (Watzlawick, Weakland, and Fisch, 1974, p. 95). Reframing does not change the facts of the situation but rather the meaning attributed to them by the individual. To illustrate, a teacher may make dispositional attributions (for example, attributions about the ability of a student) that make the problem unsolvable. By reframing the student's behaviors, the teacher becomes more confident that she or he can achieve control (Strong and Claiborn, 1982).

Reinforcement

The length of time and the amount of energy that a person is willing to expend in response to a challenging problem are related to expectations of success (Bandura, 1977). A consultee who lacks self-confidence and is uncertain about problem resolution is unlikely to expend a great deal of effort. Although certain techniques (for example, reframing) promote consultee confidence, until success is actually realized, it will be especially important to reinforce consultee efforts through moral support and encouragement. Reinforcement for personal effort is as important for adults as it is for children!

Constructive Confrontation

Confrontation may also be used to deal with resistance. Unfortunately, for those who are not familiar with the term professionally, *confrontation* tends to carry a negative connotation, conjuring up images of heated debates. However, as it is used within the context of consultative interactions, confrontation refers to a constructive interpersonal process that is used to resolve seeming contradictions in information or perceptions. Despite understandings to the contrary, confrontation is intended to be free of high emotions, particularly hostility, and of win-or-lose struggles. Both indirect and direct confrontation can be used to deal with consultee resistance.

Caplan (1970) offers indirect confrontation as an appropriate technique for consultants. With his highly psychotherapeutic orientation, Caplan is sensitive to the need to retain the defense mechanisms of the consultee if at all possible. He views indirect confrontation as a procedure for dealing with contradictions that emerge during consultation (for example, resistance to implementing strategies developed) without unnecessarily breaking down the consultee's defenses.

Indirect confrontation essentially allows the consultee an escape from the contradiction without placing the onus on the consultee. To allow the consultee's defenses to remain intact, the confrontational suggestion or inquiry is directed at another target, perhaps the client. For example, if a consultant suspects that a classroom teacher's resistance is a result of feelings of inadequacy in dealing with rather routine classroom-management situations, indirect confrontation would shift the focus away from the feelings of inadequacy and toward the children who pose the threat to the confidence of the teacher. The consultant might suggest that these particular children "aren't able to function within the limits normally allowed within classrooms." And consequently, "it might be necessary to use special procedures to help them behave appropriately." This suggestion would likely reduce the resistance of the consultee because the need for the special procedures would be seen as a result of client characteristics rather than of the inadequacies of the teacher. The consultant could then assist the teacher in developing good classroom-management techniques.

Although this method appears to protect the defenses of the consultee, the example presented merits particular caution because it tends to reinforce an internal-to-the-child attribution in the teacher. This method is not based on an ecological perspective, and it encourages the teacher to perceive children as being solely responsible for problems. It is possible to use impersonal targets, such as working conditions or scarce resources, rather than children, parents, or colleagues. And, of course, "the system" is always a popular target.

Direct confrontation also offers an alternative to internal-to-the-child attributions. However, unless this technique is used only with consultees with whom the consultant has a strong positive relationship, consultee resistance could increase.

Direct confrontation involves open discussion by the consultant and consultee of conflicts and contradictions. Despite the apparent implication of the term itself, direct confrontation should be conducted in a somewhat tentative manner rather than through statements of fact. Seeming contradictions are approached in a way that allows the consultee to consider the validity of the suggestion. For example, the consultant might broach the subject of resistance by saying, "Do you think . . . ?" Client welfare might necessitate an increase in explicitness when the consultee continues to not recognize or to deny clearly resistant behaviors. Such escalations should be used cautiously and without the attachment of highly affective messages by the consultant.

It is important to remember that the consultant's interpretation of consultee behavior as resistant is merely the consultant's perception of the situation. The validity of that perception must be verified cautiously and with sensitivity to the reactions of the consultee. As noted previously, consultants are also cautioned to examine their own behavior to ascertain its potential contribution to the situation. Furthermore, if the consultant must resort to confrontational methods regularly with the same consultee, the consultative relationship must be examined carefully. Conversely, confrontations with several consultees might suggest scrutiny of personal behaviors by the consultant.

CHAPTER TEN

Guidelines for Operating
the Program

T he decision to adopt a schoolwide intervention assistance program does not guarantee its successful establishment and operation. A large number of practical issues need to be resolved in order for the program to succeed. These practical issues are the subject of this chapter. Failure to address these issues can result in resistance to the process or inefficient program operation (or both). Although the intervention assistance team represents only one facet of the program, we devote considerable attention to teams because of the many practical issues associated with their operation. Further, while we refer to "team members" in this chapter, we want to emphasize that these people primarily provide individual consultation rather than operate on a group (team) basis. Even as individual consultants, however, they are still considered team members.

The practical issues addressed are organized into three general areas: program operation, program administration, and professional practices. Because no research suggests which methods are most effective, many of the recommendations are based on practical experiences that we and our colleagues have had with the approach. In establishing local procedures, school personnel should consider the recommendations here and make choices and adaptations based on their particular situation.

Program Operation

Meeting Times

Consumers must be able to conveniently gain access to intervention assistance services in order to use them effectively. Teachers who engage in consultation must be relieved of instructional responsibilities as necessary; consultants need to be allocated sufficient time to engage in consultation; and members of intervention assistance teams must be free to participate in individual consultation sessions and group meetings.

Intervention assistance teams pose special scheduling problems because of the number of people involved. Selecting and scheduling regular times for the intervention assistance team to meet should be done by a group composed of the principal, special services staff, and representative regular education teachers. Some schools schedule team meetings on an as-needed basis, but we have found it beneficial to hold them regularly at least once per week. The frequency of team meetings depends on the size of the school, the number of requests for assistance, and staff availability. Requests for assistance should be monitored in order to ensure maximum usage.

In setting meeting times, the schedules of all participants must be considered. Schedules of special services staff can often be changed with less difficulty than classroom teachers' schedules. However, a problem specific to special services staff is that they are often assigned to several buildings, and all may not be in the same school on a particular day. One possible strategy for dealing with this problem is for special services personnel to reschedule their time so that they can leave one school and attend the intervention assistance team meeting at another school.

If classroom teachers are to participate, their classes must be supervised when they attend meetings. Use of a substitute to cover the classes of teachers attending the meeting is helpful. In this arrangement, a single substitute employed for the time of the meeting moves from classroom to classroom while various teachers confer with the intervention assistance team. Some principals cover classes to enable teachers to participate. Another approach is for two teachers to combine their classes for short periods of time while one teacher participates in the intervention assistance process. An advantage of this method is that minimal instructional time is lost for students if teachers carefully coordinate their instructional plans.

Time of day for meetings and length of meetings are additional considerations. Some teams have found that meeting before school is most convenient because many team members do not have routine school-related responsibilities at that time. After-school hours usually present conflicts. The length of team meetings should be specified ahead of time so that participants can manage their time efficiently. A minimum of thirty minutes is usually sufficient for a team to meet with one teacher. However, sixty minutes weekly is preferable to allow in-depth discussions or to assist more than one teacher.

Scheduling sessions between the consultant and the consultee may also be problematic. Because of difficulty finding times when both participants are free, sessions are often held during planning periods, lunch, recess, and before or after school. Brief sessions may even be held in the hall outside classrooms, although such arrangements are not as conducive to effective problem solving as sessions that allow the consultant and consultee to concentrate on the problem. Providing opportunities for consultation should be the focus of the principal, special services personnel, and classroom teachers. Some of the strategies for allowing teachers to participate in team meetings may also be helpful in addressing this problem.

Team Membership

Decisions regarding the composition of the intervention assistance team are important. Possible membership configurations were discussed in Chapter Four, but there is no one "correct" composition. The length of team membership for regular education teachers must be set. A minimum two-year term has the benefits of continuity and of making the best use of the teachers' experience as team members. Decisions about adding new members as necessary (for example, to replace someone who resigns) must be made. New members need to obtain the prerequisite skills and be assimilated into the team.

Problems in team functioning are sometimes related to team composition. In this instance, it may be necessary for the group to engage in conflict resolution (see Schmuck and Runkel, 1985) to discuss concerns along with possible solutions. If conflicts cannot be resolved, it may ultimately be necessary to change team membership.

Leadership

Someone must be assigned responsibility for directing the team and for facilitating the problem-solving process. To be effective, the leader of the team must possess the skills necessary to facilitate the group process and problem solving. School administrators, by virtue of their role in the school, are usually the people most likely to assume the leadership position. Their participation provides authority and credibility and, in addition, may be important when interventions that are developed require administrative sanction or permission.

People other than school administrators or principals can also lead the team. Despite the advantages of having the principal serve as the leader, there are drawbacks. Some school personnel may be reluctant to express problems they are experiencing in the classroom when the principal is present because the principal evaluates their performance and may make recommendations regarding tenure and merit pay. Thus, participation by the principal can hinder the open and honest communication necessary for the team to function effectively. However, if most consultation and problem solving occur during individual sessions, this potential difficulty may be minimized.

Program Administration

Record Keeping

Intervention assistance programs may not attain their full potential if a systematic record-keeping system is not established to document outcomes. Documentation of intervention outcomes is important for several reasons (as highlighted in Chapter Eleven) and is especially useful if a psychoeducational evaluation is conducted later. The intervention data provide direction for the assessment process: how to proceed, methods that have been unsuccessful, and questions to be answered.

Essentially, the documentation should be data based and should include this information: definition of the problem behavior, conditions under which it exists, measurement of the behavior (including the procedure utilized and baseline data), discrepancy between current and expected behavior, intervention strategy to be used, evaluation method to determine whether the intervention was successful, the follow-up date, results and date of the follow-up evaluation. Figure 12 is a sample form for documenting the intervention process.

Incentives for Participation

Personnel who participate in individual and group problem solving devote significant energy and time to the intervention assistance process, and reinforcement for their participation is important for program initiation and maintenance. Some methods of providing incentives are described in this section.

Administrators can provide verbal reinforcement to program participants throughout the process. They can encourage team members for their efforts and support referring teachers for seeking assistance for their students. Recognition in school and community newspapers is another easy way to acknowledge staff contributions.

Because of the time they invest, team members may need special incentives. For example, one frequently used method of reinforcement for teachers who serve as team members is to relieve them of some other responsibility (for example, cafeteria or playground supervision) once or twice a week. There could also be some status associated with team membership, particularly if the program is viewed as a highly regarded and effective innovation in the district. One district obtained a state grant to provide monetary stipends to team members, similar to those given to coaches or club

Figure 12. Intervention Record.

Child's name _____ Date _____

I. *Initial intervention plan*

  1. *Definition of problem behavior:*

  What: _____

  _____

  When: _____

  _____

  2. *Measurement of behavior:*   Date _____

  Procedure: _____

  _____

  Baseline: _____

  _____

  3. *Discrepancy between expected and actual behavior:* _____

  _____

  4. *Strategy to be implemented:*   Date _____

  _____

  _____

  5. *Evaluation strategy and follow-up date:* _____

  _____

  6. *Evaluation of intervention and date:* _____

  _____

II. *Modification of intervention:* _____

  _____

  1. *Discrepancy between expected and actual behavior:* _____

  _____

  2. *Evaluation strategy and follow-up date:* _____

  _____

  3. *Evaluation of intervention and date:* _____

  _____

sponsors. However, our experience suggests that such monetary payment is rare. More commonly, it is provided through merit pay.

Many individuals who become members of the intervention assistance program engage in relatively extensive training prior to assuming team and individual consultation responsibilities. This additional training may be considered an incentive, and it also may be possible to arrange for the awarding of continuing education units or university credits for such efforts. When training is provided by a university faculty member, such an arrangement is likely. Many universities provide coursework in consultation through their school psychology, counseling, special education, or similar programs.

A related issue is the provision of incentives for teachers to participate as consultees in the process. To encourage participation, one school (noted by Brown, Pryzwansky, and Schulte, 1987) included "Makes use of available consultation sources" (p. 187) as an area of evaluation for teacher performance. However, this set-up may conflict with the voluntary nature of program participation.

Providing Appropriate Training

We have stressed repeatedly the importance of assuring that special services providers have the necessary skills to provide effective consultation. This training should be provided before the intervention assistance program is implemented. In one school that we know of, an intervention assistance program was introduced but staff had not yet been trained to assume consultant roles. Although the intervention assistance program itself was well conceived, an unintended outcome developed. Special services teachers who were not trained for consultative roles often undercut referrals to the team and encouraged teachers to request that students receive psychoeducational evaluations without systematic attempts at classroom interventions. Thus, program success is closely related to staff preparation.

A checklist of some of the skills needed by team members has been developed by the Ohio Department of Education (1985) (see Figure 13). We discussed the skills needed for effective consultation and participation on teams in Chapters Three and Four.

Figure 13. Checklist of Skills Needed by Members of Intervention
Assistance Teams.

		Yes	No	N/A
1.	Do members have knowledge of informal assessment techniques?	___	___	___
2.	Do members have knowledge of the scope and sequence of academic content areas?	___	___	___
3.	Do members have observation skills?	___	___	___
4.	Do members understand the district philosophy?	___	___	___
5.	Do members have knowledge of the various program goals?	___	___	___
6.	Do members have knowledge of various instructional strategies?	___	___	___
7.	Do members have knowledge of behavior-change strategies?	___	___	___
8.	Do members have knowledge of available resources in the building, district, or region?	___	___	___
9.	Do members have knowledge of eligibility criteria for placement in special education programs?	___	___	___
10.	Do members have good listening skills?	___	___	___
11.	Do members have conflict-resolution skills?	___	___	___
12.	Do members have collaborative decision-making skills?	___	___	___
13.	Do members have knowledge of group dynamics?	___	___	___
14.	Do members have sending and receiving communication skills?	___	___	___
15.	Does chairperson have leadership skills?	___	___	___
16.	Does chairperson have management skills?	___	___	___

Source: Ohio Department of Education, 1985.

Organizational Philosophy, Policies, and Procedures

Most schools have written philosophies of education,
although these documents tend to be general and nonspecific and
are often developed by the board of education with little teacher

input. To maximize the chances of success for an intervention assistance program, school philosophy, policies, and procedures should emphasize prevention and meeting individual needs of all students. If the prevailing philosophy (or behavior) is to deal with students experiencing problems by "getting them out of the classroom," a significant obstacle can be placed in the way of an effective intervention assistance system. Flexibility to alter the curriculum or to modify classroom programs to meet student needs must be provided and encouraged. Often, the written district or school policy has components (such as "serving the needs of all students") that can be used to support adoption of the intervention assistance process.

Professional Practices

Gaining Access to Services

Specific procedures must be developed regarding access to intervention assistance services, and all personnel must be familiarized with them. Schedules of when personnel will be available for individual consultation and information about how arrangements can be made to meet with them should be provided in writing. Arrangements must also be made for teachers to meet with the intervention assistance team. A schedule might be kept by the team leader or the school secretary. Then anyone interested in meeting with the team can initiate the process by completing a brief written form or by notifying the relevant person of their interest before a specified time. This procedure allows the team leader to cancel the meeting if no requests for assistance have been received. Keeping a schedule also facilitates monitoring usage of the intervention assistance process. Establishing a schedule and priorities ahead of time helps when there are several requests to meet with the team at the same time.

One likely reason for the overreliance on a psychometric approach to services delivery is that school personnel and parents believe that making a referral for evaluation is the only way to gain access to special services assistance. If indeed this is the sole way to obtain assistance, there is a clear need to put significant effort into promoting and marketing alternative mechanisms.

One alternative that has been used in some districts is to establish a differentiated referral system. Teachers, parents, and others may make referrals for assessment or for consultation depending on perceived need. Such a system allows consumers access to nontest-based assistance, but it does not necessarily encourage systematic attempts at intervention prior to a consideration of referral for assessment. Teachers could continue to refer students for psychoeducational evaluations before significant attempts to resolve the problem situation were made. In our experiences, this differentiated-referral model does not maximize referrals for consultative assistance.

We believe that the intervention assistance approach as described has far more potential than does the differentiated-referral model for providing needed assistance to teachers and students. In the rare instances in which assessment should be conducted immediately without attempts at intervention in the classroom, the intervention assistance system would certainly allow such assessments to take place. However, the appropriate response in most instances is to develop specific interventions within the student's current educational setting. Such an approach ensures that interventions are attempted and documented prior to consideration of a psychoeducational evaluation.

Establishing Liaisons

In addition to actively involving all relevant school personnel in the development and implementation of an intervention assistance program, it is also important to keep parents fully informed about such efforts and to consider their views. In fact, parents can serve as a resource in the operation of the program. The PTA/PTO, for example, might assist in collecting classroom norms for curriculum-based assessments or might help in monitoring student progress through CBA. Volunteer senior citizens or grandparents might be trained to provide tutoring. These kinds of efforts to encourage a broad base of support enhance the instructional opportunities provided by a school or district and ultimately may improve the school environment for the benefit of many students.

CHAPTER ELEVEN

Making Evaluation
an Integral Part
of the Process

A ccountability may help to reduce or to prevent the emergence of many sources of resistance, particularly if implemented on a proactive basis. These methods should be considered integral components of an intervention assistance program and therefore should be discussed during the initial planning process. These procedures are the focus of this chapter.

Need for Evaluation

Accountability and quality control will continue to be major issues facing educational practitioners as federal financial support for education continues to decrease and schools seek innovative methods to reduce costs. Already, for example, in an apparent effort to cut costs, many schools have made contractual arrangements with outside professionals and agencies to provide special services (Zins, 1982). Although these contracted services may be less costly than within-building services, they are also usually less comprehensive in scope. One reason for the use of these contractual services may be inadequate accountability and evaluation; good evaluation efforts could demonstrate the quality and value of various special services.

Concurrently, parents, taxpayers, and legislators are demanding increasingly higher-quality educational services. Numerous state and national commissions (for example, National Commission on Excellence in Education, 1983) have examined the state of American education, and their efforts have resulted in a call for major improvements. Accountability and evaluation efforts are critical for demonstrating that special and other services are effectively and efficiently helping students and the educational system. Evaluation of professional practices is also important in intervention assistance programs as a means to determine the impact of services through the assessment of outcome variables, to gather information about program strengths and needs and to suggest areas of modification, to obtain information about consumer satisfaction, to assist with professional development, to chart progress toward goals, and to determine patterns in the use of services (Zins and Curtis, 1984).

Although it appears obvious that evaluation should be an integral component of all programs, the reality is that a large percentage of practitioners do not engage in such efforts, as documented by several surveys of special services providers (Fairchild and Zins, 1986; Guthrie, 1982; Zins and others, 1982; Zins and Fairchild, 1986). Interestingly, however, in each of these surveys, a large number of respondents indicated a desire to obtain additional information and guidance about relevant evaluation methods that they might use to improve their services delivery. Thus, there appears to be widespread recognition of the professional responsibility to provide the "best . . . services possible given the present state of knowledge, the available information about a client's behavioral assets and deficits, and the fiscal and temporal constraints of the school organization" (Maher, 1981, p. 170).

Purposes of Program Evaluation

Accountability and evaluation efforts should focus on two general aspects of the intervention assistance process. First are the individual interventions that are developed during consultation sessions—that is, individual accountability. Second is the efficacy of the entire intervention assistance process—program evaluation. Obviously, these two evaluation areas often overlap. For example, aggregate data on the effectiveness of a number of individual interventions might be compiled to indicate overall program effectiveness. Evaluation of individual intervention effectiveness was presented as a step in the consultation process in Chapter Four. Therefore, this chapter focuses on program evaluation, and minimal discussion is devoted to individual accountability.

Essentially, the purpose of an evaluation is to provide information about the merits of various aspects of the program; this information can then be used to make judgments about further development, modification, or termination (Maher, 1981). Both the process and the outcomes of the intervention assistance program should be examined. For example, information can be provided on outcomes of individual interventions, the efficacy of the operation of the entire system, associated costs (time, energy, required

Table 9. Evaluating Intervention Assistance Goals.

Goal	Evaluation Method
1. Make consultation an integral aspect of the services delivery system and expand the range of services provided by special services staff.	1a. Determine number of requests for consultative assistance. 1b. Examine activity logs to determine time devoted to various professional tasks. 1c. Determine number of psychoeducational evaluations completed.
2. Provide assistance to students in regular education classroom to decrease special education placements.	2a. Determine number of students placed in special education. 2b. Assess consumer reactions to availability of support services. 2c. Same as 1a, 1b, 1c.
3. Increase teacher skills in meeting individual student needs.	3a. Conduct behavioral observations of the instructional environment. 3b. Evaluate student academic progress through CBA. 3c. Conduct observations of change in target behaviors. 3d. Same as 2a.
4. Increase assistance to classroom teachers.	4a. Survey teacher satisfaction with consultation services. 4b. Same as 1a, 1b.

changes), effectiveness in reducing inappropriate placements in special education, influence of the program on others (for example, students not directly involved in the program), and influence on staff morale and cohesion. The specific information that a district or school obtains depends on the goals and objectives that have been established for the program.

Domains of Information to Be Collected

A number of different types of evaluation information can be collected. Maher and Bennett (1984) suggest that outcome assessment can be organized into the categories listed here. Examples of evaluation questions are also included for each of these categories:

- Goal attainment: Have consultation goals been achieved? Goal-attainment data and methods for collecting them are listed in Table 9.
- Related effects: Were results produced that were not delineated in program goals? These effects are often found because of the reciprocal interactive nature of systems; changes in part of a system unintentionally affect other system components.
- Consumer reaction: What response did consumers (for example, teachers) have to the program or to the consultants who provided the service? Table 10 is a questionnaire that we have used to obtain such information.
- Cause-effect relationships: Were the outcomes found produced by the program or by other variables? The use of single-subject and multiple-baseline research designs may be helpful in this regard (see, for example, Barlow and Hersen, 1984).
- Cost-effectiveness: Was the intervention assistance program worthwhile considering the costs associated with it?

Framework for Program Evaluation

A problem-solving approach (similar to that described in Chapter Four for use in consultation) forms the conceptual basis for evaluation of intervention assistance programs. The following

Table 10. Psychological-Services Assessment Questionnaire.

Please check the correct response for each of the following:
1. Position:

_____ Teacher   _____ Principal, remedial reading, nurse, speech

2. Grade level:

_____ Primary   _____ Junior high
_____ Intermediate   _____ All levels

3. To what extent have you worked with the school psychologist in individual or small-goup conferences/consultation during the present school year?

_____ None   _____ One time   _____ Two times   _____ Three times
_____ Four times   _____ Five times   _____ Six or more times

For each of the following statements, circle the number on the scale that most accurately reflects your perception of the school psychologist.

0	Don't know or not applicable	3	Neutral
1	Strongly disagree	4	Agree
2	Disagree	5	Strongly agree

		DK	SD	D	N	A	SA
4.	Easy to work with	0	1	2	3	4	5
5.	Knowledgeable about the behavior of individual children	0	1	2	3	4	5
6.	Offers useful information	0	1	2	3	4	5
7.	Understands classroom and educational issues	0	1	2	3	4	5
8.	Helps identify useful resources	0	1	2	3	4	5
9.	Views her role as a facilitator rather than an authority	0	1	2	3	4	5
10.	Fits into my school environment	0	1	2	3	4	5
11.	Understands important aspects of problems I bring up	0	1	2	3	4	5
12.	Appears interested in my concerns	0	1	2	3	4	5
13.	Makes me feel comfortable when discussing sensitive issues	0	1	2	3	4	5
14.	Provides assistance in a reasonable amount of time	0	1	2	3	4	5
15.	Works effectively with parents	0	1	2	3	4	5

Table 10. Psychological-Services Assessment Questionnaire, Cont'd.

16.	Helps students through individual or group counseling or both	0 1 2 3 4 5
17.	Helped me develop a wide range of problem-solving skills	0 1 2 3 4 5
18.	Helped me see situations objectively	0 1 2 3 4 5
19.	Encouraged me to try a variety of interventions	0 1 2 3 4 5
20.	Helped me identify alternative solutions to problems	0 1 2 3 4 5
21.	Assisted me in seeing the complexities of problems	0 1 2 3 4 5
22.	Encouraged me to try out my own ideas	0 1 2 3 4 5

. . . .

23. How satisfied were you with the strategies developed during conferences you had with the school psychologist?

     Dissatisfied 1 2 3 4 5 Satisfied

24. Did you implement any of the strategies?

     _____ Yes   _____ No

     24a. If yes, how successful were they?

     Unsuccessful 1 2 3 4 5 Successful

     24b. If no, why not? _____

25. How confident are you in your ability to solve similar problems in the future?

     Not at all 1 2 3 4 5 Very confident

26. How helpful has it been to work with the school psychologist and implement interventions in the classroom before referring a student for testing?

     Not at all 1 2 3 4 5 Very helpful

27. How would you rate the overall effectiveness of the school psychologist?

     Low 1 2 3 4 5 High

28. What suggestions do you have for improving the overall quality of the psychological services being provided?

Source: Adapted from Zins, 1984. Copyright 1984 by the American Psychological Association. Reprinted by permission.

discussion of the approach relies primarily on the work of Maher and colleagues (Maher, 1981; Maher and Bennett, 1984).

Five interdependent steps characterize the problem-solving approach to evaluation. Each step is discussed in this section with examples of its application to an intervention assistance program.

The process can begin with a request for evaluation information, or it can be initiated by a special services provider. There are many advantages to a proactive approach, in which evaluation strategies are developed during initial planning phases by special services staff. For example, when special services personnel rather than others develop the evaluation, the questions and methods may be more relevant, there is more time available (and less pressure) to consider various methods of conducting the evaluation, and the results can be used to market the program to decision makers and consumers (Zins, 1984). If the evaluation is initiated at the staff level, administrative support for conducting it is still necessary. Such sanction is usually obtained during initial discussions of program implementation.

Clarification of the Evaluation Questions

Once sanction has been obtained, the initial task is to clarify the questions that need to be answered (Maher, 1981). The problem-clarification process should be a collaborative effort of administrators, special services providers, and other program planners. It is particularly advantageous to involve all special services providers and other persons who will deliver intervention assistance services, as well as recipients of the services (classroom teachers) in identifying the evaluation questions. Their participation may reduce the amount of "threat" that some experience from evaluation activities (Zins, 1985).

Essentially, the reason for implementing an intervention assistance program is to resolve a problem in services delivery or to improve the manner in which services are delivered. In order to ascertain the most salient questions to be answered, the original goals and objectives of the program should be examined. The program evaluation is intended to determine how effectively and efficiently these goals were met. Possible questions include the following: Are students with mild learning problems receiving additional support and alternative instruction and thus achieving at higher levels in their current classrooms than they did previously? Are special services providers spending more time than they did previously in consultation? Are teachers now more aware of and more frequently using alternative instructional and classroom-management strategies? Of greatest importance are questions about improvements in the educational and behavioral performance of individual students (Curtis, Zins, and Graden, 1987).

Design

In order to answer such questions, it is necessary to determine to what extent the following resources are needed or available: human (for example, data collectors), technological (for example, methods for administering questionnaires), informational (for example, records of the number of students placed in special education before and after program implementation), and financial (for example, money for monitoring student outcomes) (Maher, 1981). Furthermore, it is important to ensure that the data collected are valid, reliable, and representative.

During the design phase, it is also necessary to delineate the specific evaluation activities that will be carried out. For example, will classroom observations be conducted to evaluate student performance? Will records of the number of referrals for evaluation and of special education placements be reviewed? Will consumer satisfaction questionnaires be disseminated to determine reactions to the intervention assistance program? In other words, what types of data are necessary to answer the evaluation questions?

Finally, it often is helpful to put the evaluation plan into writing so that the goals, objectives, and activities that have been agreed on are clear to all concerned (Maher, 1981).

Implementation

The next step in the evaluation process is to implement the evaluation as planned (Maher, 1981). The evaluator must ensure that all evaluation-related activities are carried out properly. For example, data collectors must be trained in appropriate behavioral observation techniques, the intended types of data must be collected reliably, and data must be analyzed appropriately.

Another part of this step is to determine whether any negative effects might be associated with the evaluation program (Maher, 1981). It may be found, for example, that some teachers are resistant to providing data or to allowing an observer in their classrooms, or that special education teachers perceive that the data will be used to demonstrate that they are not needed and therefore to eliminate their jobs. If such effects are uncovered, efforts must be taken to eliminate them.

Dissemination of Evaluation Information

Unless the results of the program evaluation are disseminated to decision makers and to the individuals involved in the program, they will not be fully utilized. The information that has been gathered is useful not only for decision-making purposes but also for improving services delivery, marketing the intervention assistance program, and expanding intervention assistance efforts to other schools. A detailed discussion of dissemination is included in a later section of this chapter.

Written and oral reports of the program evaluation should be shared as appropriate. The people who should receive a program evaluation report as well as appropriate formats and times for the presentations have to be determined. Different audiences require varying amounts or types of information. For example, the PTA/PTO might receive a general discussion of the program and its benefits, whereas the special services staff might be given specific outcome data and information about implications for changing services.

This dissemination of evaluation results can be viewed favorably by decision makers. As an illustration, when one of us worked as a district school psychologist and presented program evaluation data to the board of education, the chair of the board made a special trip to the school psychologist's office to offer his congratulations on the report and followed up with a laudatory memo to the superintendent.

Meta-Evaluation

Maher (1981) suggests the use of a meta-evaluation—an evaluation of the evaluation process—to enhance the effectiveness of program evaluation procedures. Important meta-evaluation questions include: Were the data obtained valid, reliable, and representative? Was the information presented in a timely fashion? Was the evaluation cost-effective? Did the evaluation effectively address the original evaluation questions? How can future evaluation efforts be improved? What uses were made of the data? Were recommendations acted on or were they filed away?

In most cases, the meta-evaluation is conducted by someone in the school district, perhaps someone from the central administration or another school building or at least someone not involved in the evaluation process. Large-scale evaluations can be conducted by an external consultant such as a faculty member from a local university with expertise in program evaluation.

Potential Problems

Often a major problem is neglecting to consider evaluation when initially developing and implementing a program. Too frequently, evaluation is added as an afterthought at the end of the semester or school year, typically in response to an administrator's questions regarding operation of the program or when staff feel threatened by budget cutbacks. Unfortunately, program evaluations conducted under such conditions, and in a reactive rather than proactive manner, are usually poorly conceived and unable to address the questions that have been asked.

A second relevant problem is related to evaluation of prevention programs. With most interventions, it is a relatively straightforward process to ascertain whether problems were resolved by a particular treatment (although direct cause-and-effect relationships can be difficult to determine). However, in most prevention programs the goal is to stop a problem from arising or at least from becoming serious. Nevertheless, several goals or outcomes of the intervention assistance process, as indicated previously, are readily measurable. Also, the particular goal of preventing problems may be approximately measured by assessing changes in teachers' use of intervention techniques and by questioning teachers about the preventive impact on students.

Utilizing and Communicating Evaluation Data

As noted previously, unless some use is made of the data collected, there is little need to expend efforts in this regard. In addition to using evaluation information to make decisions about the program itself (for example, whether to continue it or expand it to other schools), there are two other primary applications: to improve services delivery and to market the intervention assistance program to consumers and decision makers.

Improving Services Delivery

Information collected through evaluation procedures can be used to improve the performance of the individual practitioner as well as to increase the effectiveness of the entire services delivery system. A few years ago one of us administered a psychological-services assessment questionnaire (containing items similar to those in Table 10) to teachers in a school district (Zins, 1981). A consultative approach was emphasized in the district, and the evaluative questionnaire distributed each year contained a number of questions regarding the psychologist's performance as a consultant. Overall, the psychologist's performance was highly regarded, although his knowledge of relevant resources was rated relatively low. After the psychologist reviewed these data, he decided to expand his knowledge of school and community resources, and his performance in this area improved, as rated on subsequent questionnaires.

Marketing the Program

Marketing, or selling consumers and decision makers on the worth and value of the intervention assistance system, is a significant component of a successful program. Although some special services providers may have a tendency to view marketing as unprofessional or unnecessary because they believe the value of their services is self-evident, for numerous reasons marketing activities must become an integral, systematic, and routine aspect of the intervention assistance program. As described at the beginning of this chapter, there is increased competition for funds within education. At the same time, federal contributions to education are decreasing. Thus, all programs must become accountable and able to demonstrate their effectiveness. Relatedly, parents have more choices of schools to which they can send their children than they did before. Schools that can clearly demonstrate the quality of their services to potential consumers will likely be able to compete and thus survive in face of increased competition in the marketplace. Similarly, in schools that contract for some services, administrators may need to be informed of the valuable services that could be provided by a school-based practitioner.

Marketing efforts can decrease client/consumer uncertainty about services that are available. For the intervention assistance program to maximize its effectiveness, services must be well known by as many potential consumers as possible. Marketing strategies enable special services providers to disseminate information regarding program operation and availability.

Another goal of marketing can be to expand services delivery. For example, a school or a school district may be unwilling to commit itself to full-scale implementation of an intervention assistance system but may sanction use of such an approach on a limited basis (for example, with several cases or in one school). Through program evaluation, special services providers may be able to demonstrate to decision makers and consumers that the approach is effective. Even if school administrators are not convinced of the merits of the approach, parents and teachers may be able to exert enough influence to convince administrators (possibly through the school board) to try the intervention assistance system on a pilot basis and to again evaluate its effectiveness. Zins (1981), for example, demonstrated that by providing accountability data to the superintendent and board of education in his district, he was able to expand the quantity of psychological services provided (with primarily a consultative emphasis) over a three-year period.

Marketing can use low-intensity or high-intensity approaches (Rothman and others, 1983), each with its advantages and limitations. As will be clear, a combination of the two approaches may be most advantageous.

Low-intensity approaches tend to be impersonal and relatively inexpensive. Examples include placing a written description of the intervention assistance program in teachers' mailboxes, making a brief announcement of the program at a faculty meeting, or writing an article about the program for the PTA/PTO newsletter. Conversely, a high-intensity approach is much more personal and therefore more costly (Rothman and others, 1983). It could include having an in-service training session on the intervention assistance program, with a demonstration of an intervention assistance team in operation, or sponsoring a visit to another school to view an intervention assistance program in operation. Both low- and high-intensity approaches can be useful in marketing intervention assistance services, but each must be examined for cost-effectiveness.

CHAPTER TWELVE

Legal and Ethical Considerations

T he purpose of this chapter is to discuss specific legal and ethical issues that may face professionals who engage in intervention assistance activities. Because of the relative newness of the intervention assistance process, many of these issues are only now being recognized and addressed in the literature. Moreover, there are few published discussions of legal rules and ethical principles as they apply to intervention assistance programs.

Legal Issues

All programs provided within public education settings must comply with pertinent federal and state rules and regulations. In view of the numerous regulations that govern professional practices in the schools, it is incumbent on practitioners to remain abreast of current legal guidelines. In this section, a number of legal considerations as well as areas of potential vulnerability are reviewed. Although legal difficulties experienced by consultants involved in such programs are quite rare, practitioners should be aware of a number of potential legal entanglements.

Public Law 94-142

P.L. 94-142 and parallel state enactments are the laws of most concern to those involved with intervention assistance programs.

One requirement of these laws is that handicapped students be educated in the least restrictive environment. Although nonhandicapped students are typically not discussed from this perspective, we believe that they too have the right to be educated in the least restrictive environment. For most students, the regular classroom is less restrictive than are remedial programs administered in segregated settings. Although most students who are the focus of consultative interventions are not classified as handicapped, a primary goal of this approach is to maintain as many students as possible within regular education settings. Without consultative intervention, many of these students might eventually be classified as mildly handicapped. Research has suggested that many of these mildly handicapped students can be educated effectively within regular classrooms if provided with alternative approaches to instruction and appropriate support (Wang and Birch, 1984). Moreover, many states and legal education agencies (LEAs) have adopted requirements that interventions be attempted before making a referral for a multifactored evaluation. Thus, intervention assistance programs are highly consistent with the intent of P.L. 94-142 as well as with state and local guidelines.

On numerous occasions, we have heard the argument that intervention assistance programs are partially or wholly intended to deny or delay the provision of special services to students who need them. Use of this approach in that way would clearly be in direct violation of P.L. 94-142 and inconsistent with the ethical guidelines of professional associations that seek to protect clients. Intervention assistance programs are not intended to divert or delay needed services; in fact, the goal is to make services readily accessible to teachers and parents and responsive to the needs of students. In other words, the purpose of the system is to expand opportunities for students rather than to narrow them, and to provide opportunities to succeed in the least restrictive environment (Curtis, Zins, and Graden, 1987).

Record Keeping

In previous chapters we noted the importance of maintaining records that document consultative interventions. A decision must be made regarding the location of such records. Among the various options are keeping them in individual student files or in a separate consultation file. If the information is not maintained in individual student files, a notation should be made in each student file indicating that the documentation exists and where it is located, as required by the Family Educational Rights and Privacy Act (FERPA).

Records from intervention assistance team meetings are accessible to parents because they are shared among team members and include identifying information about individual students. The FERPA requires that parents have access to essentially all individually identifiable information pertaining to their child. The only exception to this rule is the sole-possession exception, which refers to notes that remain in the sole possession of their creator, are not shared with anyone else, and are not used in making a decision regarding the student's educational program. This exception was intended to protect treatment notes that are created and used solely by an individual in providing services to a client. The sole-possession exception clearly pertains to notes about direct service, and it seems reasonable that it would pertain similarly to notes developed and used solely by a consultant in the provision of indirect services to a student through a teacher or another third party. The only purpose of the notes would be as a memory aid to the consultant.

Parents are not guaranteed access to such notes. However, if the notes or their content are ever shared with anyone else (including intervention assistance team members), they are automatically reclassified as educational records and as such become accessible to parents under the FERPA. It should also be noted that anything, including treatment notes, is accessible through court subpoena.

Permission for Consultation

The consultation process begins with the establishment of communication between the school and the home. It is our practice to inform parents of interventions that are contemplated before they are implemented. In fact, it is usually advantageous to involve parents (and students) in the problem-identification phase as well as in the development of problem solutions in order to gain their support, obtain relevant information, and enlist their involvement in and commitment to developing and carrying out interventions. Communication enhances parent/school partnerships and improves intervention implementation that requires collaboration. If a problem is significant enough to warrant consultation (even though the student is not suspected of being handicapped), without question, parents have a right to be informed of the precipitating concern. Furthermore, if a psychoeducational assessment that could result in placement in special education is deemed necessary at a later time, parents will be likely to understand the concerns prompting the referral.

We have found that most school districts have not interpreted the FERPA as requiring written parental permission for consultation, although practices differ. However, when consultation is part of a system that could lead to placement in special education (one possible outcome of an intervention assistance program), some authors suggest that informed consent may be necessary (Piersel, 1985). However, requiring written parental permission could be a barrier to the provision of consultative services. At a minimum it involves a time lag in services while permission is secured. The requirement for written permission might also suggest the possibility of difficult interactions with parents, a likely matter of concern to many teachers and therefore a source of resistance to consultation. We do not mean to imply that, because of the possibility of increased resistance, parents should not be informed. Rather, it is important for those involved in the intervention assistance program to be aware of this possibility. However, if the consultant is not a school employee, written parental permission is clearly needed to share personally identifiable student information.

Permission to Intervene

The necessity to obtain formal written permission to intervene with a student is often a gray area. In our opinion, clear policies regarding written permission to intervene must be established by the local school district. Permission may not be necessary for many interventions. However, it may still be good practice to obtain written permission if significant alterations are being made in a student's educational program. In any case, the student or parents or both should retain the right to withdraw their permission for the intervention.

Piersel (1985) states that if "the identified plan to resolve student problems intrudes into the educational environment, involves aversive procedures, or permits the student to be identified as different, informed consent is necessary" (p. 274). Hughes (1986) notes that parental consent may be necessary when a student is singled out for an intervention that may cause the child to be perceived negatively by her or his peers, but "procedures that are customary in the particular classroom and that are generally accepted educational practices do not require parental consent" (p. 492). Although both authors bring up important aspects of this issue, the bottom line is that there are few clear guidelines in this area, and professional judgment consequently assumes great importance.

A general rule that may prove helpful in deciding when parents must give permission for intervention relates to individualized treatment of the student. Any activity, including consultation, that results in a student's being singled out or treated differently from other students (a behavior modification program, counseling) requires parental permission. However, those interventions that focus on students in general (classroom management, group instructional methods) do not require parental permission. Whether or not parental permission is required, open and ongoing parent/professional communication is extremely important in all aspects of the educational process.

Ethical Issues

Just as practitioners must comply with legal rules regulating their performance, they are also expected to follow the ethical guidelines of their respective professions. Many ethical principles have been developed to assist professionals in avoiding legal pitfalls. In addition, they are intended to provide useful guidance to the practitioner in decision making, and they are a means of protecting the public (Brown, Pryzwansky, and Schulte, 1987).

Confidentiality

Communication tends to be more open and free when there is some assurance of confidentiality than when there is not. For this reason, confidentiality issues should be discussed explicitly with consultees before engaging in consultative interactions. Furthermore, it is essential that the special services provider obtain administrative sanction for making the contents of consultative sessions confidential. Administrators must be informed of the necessity of maintaining confidentiality to facilitate the open and free discussion of work-related difficulties with the consultant. Basically, issues discussed during consultation sessions should be shared with other people by consultants only on a need-to-know basis.

A difficult situation arises when a consultee is "chronically and stubbornly involved in unethical activities toward the client" (Conoley and Conoley, 1982, p. 216). In such cases, concern for the welfare of the student may outweigh the desire to maintain confidentiality. In such situations the consultee's behavior must be clearly detrimental to the child rather than only a case of substandard professional performance (Hughes, 1986). In most cases, the consultee should be informed beforehand that confidentiality will be breached and why.

The American Psychological Association (APA) (1981) ethical standards may be interpreted in such a way as to add some confusion to the confidentiality issue. They state that "information obtained in clinical or consulting relationships . . . is discussed only for professional purposes and only with persons clearly concerned with the case" (p. 636). Although this statement may imply that the contents of consultative sessions can be shared with administrators or parents, we suggest that consultants exercise caution before doing so. The APA code does not take fully into account the complexities of the consultative process (Brown, Pryzwansky, and Schulte, 1987). Consultee permission is needed (under most circumstances) before information generated during consultation can be shared. When the consultant believes that good professional practice, legal mandate, or organizational policy dictate that others outside the relationship be informed, the consultee should be encouraged to take the necessary action. The consultant might even help the consultee consider ways in which to do so. Also, as noted, client welfare could require disclosure even if the consultee is not in agreement.

Introducing Change

Even though there are obvious potential benefits to a school in an intervention assistance approach, some administrators may not support such programs. In these instances, it may be unethical or at least poor practice for a special services staff member to attempt to implement the system anyway, although it may be possible to continue providing consultation services on a nonsystemic basis. Conoley and Conoley (1982) note that loyalty to the school demands that the consultant not engage in unauthorized change. This is not to suggest that consultants should discontinue efforts to familiarize policy makers with the operation and benefits of an intervention assistance program and thereby seek their support for it.

If the administration severely restricts the type of services that can be provided, special services providers should attempt to resolve the issue by working within the system to bring about change. If the conflict cannot be resolved satisfactorily after a sincere and sustained effort, it may be necessary to appeal to higher authorities. As a last resort, it might become necessary to seek employment elsewhere. However, we have seen a number of new professionals become overly frustrated in a relatively short period of time and leave because they were unable to turn things around. Often they have seemed to lack an understanding of the long-term effort needed to bring about meaningful change. Consequently, they have left the responsibility for changing the system to the next person, who often then faces an even more difficult situation.

Who Is the Client?

The answer to this question has a bearing on a number of the activities of special services providers. The ethical principles of the National Association of School Psychologists (1984) specify that pupils are the school psychologist's primary clients and that these professionals therefore should advocate for pupils' rights and well-being. However, because consultants often work with parents and other school personnel rather than directly with students, they may not always recognize that the student is their primary client (Hughes, 1986). The intervention assistance approach emphasizes that consultation efforts are intended primarily to benefit students. Although consultee skill improvement often results from such interactions as well, students are expected to benefit in the long run from the enhanced skills of the consultee.

Value Dilemmas

Occasionally, special services providers and administrators, teachers, and parents may have different values regarding potential interventions. Common areas of disagreement are the use of corporal punishment and retention. Although organizations such as the National Education Association have taken an official position opposing the use of corporal punishment in schools, many teachers and administrators view the practice as a necessary component of school discipline. The school counselor who consults with a teacher who holds this view may be aware of the research and literature on corporal punishment that suggests that it is an ineffective disciplinary technique, degrading to children and teachers, an infringement of student rights, and abusive. If these two parties need to establish consequences for a student who is seriously disrupting the classroom, the teacher may suggest the use of corporal punishment, while the counselor may overtly oppose such methods or advocate alternatives such as teaching prosocial skills and improving classroom organization and management strategies. Obviously, such conflicts must be resolved in order for the two people to collaborate effectively. Recognizing and understanding value differences may be helpful in efforts to resolve such differences, but a serious barrier exists when one party views the actions of the other as unethical.

Responsibility for the Client

Although consultants make their expertise available to consultees, consultees retain primary responsibility for students.

Thus, it is important that consultants do not assume responsibility for resolving the problem situation or imply that they are willing to do so. It should be noted that an authoritative consulting style may convey the message that the consultant is responsible for resolving the presenting problem (Curtis and Anderson, 1977).

This issue of responsibility becomes complex because consultation involves an interpersonal-influence process (Meyers, Parsons, and Martin, 1979). Consultants rightfully attempt to influence consultees and may encourage them to adopt a certain perspective regarding a problem situation or to attempt one intervention rather than another. Therefore, it is important that consultants make their attempts at influence overt rather than covert and at the same time realize that the ultimate decision regarding problem solution must be made by the consultee.

Intervention Approaches

Interventions developed during consultation must be made in the student's best interest. However, interventions sometimes are implemented with little consideration of the student. For example, Winnett and Winkler (1972) describe much behavioral intervention in the classroom as having the goals of keeping students still, quiet, and docile, which they contend is inappropriate and not beneficial for the students. Classroom control should not be the sole criterion for intervention implementation. Both the short- and long-term outcomes of interventions for the student must be considered.

As another example, in Chapter Six we discussed the use of peer-mediated interventions. Such techniques can be extremely effective for a variety of student-related problems, but there is potential risk with regard to the target student's relationships with his or her peers (Hughes, 1986). Caution should be exercised so that the child who fails to attain the criterion does not suffer unnecessary negative social consequences out of proportion to potential benefits.

Furthermore, the selection of target behaviors should be decided collaboratively with teachers (or parents or both) and should involve the student whenever possible because such involvement can be helpful. Too often targets are chosen because of their reinforcing value to teachers or parents (Stolz and Associates, 1978). Therefore, all participants in consultation should consider multiple perspectives for viewing the problem (Van Someren, Rhoades, and Kratochwill, 1986).

Lack of Practitioner Training

Lack of preparation to participate in an intervention assistance program may be an ethical concern in some instances. The ethical codes of counselors and psychologists (for example, American Association for Counseling and Development, 1981; American Psychological Association, 1981; National Association of School Psychologists, 1984) specify that practice should be limited to those areas in which one has competence that has been attained through training, experience, and supervision. If a psychologist or counselor has not been taught consultation skills, the question arises as to whether that person is operating outside his or her area of expertise when involved in intervention assistance efforts.

Because there is potential for negative change as a result of consultation, competence in this area is crucial. A number of authors have argued that training in consultation should include both didactic coursework and supervised experience (for example, Crego, 1985; Curtis and Zins, 1981a; Gallessich, 1982). There is a specific body of knowledge associated with consultation proficiency. However, ethical principles do not specify the exact training or experiences necessary to practice consultation (Robinson and Gross, 1985), there are no widely held standards for training in consultation (Brown, 1985; Gallessich, 1982), and few empirical studies specify the objectives of training (Van Someren, Rhoades, and Kratochwill, 1986), thus leaving the final determination of competence to the individual practitioner. Such a judgment is clearly subjective, and specific training standards for consultation are therefore needed.

A related point concerns the practitioner whose consultation skills are not well developed. Research evidence suggests that low-skilled consultants may have a negative influence on problem identification during consultation (Curtis and Watson, 1980), which in turn may lead to detrimental outcomes since problem identification has been found to be a primary determinant of positive outcomes in consultation (Bergan and Tombari, 1976). Thus, the question remains whether poorly prepared or low-skilled people should even engage in consultation.

Appropriateness of Consultation

A related issue is whether it is always appropriate to provide consultation services. Zins and Curtis (1984) suggest that consultation should not be provided when counseling or psychotherapy is needed instead, supervision is more appropriate, the consultant's personal biases significantly impair his or her ability to work with the consultee or the problem situation, or the consultee is forced to consult. Under these circumstances, consultants need to examine whether they indeed should provide consultative assistance. If a consultee requires personal therapy and is receiving it from another professional, it may still be appropriate to provide consultation services simultaneously. However, special care should be taken by the consultant to maintain a work-related focus.

Efficacy of Special Education

The issue of the efficacy of current special education programs has been raised in the literature by a number of authors (for example, Algozzine and Maheady, 1986). As noted by Algozzine and Maheady, investigations of the effectiveness of special education programs have not yielded consistently positive results (see Carlberg and Kavale, 1980; Glass, 1983). Although there admittedly are numerous challenging methodological problems involved in researching this area, one suggestion to improve efficacy is to make special education staff (with the assistance of program evaluators) responsible for demonstrating that "high-quality, effective special instruction is being provided and that the goals of the special education program could not be achieved as effectively within the regular classroom" (Panel on Selection and Placement of Students in Programs for the Mentally Retarded, 1982, p. 105). Although such a procedure may not solve all the problems related to special education placement, it may be a major step toward improving services delivery.

Once placed in a special education program, the student has a high probability of remaining in the program for an extended period of time, even when he or she has only a mild handicap (Panel on Selection and Placement of Students in Programs for the Mentally Retarded, 1982). Student status and continuation in a program should be assessed continuously with regard to progress in meeting individual educational plan (IEP) goals as well as with regard to the student's specific need for continued assistance.

From an ethical standpoint, the lack of convincing empirical support for the efficacy of special education programs raises serious questions. Is it ethical to implement interventions that do not have empirical support when there are alternative interventions whose effectiveness has been demonstrated? Do educators have an obligation to inform parents of the limited research support for special education placement? Must parents be told of the potential detrimental effects of their child's being placed in classes or programs separate from nonhandicapped peers? Is it ethical to assure parents that a special education placement will meet the needs of their child without simultaneously telling them about the potential negative outcomes, or of the likelihood that their child will remain in such a placement for many years? It is easy to raise these and other questions but far more difficult to answer them. Nevertheless, they deserve careful consideration by special services providers.

CHAPTER THIRTEEN

Conclusion:
Future Directions
for Practice and Research

We have presented the rationale for providing intervention assistance in the classroom as well as discussion of the practical issues involved in planning, implementing, and evaluating such programs. The major contributions of our work to professional practice are threefold. First, we have provided a description of how the intervention assistance process can be made available to all students within the current educational system, regardless of presenting problem or placement. Our framework represents a substantial expansion of conceptualizations (described as prereferral intervention, preevaluation activities, and so forth) that focus primarily on delivering services to students who are in danger of special education placement.

Second, although consultation has been promoted as a services delivery system since the 1960s, ours is the first detailed discussion of how to implement and operate the approach on a systemic basis. Previously, consultation was typically a service delivered by individual practitioners, with little coordinated effort by various providers, and the educational system was not organized to directly facilitate use of this type of service.

Third, many so-called models of consultation do not include dimensions of the process critical to effective practice. The behavioral model, for example, tends to ignore interpersonal issues between the consultant and consultee, and the mental health model usually provides intrapsychic causal explanations for problems and minimizes ecological variables. Other models (for example, Teacher Assistance Teams) emphasize a more authoritative approach in contrast to the collaborative approach we advocate. We have presented an approach that includes both cognitive/problem-solving and affective/interpersonal dimensions. In addition, we have described in great detail the various practical issues involved in setting up and operating the intervention assistance program.

We do not propose this model of intervention assistance as a panacea for all the ills of education; nevertheless, it overcomes many shortcomings, and it has the potential to improve significantly the educational process for many students. Widespread adoption of this system depends on a variety of factors, both internal and external to local schools. In this chapter, we make several suggestions regarding these factors and provide ideas for future practice and applied research.

New Directions for Training and Practice

Little is to be accomplished by assigning blame for the current rather troubled state of special services delivery. Responsibility for resolving these difficulties and bringing about substantial improvement in the system clearly rests with a variety of professionals at various levels. These people must accept and pursue changes in order to institute needed improvements.

The basic premise underlying our entire discussion should be apparent to all readers by now: Schools must actively try to meet the individual needs of all students within the least restrictive setting. The intervention assistance system is designed to facilitate, organizationally and philosophically, the provision of such services and to enhance the potential of special services providers to accomplish this goal, and to do both within the current context of education. We have discussed the intervention assistance system and how to implement it in the schools; other changes, to the extent they are adopted, will facilitate implementation and will help to maximize the effectiveness of the intervention assistance process. The result is intended to be improved learning and adjustment outcomes for all students. These key ingredients for increasing the probability that intervention assistance programs will be successful are addressed here.

Training

Colleges of education bear a primary responsibility for contributing to the desired change. As Sarason (1982) notes, "It is here that they [school personnel] learn there are at least two types of human beings and if you choose to work with one of them you render yourself *legally* and conceptually incompetent to work with the others" (p. 258). The existence of separate departments within our colleges to prepare future teachers and administrators to work with regular or with special students is one way in which the differentiated treatment of so-called handicapped students is promulgated.

In order to assume the expanded roles and functions discussed in this book, future teachers and administrators will need to be exposed early in their training to alternative teaching and classroom-organization methods such as those described in Chapters Five and Six. Similarly, multidisciplinary collaboration and cooperation should be discussed and experienced at this time so that these activities become routine for future teachers and administrators. Clearly, there is a need to expand the range of instructional techniques taught to include understanding of and tolerance for individual differences, and understanding of the potential influence of a vast array of ecological factors on student learning. Issues related to providing noncategorical personnel preparation are discussed by Blackhurst, Bott, and Cross (1987). Furthermore, extensive training in areas such as classroom organization and management, behavioral and academic interventions, and methods of regularly monitoring student progress will be helpful. Along with training in these areas, future administrators also need thorough preparation in teaming strategies, systems and organizational theory, and group problem-solving skills.

Current training procedures for special services providers also require modification so that emphasis is placed on consultation, teaming strategies, systems theory, and data-based intervention techniques. Moreover, a revamping of assessment practices is called for. Traditional norm-referenced tests have many limitations, but they can be supplemented (until state education agencies cease to require traditional IQ, achievement, and other tests) with approaches that are more readily applicable to helping children in the classroom. Moreover, we must develop an understanding of how best to use various assessment data in decision making and intervention planning.

Although sufficient empirical evidence supports adoption of expanded intervention assistance efforts, we are concerned that many districts and states are jumping on the bandwagon before school personnel are adequately prepared for implementation of such an approach (Curtis, Zins, and Graden, 1987). If personnel do not have the prerequisite skills, there is great likelihood that these change efforts will result in failure, with blame erroneously attributed to the intervention assistance program's conceptual framework ("the system doesn't work").

Meeting Individual Needs

A key ingredient of successful intervention assistance programs is adaptation of regular education to accommodate individual learning characteristics and needs, an accommodation that incidentally has been advocated by special education for many years. If educational services are determined by individual student needs, there is no longer a need for two separate educational programs. Moreover, the essential characteristics that have been identified in the effective-schools research should be adopted by every school. These include "high expectations by teachers for achievement of all students" (Lipsky and Gartner, 1987, p. 71).

Laws, rules, and regulations at the state and federal levels must be altered to encourage and support financially the practice of providing a free and appropriate education for every student (Stainback and Stainback, 1987). At a minimum, some current requirements must be waived. For example, with services funded and organized noncategorically, labels, with their related detrimental effects, would no longer be necessary. Local, state, and national professional organizations, parent groups, and related organizations with interests in this area must work toward effecting changes in funding procedures to facilitate support for intervention assistance programs. Parent groups and teacher unions in particular could be pivotal in this regard.

On a local level, schools must develop philosophies that emphasize the unique learning needs of students. Requiring students to fit into a preconceived mold in order to remain in the regular education program is an archaic practice and unfair to children. School administrators must provide the necessary leadership and institute carefully planned changes within their buildings to eliminate this practice. Without their active involvement and support, little will happen. Teachers too must devote more effort than ever toward meeting individual student needs, as they are the true cornerstones of program effectiveness. A critical dimension is the desire and effort of each individual professional to provide the best possible services to each child for whom he or she has some responsibility.

Other resources must also be found. Teacher aides (who might be obtained by tapping such underutilized assets as senior citizens) somehow must be made available to supplement the efforts of the special services staff and teachers. Mobilizing the business community to support schools (for example, through adopt-a-school programs) is another potential area of assistance. Given the prediction of a critical shortage of skilled workers by the end of the century, businesses have increasing rewards to gain through such partnerships. To the extent that additional support is available, it will be easier for teachers to individualize and to implement interventions.

New Directions for Applied Research

As in most areas of psychology and education, there is a desperate need for additional applied research regarding intervention assistance programs. Although a substantial amount of empirical research supports the efficacy of consultation, significant problems with this research require resolution. For example, many studies do not contain sufficient descriptions of the consultation model used; consultant, consultee, and client characteristics; the targets and types of interventions used; methods used to evaluate consultative effectiveness (Pryzwansky, 1986; West and Idol, 1987); and strategies used to promote the development of consultation services within an organization.

Additional information is needed regarding critical variables that lead to consultative success or failure. In particular, the interpersonal-influence process has not been examined carefully enough despite the fact that it is a critical element of consultation. Although we have adequate technology for behavioral and academic interventions, this technology is of little use if it is not applied to assist students. A major goal for consultants is to encourage teachers to use this technology in the classroom. Identification of the knowledge, skills, attitudes, beliefs, and other variables that make one consultant or consultee more successful in consultation than another is needed. Likewise, school-consultation theory has tended to be somewhat narrow in that it has not borrowed much readily applicable knowledge from other areas, such as social, cognitive, educational, and organizational psychology, regarding change and interpersonal influence. Even within education, special educators, school psychologists, counselors, and so forth read narrowly and are not familiar with one another's literature.

Longitudinal studies are also needed to ascertain the impact of consultation on student outcomes. Does it result in improved learning and adjustment over time? Do students who are the focus of consultative interventions continue to be the target of consultation year after year? Are these students eventually placed in restrictive environments or are they successful in their current placements? If placement is delayed, is this necessarily a negative outcome?

Evidence suggests that some organizations are more receptive to a consultative approach than others. Are there reliable means to identify such organizations? What techniques are more effective for changing organizations so that they accept intervention assistance efforts?

These are but a few of the many types of questions that need to be answered. Without a doubt, as our knowledge base expands, additional methods of helping students will be developed. However, the need will remain to translate this empirical knowledge into daily practice through means such as intervention assistance programs.

References

Abidin, R. R. "Negative Effects of Behavioral Consultations: I Know I Ought To, But It Hurts Too Much." *Journal of School Psychology,* 1975, *13,* 51–56.

Algozzine, B., Christenson, S., and Ysseldyke, J. E. "Probabilities Associated with the Referral to Placement Process." *Teacher Education and Special Education,* 1982, *5,* 19–23.

Algozzine, B., and Maheady, L. (eds.). "In Search of Excellence: Instruction That Works in Special Education Classrooms." *Exceptional Children,* 1986, *52* (6) (entire issue).

Algozzine, B., Ysseldyke, J. E., and Christenson, S. "An Analysis of the Incidence of Special Class Placement: The Masses Are Burgeoning." *Journal of Special Education,* 1983, *17,* 141–147.

Alpert, J. L., Ludwig, L. M., and Weiner, L. "Selection of Consultees in School Mental Health Consultation." *Journal of School Psychology,* 1979, *17,* 59–66.

American Association for Counseling and Development. *Ethical Standards.* Washington, D.C.: American Association for Counseling and Development, 1981.

American Psychological Association. *Ethical Standards of Psychologists.* Washington, D.C.: American Psychological Association, 1981.

Aronson, E., and others. *The Jigsaw Classroom.* Beverly Hills, Calif.: Sage, 1978.

Bandura, A. *Social Learning Theory.* Englewood Cliffs, N.J.: Prentice-Hall, 1977.

Bandura, A. *Social Foundations of Thought and Action: A Social Cognitive Theory.* Englewood Cliffs, N.J.: Prentice-Hall, 1986.

Barker, R. "On the Nature of Environment." In H. M. Proshansky, W. Ittelson, and L. Rivlin (eds.), *Environmental Psychology.* New York: Holt, Rinehart & Winston, 1976.

Barlow, D. H., Hayes, S. C., and Nelson, R. O. *The Scientist Practitioner: Research and Accountability in Clinical and Educational Settings.* Elmsford, N.Y.: Pergamon Press, 1984.

Barlow, D. H., and Hersen, M. *Single Case Experimental Designs: Strategies for Studying Behavior Change.* Elmsford, N.Y.: Pergamon Press, 1984.

Barrish, H. H., Saunders, M., and Wolf, M. M. "Good Behavior Game: Effects of Individual Contingencies for Group Consequences on Disruptive Behavior in a Classroom." *Journal of Applied Behavior Analysis,* 1969, *2,* 119–124.

Barron, B. G., and others. "Study Skills: A New Look." *Reading Improvement,* 1983, *20,* 329–332.

Becker, W. C. "Teaching Reading and Language to the Disadvantaged—What We Have Learned from Field Research." *Harvard Educational Review,* 1977, *47,* 518–543.

Becker, W. C. "The National Evaluation of Follow Through: Behavior-Theory-Based Programs Come Out on Top." *Education and Urban Society,* 1978, *10,* 431–458.

Becker, W. C., and Carnine, D. W. "Direct Instruction: A Behavior Theory Model for Comprehensive Educational Intervention with the Disadvantaged." In S. W. Bijou and R. Ruiz (eds.), *Behavior Modification: Contributions to Education.* Hillsdale, N.J.: Erlbaum, 1981.

Beer, M. *Organizational Change and Development: A Systems View.* Santa Monica, Calif.: Goodyear, 1980.

Benjamin, A. *The Helping Interview.* Boston: Houghton Mifflin, 1969.

Bergan, J. R. *Behavioral Consultation.* Columbus, Ohio: Merrill, 1977.

Bergan, J. R., and Tombari, M. L. "Consultant Skill and Efficiency and the Implementation and Outcomes of Consultation." *Journal of School Psychology*, 1976, *14*, 3–14.

Blackhurst, A. E., Bott, D. A., and Cross, D. P. "Noncategorical Special Education Personnel Preparation." In M. C. Wang, M. C. Reynolds, and H. J. Walberg (eds.), *The Handbook of Special Education: Research and Practice*. Oxford, England: Pergamon Press, 1987.

Blaney, N. F., and others. "Interdependence in the Classroom: A Field Study." *Journal of Educational Psychology*, 1977, *69*, 121–128.

Block, P. *Flawless Consulting*. Austin, Tex.: Learning Concepts, 1981.

Bohlmeyer, E., and Burke, J. P. "Selecting Cooperative Learning Techniques: A Consultative Strategy Guide." *School Psychology Review*, 1987, *16* (1), 36–49.

Bornstein, P. H., and Quevillon, R. P. "The Effects of a Self-Instructional Package on Overactive Preschool Boys." *Journal of Applied Behavior Analysis*, 1976, *9*, 179–188.

Bragstad, B. J., and Stumpf, S. M. *A Guidebook for Teaching Study Skills and Motivation*. Boston: Allyn & Bacon, 1982.

Brown, D. "The Preservice Training and Supervision of Consultants." *The Counseling Psychologist*, 1985, *13* (3), 410–425.

Brown, D., Pryzwansky, W. B., and Schulte, A. C. *Psychological Consultation: Introduction to Theory and Practice*. Boston: Allyn & Bacon, 1987.

Camp, B., and Bash, M. *Think Aloud: Improving Social and Cognitive Skills*. Champaign, Ill.: Research Press, 1981.

Camp, B., and Ray, R. S. "Aggression." In A. Meyers and W. E. Craighead (eds.), *Cognitive Behavior Therapy with Children*. New York: Plenum, 1984.

Camp, B., and others. "Think Aloud: A Program for Developing Self-Control in Young Aggressive Boys." *Journal of Abnormal Child Psychology*, 1977, *5*, 157–169.

Caplan, G. *The Theory and Practice of Mental Health Consultation*. New York: Basic Books, 1970.

Carkhuff, R. R., and Berenson, B. G. *Beyond Counseling and Therapy*. New York: Holt, Rinehart & Winston, 1967.

Carlberg, C., and Kavale, K. "The Efficacy of Special Versus

Regular Class Placement for Exceptional Children: A Meta-Analysis." *Journal of Special Education,* 1980, *14,* 295–309.

Carnine, D. "Effects of Two Teacher-Presentation Rates on Off-Task Behavior, Answering Correctly, and Participation." *Journal of Applied Behavior Analysis,* 1976, *9* (2), 199–206.

Chalfant, J. C., Pysh, M. V., and Moultrie, R. "Teacher Assistance Teams: A Model for Within Building Problem Solving." *Learning Disability Quarterly,* 1979, *2,* 85–96.

Christenson, S., and others. "Teachers' Attributions for Problems That Result in Referral for Psychoeducational Evaluation." *Journal of Educational Research,* 1983, *76,* 174–180.

Cohen, P. A., Kulik, J. A., and Kulik, C. C. "Educational Outcomes of Tutoring: A Meta-Analysis of Findings." *American Educational Research Journal,* 1982, *19,* 237–248.

Cohen, R. "Self-Generated Questions as an Aid to Reading Comprehension." *The Reading Teacher,* 1983, *36,* 770–775.

Conoley, J. C. "Contributions of Psychology to Mental Health Consultation." In F. V. Mannino and others (eds.), *Handbook of Mental Health Consultation.* Washington, D.C.: U.S. Government Printing Office, 1986.

Conoley, J. C., and Conoley, C. W. *School Consultation: Guide to Practice and Training.* Elmsford, N.Y.: Pergamon Press, 1982.

Conyne, R. K., Zins, J. E., and Vedder-Dubocq, S. "Primary Prevention in the Schools: Enhancing Student Competence." In J. L. Graden, J. E. Zins, and M. J. Curtis (eds.), *Alternative Educational Delivery Systems: Enhancing Instructional Options for All Students.* Washington, D.C.: National Association of School Psychologists, 1988.

Cosden, M., Pearl, R., and Bryan, T. "The Effects of Cooperative and Individual Goal Structures on Learning Disabled and Nondisabled Students." *Exceptional Children,* 1985, *52* (2), 103–114.

Council for Exceptional Children. *A Statement by the Teacher Education Division, Council for Exceptional Children, on the Regular Education Initiative.* Reston, Va.: Council for Exceptional Children, 1986.

Cowan, R., Jones, R., and Bellack, A. "Grandma's Rule with

Group Contingencies: A Cost-Efficient Means of Classroom Management." *Behavior Modification,* 1979, *3,* 397-418.

Crego, C. A. "Ethics: The Need for Improved Consultation Training." *The Counseling Psychologist,* 1985, *13* (3), 473-476.

Crouch, P. M., Gresham, F., and Wright, W. "Interdependent and Independent Group Contingencies with Immediate and Delayed Reinforcement for Controlling Classroom Behavior." *Journal of School Psychology,* 1985, *23,* 177-187.

Csapo, M. "Peer Models Reverse the 'One Bad Apple Spoils the Barrel' Theory." *Teaching Exceptional Children,* 1972, *4,* 20-24.

Curtis, M. J., and Anderson, T. E. *Consulting in Educational Settings: Demonstrating Collaborative Techniques.* Cincinnati, Ohio: Faculty Resource Center, University of Cincinnati, 1977. Videotape.

Curtis, M. J., and Meyers, J. "Best Practices in School-Based Consultation." In A. Thomas and J. Grimes (eds.), *Best Practices in School Psychology.* Washington, D.C.: National Association of School Psychologists, 1985.

Curtis, M. J., and Watson, K. "Changes in Consultee Problem Clarification Skills Following Consultation." *Journal of School Psychology,* 1980, *18,* 210-221.

Curtis, M. J., and Zins, J. E. "The Experiential Component in Training for Consultation." Paper presented at the annual meeting of the National Association of School Psychologists, Houston, Texas, Apr. 1981a.

Curtis, M. J., and Zins, J. E. (eds.). *The Theory and Practice of School Consultation.* Springfield, Ill.: Charles C. Thomas, 1981b.

Curtis, M. J., and Zins, J. E. "The Organization and Structuring of Psychological Services Within Educational Settings." In S. N. Elliott and J. C. Witt (eds.), *The Delivery of Psychological Services in Schools: Concept, Processes, and Issues.* Hillsdale, N.J.: Erlbaum, 1986.

Curtis, M. J., Zins, J. E., and Graden, J. L. "Prereferral Intervention Programs: Enhancing Student Performance in Regular Education Settings." In C. A. Maher and J. E. Zins (eds.), *Psychoeducational Interventions in the Schools: Methods and Procedures for*

Enhancing Student Competence. Elmsford, N.Y.: Pergamon Press, 1987.

Darch, C. B., and Thorpe, H. W. "The Principal Game: A Group Consequence Procedure to Increase Classroom On-Task Behavior." *Psychology in the Schools,* 1977, *14,* 341–347.

Deno, S. L. "Curriculum-Based Measurement: The Emerging Alternative." *Exceptional Children,* 1985, *52,* 219–232.

Deno, S. L. "Formative Evaluation of Individual Student Programs: A New Role for School Psychologists." *School Psychology Review,* 1986, *15,* 346–358.

Deno, S. L., and Mirkin, P. K. *Data-Based Program Modification: A Manual.* Reston, Va.: Council for Exceptional Children, 1977.

Deno, S. L., and others. "Oral Reading Fluency: A Simple Datum for Scaling Reading Disability." *Topics and Teaching in Learning Disabilities,* 1983, *2,* 53–59.

Derr, C. B. "OD Won't Work in Schools." *Education and Urban Society,* 1976, *8,* 227–241.

Devine, T. G. *Teaching Study Skills.* Boston: Allyn & Bacon, 1981.

DeVries, D., and others. *Teams-Games-Tournaments: The Team Learning Approach.* Englewood Cliffs, N.J.: Educational Technology Publications, 1980.

Dustin, D., and Blocher, D. H. "Theories and Models of Consultation." In S. D. Brown and R. W. Lent (eds.), *Handbook of Counseling Psychology.* New York: Wiley, 1984.

Edelstein, B. A., and Michelson, L. (eds.). *Handbook of Prevention.* New York: Plenum Press, 1986.

Edgar, E., and Hayden, A. H. "Who Are the Children Special Education Should Serve and How Many Children Are There?" *Journal of Special Education,* 1984–1985, *18,* 523–539.

Ehly, S. *Peer Tutoring: A Guide for School Psychologists.* Washington, D.C.: National Association of School Psychologists, 1986.

Ehly, S., and Larsen, S. C. *Peer Tutoring for Individual Instruction.* Boston: Allyn & Bacon, 1980.

Elias, M. J., and Clabby, J. F. "Social Problem Solving Curriculum for Enhancing Critical Thinking Skills." Unpublished manuscript, Department of Psychology, Rutgers University, New Brunswick, N.J., 1980.

Elias, M. J., and others. *The Improving Social Awareness–Social Problem Solving Project.* Action Research Workshop Report 4. New York: W. T. Grant Foundation, 1982.

Elias, M. J., and others. "Impact of a Preventive Social Problem Solving Intervention on Children's Coping with Middle-School Stressors." *American Journal of Community Psychology,* 1986, *14,* 259-275.

Elliott, S., Gresham, F., and Heffer, R. "Social Skills Interventions: Research Findings and Training Techniques." In C. A. Maher and J. E. Zins (eds.), *Psychoeducational Interventions in the Schools: Methods and Procedures for Enhancing Student Competence.* Elmsford, N.Y.: Pergamon Press, 1987.

Fairchild, T. N., and Zins, J. E. "Accountability Practices of School Counselors: A National Survey." *Journal of Counseling and Development,* 1986, *65,* 196-199.

French, J., and Raven, B. "The Bases of Social Power." In D. Cartwright (ed.), *Studies in Social Power.* Ann Arbor, Mich.: Institute for Social Research, 1959.

Fuchs, L. S., and Fuchs, D. "Linking Assessment to Instructional Interventions: An Overview." *School Psychology Review,* 1986, *15,* 318-323.

Fullan, M., Miles, M. B., and Taylor, G. "Organization Development in Schools: The State of the Art." *Review of Educational Research,* 1980, *50,* 121-183.

Gallagan, J. E. "Psychoeducational Testing: Turn Out the Light, the Party's Over." *Exceptional Children,* 1985, *52,* 288-299.

Gallessich, J. "Training the School Psychologist for Consultation in the Schools." *Journal of School Psychology,* 1973, *11,* 57-65.

Gallessich, J. *The Profession and Practice of Consultation: A Handbook for Consultants, Trainers of Consultants, and Consumers of Consultation Services.* San Francisco: Jossey-Bass, 1982.

Gelfand, D. M., and Hartmann, D. P. *Child Behavior Analysis and Therapy.* Elmsford, N.Y.: Pergamon Press, 1984.

Gerber, M. M. "The Department of Education's Sixth Annual Report to Congress on PL 94-142: Is Congress Getting the Full Story?" *Exceptional Children,* 1984, *51,* 209-224.

Gerber, M. M., and Semmel, M. I. "Teacher as Imperfect Test:

Reconceptualizing the Referral Process." *Educational Psychologist*, 1984, *19*, 137–148.

Gesten, E., and others. "Social Problem Solving Training: A Skills Based Approach to Prevention and Treatment." In C. A. Maher and J. E. Zins (eds.), *Psychoeducational Interventions in the Schools: Methods and Procedures for Enhancing Student Competence*. Elmsford, N.Y.: Pergamon Press, 1987.

Gickling, E., and Thompson, V. "A Personal View of Curriculum-Based Assessment." *Exceptional Children*, 1985, *52*, 205–219.

Glass, G. V. "Effectiveness of Special Education." *Policy Studies Review*, 1983, *2*, 65–78.

Goldstein, A. P., and others. *Skillstreaming the Adolescent: A Structured Learning Approach to Teaching Prosocial Skills*. Champaign, Ill.: Research Press, 1980.

Goldstein, A. P., and others. "The Adolescent: Social Skills Training Through Structured Learning." In G. Cartledge and J. F. Milburn (eds.), *Teaching Social Skills to Children: Innovative Approaches*. (2nd ed.) Elmsford, N.Y.: Pergamon, 1986.

Goodstein, L. D. *Consulting in Human Service Organizations*. Reading, Mass.: Addison-Wesley, 1978.

Gordon, T. *Teacher Effectiveness Training*. New York: Peter Wyden, 1974.

Gould, R., and Sigall, H. "The Effects of Empathy and Outcome on Attribution: An Examination of the Divergent-Perspectives Hypothesis." *Journal of Experimental Social Psychology*, 1977, *13*, 480–491.

Graden, J. L., Casey, A., and Bonstrom, O. "Implementing a Prereferral Intervention System. Part II: The Data." *Exceptional Children*, 1985, *51*, 487–496.

Graden, J. L., Casey, A., and Christenson, S. L. "Implementing a Prereferral Intervention System. Part I: The Model." *Exceptional Children*, 1985, *51*, 377–384.

Graebner, J., and Dobbs, S. "A Team Approach to Problem Solving in the Classroom." *Phi Delta Kappan*, 1984, *66*, 138–141.

Graziano, A. M., and others. "Self-Control Instruction for Children's Fear-Reduction." *Journal of Behavior Therapy and Experimental Psychiatry*, 1979, *10*, 221–227.

Greenwood, C. R., Delquadri, J., and Hall, R. V. "Opportunity to Respond and Student Academic Performance." In V. L. Heward and others (eds.), *Focus on Behavior Analysis in Education*. Columbus, Ohio: Merrill, 1984.

Gresham, F. M. "Assessment of Children's Social Skills." *Journal of School Psychology*, 1981, *19*, 120-133.

Gresham, F. M. "Social Validity in the Assessment of Children's Social Skills: Establishing Standards for Social Competency." *Journal of Psychoeducational Assessment*, 1983, *1*, 299-307.

Gresham, F. M. "Best Practices in Social Skills Training." In A. Thomas and J. Grimes (eds.), *Best Practices in School Psychology*. Washington, D.C.: National Association of School Psychologists, 1985a.

Gresham, F. M. "Research in School Consultation: Checkered Past, Present Status, and Future Directions." Paper presented at symposium, Research Methodology: State-of-the-Art. Annual meeting of the American Psychological Association, Los Angeles, Aug. 1985b.

Gresham, F. M., and Elliott, S. N. "Assessment and Classification of Children's Social Skills: A Review of Methods and Issues." *School Psychology Review*, 1984, *14*, 292-301.

Gresham, F. M., and Gresham, G. N. "Interdependent, Dependent, and Independent Group Contingencies for Controlling Disruptive Behavior." *Journal of Special Education*, 1982, *16*, 101-110.

Gresham, F. M., and Kendell, G. K. "School Consultation Research: Methodological Critique and Future Directions." *School Psychology Review*, 1987, *16*, 306-316.

Gross, S. J. "Interpersonal Threat as a Basis for Resistance in Consultation." Paper presented at the annual meeting of the American Psychological Association, Montreal, Aug. 1980.

Guthrie, P. *Survey of State Consultants Regarding Accountability Practices*. Washington, D.C.: National Association of School Psychologists, 1982.

Gutkin, T. B. "Teacher Perceptions of Consultation Services Provided by School Psychologists." *Professional Psychology: Research and Practice*, 1980, *11*, 637-642.

Gutkin, T. B., and Clark, J. H. "Resistance to School-Based Consultation: An Empirical Investigation." Paper presented at the annual meeting of the American Psychological Association, Toronto, Aug. 1984.

Gutkin, T. B., and Curtis, M. J. "School-Based Consultation: The Indirect Service Delivery Concept." In M. J. Curtis and J. E. Zins (eds.), *The Theory and Practice of School Consultation.* Springfield, Ill.: Charles C. Thomas, 1981.

Gutkin, T. B., and Curtis, M. J. "School-Based Consultation: Theory and Techniques." In C. R. Reynolds and T. B. Gutkin (eds.), *The Handbook of School Psychology.* New York: Wiley, 1982.

Gutkin, T. B., Singer, J. H., and Brown, R. "Teacher Reactions to School-Based Consultation Services: A Multivariate Analysis." *Journal of School Psychology,* 1980, *18,* 126–134.

Gutkin, T. B., and Tieger, A. G. "Funding Patterns for Exceptional Children: Current Approaches and Suggested Guidelines." *Professional Psychology: Research and Practice,* 1979, *10,* 670–680.

Hall, R. J. "Cognitive Behavior Modification and Information-Processing Skills of Exceptional Children." *Exceptional Education Quarterly,* 1980, *1,* 9–15.

Hallahan, D. P., Marshall, K. J., and Lloyd, J. W. "Self-Recording During Group Instruction: Effects on Attention to Task." *Learning Disability Quarterly,* 1981, *4,* 413.

Halpin, A. *Theory and Research in Administration.* New York: Macmillan, 1966.

Harris, V. W., and Sherman, J. A. "Use and Analysis of the Good Behavior Game to Reduce Disruptive Classroom Behavior." *Journal of Applied Behavior Analysis,* 1973, *6,* 405–417.

Hawkins, R. P. "The Function of Assessment: Implications for Selection and Development of Devices for Assessing Repertoires in Clinical, Educational, and Other Settings." *Journal of Applied Behavior Analysis,* 1979, *12,* 501–516.

Heller, K. A., Holtzman, W. H., and Messick, S. (eds.). *Placing Children in Special Education: A Strategy for Equity.* Washington, D.C.: National Academy of Sciences Press, 1982.

Hersey, P., and Blanchard, K. *Management of Organizational Behavior.* Englewood Cliffs, N.J.: Prentice-Hall, 1977.

Hobbs, N. *Issues in the Classification of Children: A Sourcebook on*

Categories, Labels, and Their Consequences. Vols. 1 and 2. San Francisco: Jossey-Bass, 1975.

Homme, L., and others. *How to Use Contingency Contracting in the Classroom.* Champaign, Ill.: Research Press, 1970.

Hughes, J. "Ethical Issues in School Consultation." *School Psychology Review,* 1986, *15,* 489–499.

Humphrey, L. L., Karoly, P., and Kirschenbaum, D. S. "Self-Management in the Classroom: Self-Imposed Response Cost Versus Self-Reward." *Behavior Therapy,* 1978, *9,* 592–601.

Idol, L., Paolucci-Whitcomb, P., and Levin, A. *Collaborative Consultation.* Rockville, Md.: Aspen, 1986.

Illback, R. J., and Zins, J. E. "Organizational Interventions in Educational Settings." In C. A. Maher, R. J. Illback, and J. E. Zins (eds.), *Organizational Psychology in the Schools: A Handbook for Professionals.* Springfield, Ill.: Charles C. Thomas, 1984.

Iowa Department of Education. *Preevaluation.* Des Moines: Iowa Department of Education, 1986.

Jackson, R. M., Cleveland, J. C., and Merenda, P. F. "The Longitudinal Effects of Early Identification and Counseling of Underachievers." *Journal of School Psychology,* 1975, *13,* 119–128.

Jason, L. A., and Ferone, L. "Behavioral Versus Process Consultation Interventions in School Settings." *American Journal of Community Psychology,* 1978, *6,* 531–543.

Jason, L. A., Ferone, L., and Soucy, G. "Teaching Peer-Tutoring Behaviors in First- and Third-Grade Classrooms." *Psychology in the Schools,* 1979, *16* (2), 261–269.

Jenkins, J., and Jenkins, C. "Peer Tutoring in Elementary and Secondary Programs." *Focus on Exceptional Children,* 1985, *17,* 1–12.

Johnson, D. W., and Johnson, R. T. *Learning Together and Alone.* Englewood Cliffs, N.J.: Prentice-Hall, 1975.

Johnson, D. W., and Johnson, R. T. "Cooperative, Competitive, and Individualistic Learning." *Journal of Research and Development in Education,* 1978, *12,* 3–15.

Johnson, D. W., and others. "Effects of Cooperative, Competitive, and Individualistic Goal Structures on Achievement: A Meta-Analysis." *Psychological Bulletin*, 1981, *89*, 47–62.

Johnson, D. W., and others. "Different Cooperative Learning Procedures and Cross-Handicap Relationships." *Exceptional Children*, 1986, *53*, 247–252.

Jones, E. E., and Nisbett, R. "The Actor and the Observer: Divergent Perceptions of the Causes of Behavior." In E. E. Jones and others (eds.), *Attributions: Perceiving the Causes of Behavior*. Morristown, N.J.: General Learning Press, 1972.

Kanfer, F. H., and Gaelick, L. "Self-Management Methods." In F. H. Kanfer and A. P. Goldstein (eds.), *Helping People Change: A Textbook of Methods*. (3rd ed.) Elmsford, N.Y.: Pergamon Press, 1986.

Karoly, P., and Harris, A. "Operant Methods." In F. H. Kanfer and A. P. Goldstein (eds.), *Helping People Change: A Textbook of Methods*. (3rd ed.) Elmsford, N.Y.: Pergamon Press, 1986.

Karoly, P., and Kanfer, F. H. (eds.). *Self-Management and Behavior Change: From Theory to Practice*. Elmsford, N.Y.: Pergamon Press, 1982.

Kazdin, A. E. *Behavior Modification in Applied Settings*. Homewood, Ill.: Dorsey Press, 1980.

Kelley, H. H. *Personal Relationships: Their Structures and Processes*. Hillsdale, N.J.: Erlbaum, 1979.

Kendall, P., and Braswell, L. *Cognitive-Behavioral Therapy for Impulsive Children*. New York: Guilford Press, 1985.

Kendall, P. C., and Williams, C. L. "Assessing the Cognitive and Behavioral Components of Children's Self-Management." In P. Karoly and F. Kanfer (eds.), *Self-Management and Behavior Change: From Theory to Practice*. Elmsford, N.Y.: Pergamon Press, 1982.

Kerr, M. M., and Nelson, C. M. *Strategies for Managing Behavior Problems in the Classroom*. Columbus, Ohio: Merrill, 1983.

Kirschenbaum, H., and Glasser, B. *Developing Support Groups*. Vol. 3. La Jolla, Calif.: University Associates, 1978.

Kratochwill, T. R. "Selection of Target Behaviors in Behavioral Consultation." *Behavioral Assessment*, 1985, *7*, 49–61.

Kuehnel, J. *Faculty, School, and Organizational Characteristics, and Schools' Openness to Mental Health Resources*. Unpublished doctoral dissertation, Department of Educational Psychology, University of Texas, Austin, 1975.

Lentz, F. E. "Designing and Implementing Academic Interventions: Linkage to Functional Assessment." Workshop presented for the Hamilton County Office of Education, Cincinnati, Ohio, Mar. 1987a.

Lentz, F. E. "Functional Assessment of Academic Problems." Workshop presented for the Hamilton County Office of Education, Cincinnati, Ohio, Jan. 1987b.

Lentz, F. E., and Shapiro, E. S. "Behavioral School Psychology: A Conceptual Model for the Delivery of Psychological Services." In T. Kratochwill (ed.), *Advances in School Psychology.* Vol. 4. Hillsdale, N.J.: Erlbaum, 1985.

Lentz, F. E., and Shapiro, E. S. "Functional Assessment of the Academic Environment." *School Psychology Review,* 1986, *15,* 346–357.

Linn, N., and Zaltman, G. "Dimensions in Innovations." In G. Zaltman (ed.), *Processes and Phenomenons of Social Change.* New York: Wiley, 1973.

Lippitt, G. L., Langseth, P., and Mossop, J. *Implementing Organizational Change: A Practical Guide to Managing Change Efforts,* San Francisco: Jossey-Bass, 1985.

Lipsky, D. K., and Gartner, A. "Capable of Achievement and Worthy of Respect: Education for Handicapped Students as If They Were Full-Fledged Human Beings." *Exceptional Children,* 1987, *54* (1), 69–74.

Litow, L., and Pumroy, D. K. "A Brief Review of Classroom Group-Oriented Contingencies." *Journal of Applied Behavior Analysis,* 1975, *8,* 341–347.

Lloyd, J. "Academic Instruction and Cognitive Behavior Modification: The Need for Attack Strategy Training." *Exceptional Education Quarterly,* 1980, *1* (1), 53–63.

Lloyd, J., Kosiewicz, M. M., and Hallahan, D. P. "Reading Comprehension: Cognitive Training Contributions." *School Psychology Review,* 1982, *11* (1), 35–41.

Lovitt, T. C., and Esvelt, K. A. "The Relative Effects on Math Performance of Single Versus Multiple-Ratio Schedules: A Case Study." *Journal of Applied Behavior Analysis,* 1970, *3,* 261–270.

McAndrew, D. "Underlining and Notetaking: Some Suggestions from Research." *Journal of Reading*, 1983, *27* (2), 103-108.

Mace, F., Brown, D., and West, B. "Behavioral Self-Management in Education." In C. A. Maher and J. E. Zins (eds.). *Psychoeducational Interventions in the Schools: Methods and Procedures for Enhancing Student Competence.* Elmsford, N.Y.: Pergamon Press, 1987.

McGinnis, E., and others. *Skill-Streaming the Elementary School Child: A Guide for Teaching Prosocial Skills.* Champaign, Ill.: Research Press, 1984.

McGlothlin, J. E. "The School Consultation Committee: An Approach to Implementing a Teacher Consultation Model." *Behavioral Disorders*, 1981, *6*, 101-107.

McKay, M., Davis, M., and Fanning, P. *Thoughts and Feelings: The Art of Cognitive Stress Intervention.* Richmond, Calif.: New Harbinger, 1981.

Madden, N. A., and Slavin, R. E. "Mainstreaming Students with Mild Handicaps: Academic and Social Outcomes." *Review of Educational Research*, 1983, *53*, 519-569.

Maher, C. A. "Program Evaluation and School Psychology: Perspectives, Principles, Procedures." In T. R. Kratochwill (ed.), *Advances in School Psychology.* Vol. 1. Hillsdale, N.J.: Erlbaum, 1981.

Maher, C. A. "An Approach to Implementing Programs in Organizational Settings." *Journal of Organizational Behavior Management*, 1984, *6*, 53-61.

Maher, C. A. "Providing Prereferral Support Services to Regular Classroom Teachers: The Teacher Resource Team." *Education and Treatment of Children*, in press.

Maher, C. A., and Bennett, R. E. *Planning and Evaluating Special Education Services.* Englewood Cliffs, N.J.: Prentice-Hall, 1984.

Maher, C. A., and Illback, R. J. "Implementing School Psychological Service Programs: Description and Application of the DURABLE Approach." *Journal of School Psychology*, 1985, *23*, 81-89.

Maher, C. A., Illback, R. J., and Zins, J. E. "Applying Organizational Psychology in the Schools: Perspectives and Framework." In C. A. Maher, R. J. Illback, and J. E. Zins (eds.), *Organizational*

Psychology in the Schools: A Handbook for Professionals. Springfield, Ill.: Charles C. Thomas, 1984a.

Maher, C. A., Illback, R. J., and Zins, J. E. (eds.). *Organizational Psychology in the Schools: A Handbook for Professionals.* Springfield, Ill.: Charles C. Thomas, 1984b.

Manley, T. R., and Manley, E. T. "A Comparison of the Personal Values and Operative Goals of School Psychologists and School Superintendents." *Journal of School Psychology,* 1978, *16,* 99–109.

Mannino, F. V., and Shore, M. F. "Effecting Change Through Consultation." In F. V. Mannino, B. W. MacLennan, and M. F. Shore (eds.), *The Practice of Mental Health Consultation.* New York: Gardner Press, 1975.

Martin, R. "Expert and Referent Power: A Framework for Understanding and Maximizing Consultant Effectiveness." *Journal of School Psychology,* 1978, *16,* 49–55.

Martin, R. "Consultant, Consultee, and Client Explanations of Each Others' Behavior in Consultation." *School Psychology Review,* 1983, *12,* 35–41.

Martin, R., and Curtis, M. J. "Effects of Age and Experience of Consultant and Consultee on Consultation Outcome." *American Journal of Community Psychology,* 1981, *8* (6), 733–736.

Medway, F. J. "Causal Attributions for School-Related Problems: Teacher Perceptions and Teacher Feedback." *Journal of Educational Psychology,* 1979a, *71,* 809–818.

Medway, F. J. "How Effective Is School Consultation? A Review of Recent Research." *Journal of School Psychology,* 1979b, *17,* 275–282.

Medway, F. J. "School Consultation Research: Past Trends and Future Directions." *Professional Psychology: Research and Practice,* 1982, *13,* 422–430.

Medway, F. J., and Updyke, J. F. "Meta-Analysis of Consultation Outcome Studies." *American Journal of Community Psychology,* 1985, *13* (5), 489–505.

Meichenbaum, D. H. *Cognitive Behavior Modification: An Integrative Approach.* New York: Plenum, 1977.

Meichenbaum, D. H. "Cognitive Behavior Modification." In F. H. Kanfer and A. P. Goldstein (eds.), *Helping People Change: A*

Textbook of Methods. (3rd ed.), Elmsford, N.Y.: Pergamon Press, 1986a.

Meichenbaum, D. H. "Cognitive Behavioral Treatment." Paper presented at the fall conference of the Ohio School Psychologists Association, Columbus, Oct. 1986b.

Meichenbaum, D. H., and Goodman, J. "Training Impulsive Children to Talk to Themselves: A Means of Developing Self-Control." *Journal of Abnormal Psychology,* 1971, 77, 115–126.

Meyers, J. "Consultee-Centered Consultation with a Teacher as a Technique in Behavior Management." *American Journal of Community Psychology,* 1975, 3, 111–121.

Meyers, J., and Lytle, S. "Assessment of the Learning Process." *Exceptional Children,* 1986, 53 (2), 138–144.

Meyers, J., Palladino, D., and Devenpeck, G. "Think-Aloud Assessment of Reading Comprehension: An Empirical Investigation of Fourth and Fifth Grade Students." Paper presented at the meeting of the National Association of School Psychologists, New Orleans, Mar. 1987.

Meyers, J., Parsons, R. D., and Martin, R. *Mental Health Consultation in the Schools: A Comprehensive Guide for Psychologists, Social Workers, Psychiatrists, Counselors, Educators, and Other Human Service Professionals.* San Francisco: Jossey-Bass, 1979.

Michelson, L., and others. *Social Skills Assessment and Training with Children.* New York: Plenum, 1983.

Miller, J. A., and Peterson, D. W. "Peer Influenced Academic Interventions." In C. A. Maher and J. E. Zins (eds.), *Psychoeducational Interventions in the Schools: Methods and Procedures for Enhancing Student Competence.* Elmsford, N.Y.: Pergamon Press, 1987.

Millman, J., Bishop, C. H., and Ebel, R. "An Analysis of Test Wiseness." *Educational and Psychological Measurement,* 1965, 25, 707–726.

Morsink, C. V., Thomas, C. C., and Smith-Davis, J. "Noncategorical Special Education Programs: Process and Outcomes." In M. C. Reynolds, M. C. Wang, and H. J. Walberg (eds.), *The Handbook of Special Education: Research and Practice.* Oxford, England: Pergamon Press, 1987.

National Association of School Psychologists. *Principles for*

Professional Ethics. Washington, D.C.: National Association of School Psychologists, 1984.

National Association of School Psychologists/National Coalition of Advocates for Students. *Position Statement: Advocacy for Appropriate Educational Services for All Children.* Washington, D.C.: National Association of School Psychologists, 1985.

National Commission on Excellence in Education. *A Nation at Risk.* Washington, D.C.: U.S. Department of Education, 1983.

Nolte, R., and Singer, H. "Active Comprehension: Teaching a Process of Reading Comprehension and Its Effects on Reading Achievement." *The Reading Teacher,* 1985, *38,* 24–31.

Ohio Department of Education. *Intervention Assistance Teams.* Columbus: Ohio Department of Education, 1985.

Okun, B. F. *Effective Helping: Interviewing and Counseling Techniques.* Boston: Duxbury Press, 1976.

Otto, W. "Metacognition and Reading Instruction." *Journal of Reading,* 1985, *28* (6), 573–575.

Paine, S., and others. *Structuring Your Classroom for Academic Success.* Champaign, Ill.: Research Press, 1983.

Panel on Selection and Placement of Students in Programs for the Mentally Retarded. "New Approaches to Assessment and Instruction." In K. A. Heller, W. H. Holtzman, and S. Messick (eds.), *Placing Children in Special Education: A Strategy for Equity.* Washington, D.C.: National Academy of Sciences Press, 1982.

Parsons, R. D., and Meyers, J. *Developing Consultation Skills: A Guide to Training, Development, and Assessment for Human Services Professionals.* San Francisco: Jossey-Bass, 1984.

Pfeiffer, S. I., and Heffernan, L. "Improving Multidisciplinary Team Functions." In C. A. Maher, R. J. Illback, and J. E. Zins (eds.), *Organizational Psychology in the Schools: A Handbook for Professionals.* Springfield, Ill.: Thomas, 1984.

Pfeiffer, S. I., and Tittler, B. I. "Utilizing a Multidisciplinary Team to Facilitate a School-Family Systems Orientation." *School Psychology Review,* 1983, *12,* 168–173.

Piersel, W. C. "Behavioral Consultation: An Approach to Problem Solving in Educational Settings." In J. Bergan (ed.), *School*

Psychology in Contemporary Society. Columbus, Ohio: Merrill, 1985.

Piersel, W. C., and Gutkin, T. B. "Resistance to School Based Consultation: A Behavioral Analysis of the Problem." *Psychology in the Schools,* 1983, *30,* 311–320.

Piersel, W. C., and Kratochwill, T. R. "Self-Observation and Behavior Change: Applications to Academic and Adjustment Problems Through Behavioral Consultation." *Journal of School Psychology,* 1979, *17,* 151–161.

Ponti, C. R. "Attributions in the Classroom: Implications for School Psychologists." Paper presented at the annual meeting of the National Association of School Psychologists, Detroit, Mar. 1983.

Ponti, C. R., and Curtis, M. J. "Effects of Consultation on Teachers' Attributions for Children's School Problems." Paper presented at the annual meeting of the American Psychological Association, Toronto, Aug. 1984.

Ponti, C. R., Zins, J. E., and Graden, J. L. "Implementing a Consultation-Based Service Delivery System to Decrease Referrals for Special Education: A Case Study of Organizational Considerations." *School Psychology Review,* 1988, *17* (1), 89–100.

Pryzwansky, W. B. "Indirect Service Delivery: Considerations for Future Research in Consultation." *School Psychology Review,* 1986, *15* (4), 479–488.

Pugach, M. C. "The Limitations of Special Education Policy: The Role of Classroom Teachers in Determining Who Is Handicapped." *Journal of Special Education,* 1985, *19,* 123–137.

Raffaniello, E. M. "Competent Consultation: The Collaborative Approach." In M. J. Curtis and J. E. Zins (eds.), *The Theory and Practice of School Consultation.* Springfield, Ill.: Charles C. Thomas, 1981.

Regan, D., and Totten, J. "Empathy and Attribution: Turning Observers into Actors." *Journal of Personality and Social Psychology,* 1975, *32,* 850–856.

Reimers, T. M., Wacker, D. P., and Koeppl, G. "Acceptability of Behavioral Interventions: A Review of the Literature." *School Psychology Review,* 1987, *16* (2), 212–227.

Reinking, R. H., Livesay, G., and Kohn, M. "The Effects of

Consultation Style on Consultee Productivity." *American Journal of Community Psychology*, 1978, *6*, 283-290.

Reis, R., and Leone, P. E. "Teaching Text Lookbacks to Mildly Handicapped Students." *Journal of Reading*, 1985, *28* (5), 416-420.

Reynolds, M. C., Wang, M. C., and Walberg, H. J. "The Necessary Restructuring of Special and Regular Education." *Exceptional Children*, 1987, *53*, 391-398.

Rhode, G., Morgan, D. P., and Young, K. "Generalization and Maintenance of Treatment Gains of Behaviorally Handicapped Students from Resource Room to Regular Classrooms Using Self-Evaluation Procedures." *Journal of Applied Behavior Analysis*, 1983, *16*, 171-188.

Rinn, R., and Markle, A. "Modification of Social Skill Deficits in Children." In A. Bellack and M. Hersen (eds.), *Practice in Social Skills Training*. New York: Plenum, 1979.

Ritter, D. "Effects of a School Consultation Program upon Referral Patterns of Teachers." *Psychology in the Schools*, 1978, *15*, 239-243.

Roberts, M. C., and Peterson, L. (eds.). *Prevention of Problems in Childhood: Psychological Research and Applications*. New York: Wiley, 1984.

Robinson, S. E., and Gross, D. R. "Ethics of Consultation: The Canterville Ghost." *The Counseling Psychologist*, 1985, *13* (3), 444-465.

Rosenshine, B. V., and Berliner, D. C. "Academic Engaged Time." *British Journal of Teacher Education*, 1978, *4*, 3-16.

Ross, L. "The Intuitive Psychologist and His Shortcomings: Distortions in the Attributional Process." In L. Berkowitz (ed.), *Advances in Experimental Social Psychology*. Vol. 10. New York: Academic Press, 1977.

Rothman, J., and others. *Marketing Human Services*. Beverly Hills, Calif.: Sage, 1983.

Russell, T., and Ford, D. "Effectiveness of Peer Tutors vs. Resource Teachers." *Psychology in the Schools*, 1983, *20*, 436-441.

Sandoval, J., Lambert, N. M., and Davis, J. M. "Consultation from the Consultee's Perspective." *Journal of School Psychology*, 1977, *15*, 334-342.

Sarason, I. G., and Sarason, B. R. "Teaching Cognitive and Social Skills to High School Students." *Journal of Consulting and Clinical Psychology,* 1981, *49,* 908–918.

Sarason, S. *The Culture of the School and the Problem of Change.* (2nd ed.) Boston: Allyn & Bacon, 1982.

Sarason, S. B., and Doris, J. *Educational Handicap, Public Policy, and Social History.* New York: Macmillan, 1979.

Saudargas, R. A., and Creed, V. *State-Event Classroom Observation System.* Knoxville, Tenn.: University of Tennessee, Department of Psychology, 1980.

Schein, E. H. *Process Consultation: Its Role in Organizational Development.* Reading, Mass.: Addison-Wesley, 1969.

Schmuck, R. A., and Runkel, P. J. *The Handbook of Organization Development in Schools.* (3rd ed.) Mountain View, Calif.: Mayfield, 1985.

Scott, J. W., and Bushell, D. "The Length of Teacher Contacts and Students' Off-Task Behavior." *Journal of Applied Behavior Analysis,* 1974, *7,* 39–44.

Scruggs, T. E., and Osguthorpe, R. T. "Tutoring Interventions Within Special Education Settings: A Comparison of Cross-Age and Peer Tutoring." *Psychology in the Schools,* 1986, *23,* 187–193.

Shapiro, E. S. *Behavioral Assessment in School Psychology.* Hillsdale, N.J.: Erlbaum, 1987.

Shapiro, E. S., and Goldberg, R. "A Comparison of Group Contingencies for Increasing Spelling Performance Among Sixth Grade Students." *School Psychology Review,* 1986, *15,* 546–557.

Sharan, S., and Sharan, Y. *Small-Group Teaching.* Englewood Cliffs, N.J.: Educational Technology Publications, 1976.

Shinn, M. R., Tindal, G. A., and Spira, D. A. "Special Education Referral as an Index of Teacher Tolerance: Are Teachers Imperfect Tests?" *Exceptional Children,* 1987, *54* (1), 32–40.

Singer, H. "Active Comprehension: From Answering to Asking Questions." *The Reading Teacher,* 1978, *31,* 901–908.

Slavin, R. E. "'Student Teams and Achievement Divisions." *Journal of Research and Development in Education,* 1978, *12,* 39–49.

Slavin, R. E. "Cooperative Learning." *Review of Educational Research,* 1980, *50,* 315–342.

Slavin, R. E. *Cooperative Learning.* New York: Longman, 1983.

Slavin, R. E., Leavy, M., and Madden, N. A. "Effects of Student Teams and Individualized Instruction on Student Mathematics Achievement, Attitudes, and Behaviors." Paper presented at the annual meeting of the American Educational Research Association, New York, Apr. 1982.

Smith, D. K. "Practicing School Psychologists: Their Characteristics, Activities, and Populations Served." *Professional Psychology: Research and Practice,* 1984, *15,* 798–810.

Spivack, G., Platt, J. J., and Shure, M. B. *The Problem-Solving Approach to Adjustment: A Guide to Research and Intervention.* San Francisco: Jossey-Bass, 1976.

Spivack, G., and Shure, M. B. *Social Adjustment of Young Children.* San Francisco: Jossey-Bass, 1974.

Stainback, S., and Stainback, W. "Integration Versus Cooperation: A Commentary on 'Educating Children with Learning Problems: A Shared Responsibility.'" *Exceptional Children,* 1987, *54* (1), 66–68.

Stainback, W., and Stainback, S. "A Rationale for the Merger of Special and Regular Education." *Exceptional Children,* 1984, *51,* 102–111.

Stokes, S. (ed.). *School-Based Staff Support Teams: A Blueprint for Action.* Reston, Va.: Council for Exceptional Children, 1982.

Stokes, T. F., and Baer, D. M. "An Implicit Technology of Generalization." *Journal of Applied Behavior Analysis,* 1977, *10,* 349–367.

Stolz, S. B. "Adoptions of Innovations from Applied Behavioral Research: 'Does Anybody Care?'" *Journal of Applied Behavior Analysis,* 1981, *14,* 491–505.

Stolz, S. B. "Dissemination of Standardized Human Service Models: A Behavior Analyst's Perspective." In S. C. Paine, C. T. Bellamy, and B. Wilcox (eds.), *Human Services That Work.* Baltimore: Brooks, 1984.

Stolz, S. B., and Associates. *Ethical Issues in Behavior Modification: Report of the American Psychological Association Commission.* San Francisco: Jossey-Bass, 1978.

Storms, M. "Videotape and the Attributional Process: Reversing Actors' and Observers' Points of View." *Journal of Personality and Social Psychology,* 1973, *27,* 165–175.

Strain, P. S., Shores, R. E., and Timm, M. A. "Effects of Peer Social Initiations on the Behavior of Withdrawn Preschool Children." *Journal of Applied Behavior Analysis,* 1977, *10,* 289–298.

Strong, S. R., and Claiborn, C. D. *Changing Through Interaction: The Social Psychology of Counseling and Psychotherapy.* New York: Wiley-Interscience, 1982.

Sulzer-Azaroff, B., and Mayer, G. R. *Applying Behavior Analysis Procedures with Children and Youth.* New York: Holt, Rinehart & Winston, 1986.

Thurlow, M. L., and Ysseldyke, J. E. "Instructional Planning: Information Collected by School Psychologists vs. Information Considered Useful by Teachers." *Journal of School Psychology,* 1982, *20,* 3–10.

Tombari, M. L., and Bergan, J. R. "Consultant Cues and Teacher Verbalizations, Judgments, and Expectancies Concerning Children's Adjustment Problems." *Journal of School Psychology,* 1978, *16,* 212–219.

Towle, M. "Learning How to Be a Student When You Have a Learning Disability." *Journal of Learning Disabilities,* 1982, *15* (2), 90–93.

Tucker, J. A. (ed.). "Curriculum-Based Assessment." *Exceptional Children,* 1985, *52* (entire issue).

Tyler, F. B., Pargament, K. I., and Gatz, M. "The Resource Collaborator Role: A Model for Interactions Involving Psychologists." *American Psychologist,* 1983, *38* (4), 388–398.

Ulschak, F. L., Nathanson, L., and Gillan, P. G. *Small Group Problem Solving: An Aid to Organizational Effectiveness.* Reading, Mass.: Addison-Wesley, 1981.

Von Someren, K. R., Rhoades, M. M., and Kratochwill, T. R. "Ethical Issues in Behavioral Consultation." Paper presented at the annual meeting of the American Psychological Association, Washington, D.C., Aug. 1986.

Wang, M. C., and Birch, J. W. "Effective Special Education in Regular Classes." *Exceptional Children,* 1984, *50,* 371–398.

Wang, M. C., Levine, L. J., and Reynolds, M. C. "Adaptive

Instruction: An Alternative Approach to Providing for Special Needs in Education." In J. L. Graden, J. E. Zins, and M. J. Curtis (eds.), *Alternative Education Delivery Systems: Enhancing Instructional Options for All Students*. Washington, D.C.: National Association of School Psychologists, 1988.

Wang, M. C., Reynolds, M. C., and Walberg, H. J. (eds.). *The Handbook of Special Education: Research and Practice*. Oxford, England: Pergamon Press, 1987.

Watzlawick, P., Weakland, J., and Fisch, R. *Change: Principles of Problem Formation and Problem Resolution*. New York: Norton, 1974.

Weissberg, R. P., and others. *The Rochester Social Problem-Solving (SPS) Program: A Training Manual for Teachers of 2nd-4th Grade Children*. Rochester, N.Y.: Primary Mental Health Project, University of Rochester, 1980.

Wenger, R. D. "Teacher Responses to Collaborative Consultation." *Psychology in the Schools*, 1979, *16*, 127-131.

West, J. F., and Idol, L. "School Consultation (Part I): An Interdisciplinary Perspective on Theory, Models, and Research." *Journal of Learning Disabilities*, 1987, *20* (7), 388-408.

Wielkiewicz, R. M. *Behavior Management in the Schools: Principles and Procedures*. Elmsford, N.Y.: Pergamon Press, 1986.

Will, M. *Breaking Down the Barriers: A White Paper on Educating Students with Learning Problems*. Washington, D.C.: U.S. Department of Education, 1986.

Winnett, R. A., and Winkler, R. C. "Current Behavior Modification in the Classroom: Be Still, Be Quiet, Be Docile." *Journal of Applied Behavior Analysis*, 1972, *5*, 499-504.

Wise, P., Genshaft, J., and Byrley, M. "Study Skills Training: A Comprehensive Approach." In C. A. Maher and J. E. Zins (eds.), *Psychoeducational Interventions in the Schools: Methods and Procedures for Enhancing Student Competence*. Elmsford, N.Y.: Pergamon Press, 1987.

Witt, J. C. "Teachers' Resistance to the Use of School-Based Interventions." *Journal of School Psychology*, 1986, *24*, 37-44.

Witt, J. C., and Elliott, S. N. "The Response Cost Lottery: A Time Efficient and Effective Classroom Intervention." *Journal of School Psychology*, 1982, *20*, 155-161.

Witt, J. C., and Elliott, S. N. "Acceptability of Classroom Interventions Strategies." In T. R. Kratochwill (ed.), *Advances in School Psychology*. Vol. 6. Hillsdale, N.J.: Erlbaum, 1985.

Wittrock, M. C. (ed.). *Handbook of Research on Teaching*. (3rd ed.) New York: Macmillan, 1986.

Wolf, N. M. "Social Validity: The Case for Subjective Measurement, or How Applied Behavior Analysis Is Finding Its Heart." *Journal of Applied Behavior Analysis*, 1978, *11*, 203-214.

Wurtle, S. K., and Drabman, R. S. " 'Beat the Buzzer' for Classroom Dawdling: A One Year Trial." *Behavior Therapy*, 1984, *15*, 403-409.

Yoshida, R. K. "Are Multidisciplinary Teams Worth the Investment?" *School Psychology Review*, 1983, *12*, 137-143.

Ysseldyke, J. E. "Classification of Handicapped Students." In M. C. Reynolds, M. C. Wang, and H. J. Walberg (eds.), *The Handbook of Special Education: Research and Practice*. Oxford, England: Pergamon Press, 1987.

Ysseldyke, J. E., and Christenson, S. L. *The Instructional Environment Scale*. Austin, Tex.: Pro Ed, 1987.

Ysseldyke, J. E., and others. "An Analysis of Teachers' Reasons and Desired Outcomes for Students Referred for Psychoeducational Assessment." *Journal of Psychoeducational Assessment*, 1983a, *1*, 73-83.

Ysseldyke, J. E., and others. "Generalizations from Five Years of Research on Assessment and Decision Making: The University of Minnesota Institute." *Exceptional Education Quarterly*, 1983b, *4*, 75-93.

Zins, J. E. "Using Data-Based Evaluation in Developing School Consultation Services." In M. J. Curtis and J. E. Zins (eds.), *The Theory and Practice of School Consultation*. Springfield, Ill.: Charles C. Thomas, 1981.

Zins, J. E. "Contractual Services Becoming a Concern for School Psychologists." *Communique*, 1982, *10* (5), 7.

Zins, J. E. "A Scientific Problem-Solving Approach to Developing Accountability Procedures for School Psychologists." *Professional Psychology: Research and Practice*, 1984, *15*, 56-66.

Zins, J. E. "Work Relations Management." In C. A. Maher (ed.), *Professional Self-Management*. Baltimore: Brooks, 1985.

Zins, J. E. "In Search of the Theory Underlying the Practice of Consultation." In J. F. West (ed.), *School Consultation: Interdisciplinary Perspectives.* Austin: University of Texas Press, in press.

Zins, J. E., and Barnett, D. W. "Report Writing: Legislative, Ethical, and Professional Challenges." *Journal of School Psychology,* 1983, *21* (3), 219-227.

Zins, J. E., and Curtis, M. J. "Teacher Preferences for Differing Consultation Models." In M. J. Curtis and J. E. Zins (eds.), *The Theory and Practice of School Consultation.* Springfield, Ill.: Thomas, 1981.

Zins, J. E., and Curtis, M. J. "Building Consultation into the Educational Services Delivery System." In C. A. Maher, R. J. Illback, and J. E. Zins (eds.), *Organizational Psychology in the Schools: A Handbook for Professionals.* Springfield, Ill.: Thomas, 1984.

Zins, J. E., and Curtis, M. J. "Current Status of Professional Training and Practice: Implications for Future Directions." In T. R. Kratochwill (ed.), *Advances in School Psychology,* Vol. 6. Hillsdale, N.J.: Erlbaum, 1988.

Zins, J. E., and Fairchild, T. N. "An Investigation of the Accountability Practices of School Psychologists." *Professional School Psychology,* 1986, *1* (3), 193-204.

Zins, J. E., Graden, J. L., and Ponti, C. R. "Prereferral Intervention to Improve Special Services Delivery." *Special Services in the Schools,* in press.

Zins, J. E., and Ponti, C. R. "Strategies for Promoting Child and Adolescent Mental Health." *Special Services in the Schools,* 1985, *1* (3), 49-60.

Zins, J. E., and Ponti, C. R. "Prereferral Consultation: A System to Decrease Special Education Referral and Placement." *The Community Psychologist,* 1987, *20,* 10-12.

Zins, J. E., and others. *Accountability for School Psychologists: Developing Trends.* Washington, D.C.: National Association of School Psychologists, 1982.

Zins, J. E., and others. "The Peer Support Group: A Means to Facilitate Professional Development." *School Psychology Review,* 1988, *17* (1), 138-146.

Name Index

Subject Index

management, 113-114; peer-
mediated, 114-121; and peer tutoring, 115-117; and problem
definition, 54-55; reinforcement
for, 73-79; and resistance, 156-
157; and response cost, 83-85;
strategies for, 106-107; and study-
skills training, 110-113
Building level; resistance at, 161-
165; sanction and support at,
144-151

C

Categorical placement decisions, in
special education, 18
Client: ethical issues of, 205-206;
participation by, 28; responsibility for, 34, 148, 206-207
Coaching, for social competence, 92
Cognitive behavioral interventions:
covert assertion as, 89-90; methods for, 85-90; self-instruction as,
88-89; for self-management, 86-
88
Collaboration: in consultation, 29-
31; and expert/authoritative style,
39-41; purpose of, 29; and resistance, 169-171
Communication: consultant skill in,
43; for problem solving, 46-48
Confidentiality: in consultation, 33-
34; ethical issues of, 204-205; issue
of, 148
Confrontation: constructive, and resistance, 173-175; direct, 174-175;
indirect, 173-174
Consultant: consultee in relationship with, 29-34; expert and referent power of, 45; influence of, 42-
43; participation by, 27; professional specialty of, 42; skills of,
42-45. *See also* Practitioners
Consultation: affective component
of, 39-41; analysis of, 26-45; appropriateness of, as ethical issue,
209; aspects of, 27-45; cognitive
component of, 41, 46-68; collaboration in, 29-31; concept of, 4, 26-
27; confidentiality in, 33-34; em-

pirical support for, 22-23; as
framework, 4-5; goals of, 37;
implementation of, 31-32; as indirect assistance, 28-29; individual, and problem solving, 48-49;
intervention assistance related to,
5, 22; legal issues of permission
for, 201-202; participants in, 27-
28; for preventive services, 23-24;
problem solving in, 46-68; and responsibility for client, 34; and
social learning theory, 24-25, 39;
supervision distinct from, 30; systems theory of, 37-38; as voluntary, 32-33; work-related focus of,
34-36
Consultee: consultant in relationship with, 29-34; involvement of,
31, 166; participation by, 27; personal problems of, 35-36; problem solving by, 48; resistance by,
165-167. *See also* Staff
Contingency contracting, in behavioral interventions, 81-83
Cooperative learning, and peers,
117-121
Council for Exceptional Children, 21
Covert assertion, technique of, 89-
90
Curriculum-based assessment (CBA),
technique of, 103-104

D

District level: resistance at, 161-165;
sanction and support at, 144-145

E

Ethical issues: and appropriateness
of consultation, 209; of client,
205-206; of confidentiality, 204-
205; of efficacy, 209-210; of intervention assistance, 203-210; and
introducing change, 205; of responsibility for client, 206-207;
of training, 208-209; of value
dilemmas, 206
Evaluation: and group problem
solving, 68; perceived, 161, 166-

42; evaluation in, 59–60; exploring options in, 56; by groups, 49–50, 60–68; implementation in, 58–59; and individual consultation, 48–49; and next steps, 60; options for, 47; and organizational level for intervention, 52–53; process of, 46–50; real problem identified for, 53–54; and request for assistance, 48; selecting interventions in, 56–57; social, 93–95; steps in, 50–56; systems theory for, 51–53; by teacher, 48

Program: access to, 184–185; administration of, 179–184; design of, 137–138; guidelines for, 176–185; and incentives for participation, 180, 182; and liaisons, 185; and meeting times, 177–178; operation of, 177–179; and organizational philosophy, policies, and procedures, 183–184; and professional practices, 184–185; record keeping for, 179–181; and team membership, 178–179; and training, 182–183

Program evaluation: analysis of, 186–198; and clarification of question, 192–193; for delivery, 196; design of, 193; dissemination of results of, 194, 196–198; and domains for data collection, 188–191; framework for, 189, 192–195; and implementation, 153, 193–194; for marketing, 196–198; and meta-evaluation, 195; need for, 186–187; problems of, 195–196; purposes of, 187–189; utilization of, 196–198. *See also* Evaluation

Psychological Services Assessment Questionnaire, 190–191

Public Law 94-142, 2, 162, 199–200

Q

Questionnaires and surveys, on organizations, 134–135

R

Reciprocal interactions: and consultation, 24–25; and organizations, 129–130

Records: legal issues of, 200–201; of organizations, 133–134; for programs, 179–181

Referral, in special education, 15–17

Reframing: consultant skill in, 44–45; and problem identification, 172–173

Reinforcement: for academic performance, 107–109; for behavioral interventions, 73–79; differential, 78–79; with individual contingency, 74–76; and peers, 75, 77–78; and resistance, 173; by self, 87–88; for staff, 149

Relaxation strategies, technique for, 90

Research, future for, 215–216

Resistance: and acceptability of intervention, 159–160; analysis of, 154–175; and attributions, 157–159, 171–172; and behavioral interventions, 156–157; and collaboration, 169–171; and constructive confrontation, 173–175; by consultee, 165–167; and educational philosophy, 163–164; ethical issues of, 205; and external pressures, 162–163; identifying, 169; and internal pressures, 161–162; and ownership lacking, 164; and perceived evaluation, 161, 166–167; and practitioners, 167–168; preventing and overcoming, 168–175; and problem identification, 172–173; and reinforcement, 173; understanding, 154–160, 164

Response cost, and behavioral interventions, 83–85

Responsibility for client: and consultation, 34; ethical issue of, 206–207; issue of, 148

Rights Without Labels, 21

Rochester Social Problem Solving Program, 94

Role play, for assessment, 72